D0200081

MICHAEL PALIN established his reputation with *Monty Python's Flying Circus* and *Ripping Yarns*. His work also includes several films with Monty Python, as well as *The Missionary*, *A Private Function*, an award-winning performance as the hapless Ken in *A Fish Called Wanda*, *American Friends* and *Fierce Creatures*. His television credits include two films for the BBC's *Great Railway Journeys*, the plays *East of Ipswich* and *Number 27*, and Alan Bleasdale's *GBH*. He has written books to accompany his seven very successful travel series *Around the World in 80 Days*, *Pole to Pole*, *Full Circle*, *Hemingway Adventure*, *Sahara*, *Himalaya* and *New Europe*. He is also the author of a number of children's stories, the play *The Weekend* and the novel *Hemingway's Chair*. In 2006 the first volume of his diaries, *1969–1979: The Python Years,* spent many weeks on the bestseller lists. Visit his website at www.palinstravels.co.uk.

BASIL PAO began his photographic career in 1980 on his return to Hong Kong after ten years in the United States, where he was an art director for Atlantic, Polygram and Warner Bros. He first worked with Michael Palin on the design for the book accompanying Monty Python's *Life of Brian*. They have since collaborated on the books based on his seven travel series. In 2007 he wrote and photographed *China Revealed: A Portrait of the Rising Dragon*.

NEW EUROPE

MICHAEL PALIN

Photographs by Basil Pao

PHOENIX

A PHOENIX PAPERBACK

First published in Great Britain in 2007
by Weidenfeld & Nicolson
This paperback edition published in 2008
by Phoenix,
an imprint of Orion Books Ltd,
Orion House, 5 Upper St Martin's Lane,
London WC2H 9EA

An Hachette Livre UK company

1 3 5 7 9 10 8 6 4 2

A CIP catalogue record for this book
is available from the British Library.

ISBN 978-0-7538-2397-2

Printed and bound in Great Britain by Clays Ltd, St Ives plc

The Orion Publishing Group's policy is to use papers that
are natural, renewable and recyclable products and
made from wood grown in sustainable forests. The logging
and manufacturing processes are expected to conform to
the environmental regulations of the country of origin.

www.orionbooks.co.uk

www.palinstravels.co.uk

For Archie

Contents

Introduction

M ANY TIMES, too many times, I've woken, 35,000 feet in the air, in that limbo-land between the end of an old day and the start of a new one, after a long flight from somewhere far away. I've pushed up the window shutter and peered out at the twinkling lights below and wanted to be down there, in a real house with a kitchen table and eggs on the stove and coffee on the hob.

More often than not, it's eastern Europe that I see waking up below me and though it's only two hours from where I live, I realise with a jolt that I know more about Hong Kong or the Hindu Kush than what it's really like down there.

Of all the continents I've touched in the nineteen heady years since we started out on *Around the World in Eighty Days*, Europe is the one in which I've lingered least, partly because it is so close to home, and partly because much of it has been in serious disarray. Our planes were bombing Serbia only eight years ago.

But since the start of the twenty-first century Europe has begun to sort itself out. East and West have drawn closer. There have been no major conflicts. Countries once suspicious of visitors now welcome them with open arms.

So when it came to reuniting Saga Platoon for one more adventure it seemed that there was a gap to be filled. The continent I had flown over on so many dark mornings could not be ignored any longer. It was time for Europe. And time to get out my trusty, increasingly tattered, *Penguin Encyclopaedia of Places*.

'Europe: Apart from Australia, the smallest of the continents. It occupies about seven per cent of the earth's land surface. On the other hand it is second to Asia for size of population, containing over 20 per cent of the world total.'

And therein lay the first problem. An awful lot of people to meet.

It became clear that it would take us too long to cover the whole of Europe. Most interesting to me was that half of my own continent which, for most of my lifetime, was chilled by a Cold War and concealed behind an Iron Curtain. Now, with the Cold War over and the Iron Curtain lifted, there was the prospect of being able to travel through once-forbidden lands; of making a voyage of discovery on my very own doorstep.

Trying to describe such a journey in purely geographical terms didn't seem quite right. Some countries were clearly part of Eastern Europe, others very definitely Central Europe, while others, like Turkey, Moldova or Ukraine, didn't fit into either category. What they all seemed to have in common was a sense of rapid change, an opening-up of new horizons. It wasn't just names that were changing. Opportunities were being seized, old systems challenged, economic and political alliances entirely rethought. Nothing was quite as it had been before. Peoples, cultures and traditions with long historical roots were being shaken up and re-energised. Compared to the relatively secure and settled shape of Western Europe, the realignment of the eastern half of the continent was hurtling along. What was taking shape, both on the map and in the head was a new Europe. Or as we say on television, a New Europe.

If I'd made this journey eighteen years ago, instead of haring off around the world, it would have taken me through ten countries. Today there are twenty. More than all the countries in our Himalaya and Sahara journeys put together.

Many of these new nations are tiny, some with total populations smaller than that of London, but despite their size they have a very clear sense of their own identity, reinforced and defined by their own language, culture, history and currency. What makes their existence viable is the supportive hand of the European Union. Not all are part of it yet, but all feel that its benefits are worth taking seriously. After a century of power struggles which have visited unimaginable horrors upon the continent this coming-together is breathtakingly fresh and promising.

So I set out with considerable excitement in May 2006, and, a year later I find myself neither disillusioned nor cynical. The spirit of New Europe does exist, the hopes and dreams still burn and the future is full of opportunity. Our journey might just have been through a very small window in history and my natural tendency to optimism and half-full glasses may have misled me, but whatever the future holds I think it is important to have marked this moment when, for the first time in a thousand years, the old Europe of domination and conflict has been replaced by a new Europe of co-operation.

Let's, for all our sakes, hope that we can make it work.

Michael Palin, London, June 2007

The Journey

We filmed over a period of twenty-two weeks between 16 May 2006 and 4 May 2007, generally avoiding the very depths of winter, though snow and ice caught up with us in Turkey. My formative impressions of Eastern Europe had been in monochrome, as if the people there lived in concrete apartment blocks under permanently grey skies. Basil Pao's pictures for the book and Nigel Meakin's photographs for the BBC series are an eloquent corrective. The sun shone throughout most of our journey. Though there are far too many concrete blocks, we also saw well-kept, elegant, ancient and very beautiful cities and villages, as well as swathes of countryside farmed by the traditional methods fast disappearing from west European landscapes.

And though the mountains may not be the Himalayas, there was snow on the tops of the Carpathians and the Julian Alps in the middle of summer.

The book is made up from my diary notes, with one exception. For the first time on any of my travels I had my shoulder bag stolen. It happened on my arrival in Budapest and though I lost phone and money neither mattered a damn compared to the loss of my little black book containing all my notes on the Baltic states. There was nothing I could do but sit in my hotel room overlooking the Danube and recreate it all from memory and from muttered observations on my voice recorder. It's a tribute to the Baltics that so much came back so vividly.

If some days are missed out, it's because they were rest days.

Postscript

ROMANIA AND Bulgaria have joined the European Union since I set out, but the delicate balance of Balkan politics has been shaken by Kosovo's declaration of independence. On the other hand, those who disagreed with Poland's new anti-communist vetting laws (which tarnished, among others, the reputation of Ryszard Kapuscinski, one of their country's finest travellers and journalists) will have been encouraged by the victory of Donald Tusk and his liberal oppostion party in the Polish elections of October 2007. Turkey is having increasing difficulty balancing its secular tradition with Islamist aspirations, and Ukrainian politicians are still nowhere near resolving the rift between the eastern- and western-oriented halves of the country. There have been student riots in Hungary, and Russia and Estonia have come to serious blows after the relocation of a war memorial.

At least these are problems the countries of the region will have to sort out themselves. Far more worrying is that super-power politics, from whose corrosive influence Europe looked to have been mercifully released, is back on the agenda. At the time of writing the Americans and the Russians seem hell-bent on resurrecting the Cold War. But this is the year Putin and Bush both step down, so, as they say, anything could happen, but probably won't.

My advice would be, as you might expect, not to stay at home and worry, but to go to the countries and find out for yourselves.

Michael Palin, London, April 2008

A Note on Names

I have attempted to reduce the number of accents and unfamiliar spelling.

Paul Woodman, the Secretary of the Permanent Committee on Geographical Names, kindly advised which place-name accents were essential to retain. I have been more cavalier with the names of people as they are generally, apart from German umlauts, rendered accentless when encountered in English-language newspapers and magazines.

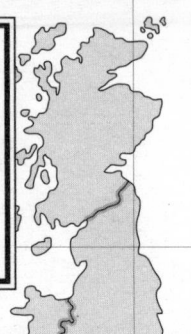
A PRACTICAL MAP OF
NEW EUROPE

---- Denotes route taken by Mr Palin
➤ Denotes direction of travel

North Sea

Germany

1. The Julian Alps, Slovenia	35. Esztergom, Hungary
2. Lake Bled, Slovenia	36. Visegrad, Hungary
3. Istria, Croatia	37. Budapest, Hungary
4. Rijeka, Croatia	38. Hortobagy, Hungary
5. Split, Croatia	39. L'viv, Ukraine
6. Hvar, Croatia	40. Yalta, Ukraine
7. Medugorje, Bosnia & Herzegovina	41. Kiev, Ukraine
8. Mostar, Bosnia & Herzegovina	42. Tallinn, Estonia
9. Sarajevo, Bosnia & Herzegovina	43. Aluksne, Latvia
10. Dubrovnik, Croatia	44. Riga, Latvia
11. Durres, Albania	45. Palanga, Lithuania
12. Tirana, Albania	46. Vilnius, Lithuania
13. Kruja, Albania	47. Nida, Lithuania
14. Lake Ohrid, Macedonia	48. Kaliningrad, Russia
15. Ohrid, Macedonia	49. Gdansk, Poland
16. Prilep, Macedonia	50. Elblag, Poland
17. The Rila Mountains, Bulgaria	51. Warsaw, Poland
18. Godec, Bulgaria	52. Poznan, Poland
19. Sofia, Bulgaria	53. Czestochowa, Poland
20. Plovdiv, Bulgaria	54. Oswiecim, Poland
21. Zlatograd, Bulgaria	55. Krakow, Poland
22. Edirne, Turkey	56. Bialka Tatrzanska, Poland
23. Istanbul, Turkey	57. The Dunajec Gorge, Slovakia/Poland
24. Selcuk, Turkey	58. The Tatra Mountains, Slovakia
25. Goreme, Turkey	59. Brno, Czech Republic
26. Chisinau, Moldova	60. Prague, Czech Republic
27. Tiraspol, Transdniester	61. Terezin, Czech Republic
28. Sulina, Romania	62. Karlovy Vary, Czech Republic
29. Tulcea, Romania	63. Dresden, Germany
30. Viseu de Sus, Romania	64. Meissen, Germany
31. Sapanta, Romania	65. Leipzig, Germany
32. Sighisoara,Transylvania	66. Bitterfeld, Germany
33. Bucharest, Romania	67. Berlin, Germany
34. Belgrade, Serbia	68. Rugen Island, Germany

Mediterranean

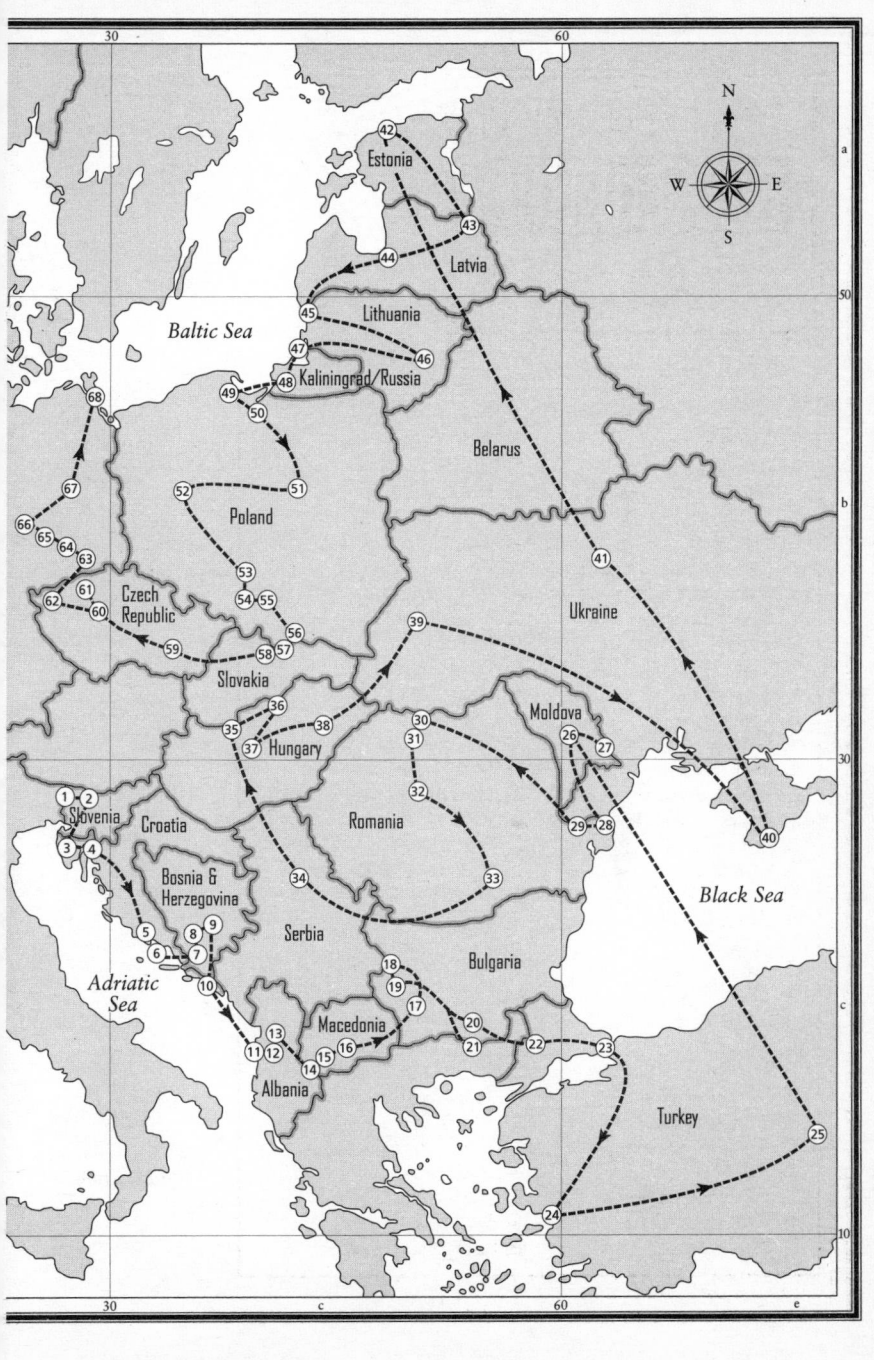

Slovenia

Day One: *The Julian Alps*

The mountain hut has been opened specially. The climbing and hiking season hasn't yet begun. There is snow all around us, but, more worryingly for our purposes, there is cloud all around us. What should be one of the most spectacular views in the eastern Alps could just as well be someone's back garden. I nurse a mug of herbal tea, personally mixed by our guide. It's a dense, intense brew, a grappa of herbal teas. He spreads his hands apologetically, and looks up at where the sky would probably be if we could see it. It's Slovenia's fault, he says, for being where it is. Moist Mediterranean air is meeting cool, dry air from Central Europe, condensing and covering the monumental landscape like dust-sheets over fine furniture.

There's a map on the wall of the hut and he points out where we are. Almost exactly on the border between Italy and Slovenia, and between what I have grown up to know as Western and Eastern Europe.

For forty-five years of my life the Soviet Union, with its satellite states, had turned half the continent into an alien place; unwelcoming, bureaucratic, grey. For forty-five years Iron Curtains and Cold Wars (sustained for the convenience of both sides) sowed division and mistrust amongst Europeans who should have been friends.

It's been eighteen years now since the fall of the Berlin Wall signalled a new direction for the continent into which I was born. Which is why I'm here 8,000 feet up in the Julian Alps, looking optimistically east, waiting for the cloud to lift so that I can see what the new Europe looks like.

Two hours later, the clouds start to wither, and we begin to make out solid objects: rocks and boulders peeking out above the snow, the outline of slopes soaring above and below us. Then with a sudden, dizzying effect a final stack of cloud falls off the mountain like an avalanche and the sun strikes buttresses of pink-tinged limestone, cracked and jagged and pointing at the sky. I head off along the path that leads east.

Day Two: *Bled*

Wake early. Beyond the trees I can see grey light reflected on an eerily still water. Nothing is moving. There is silence apart from the muted chimes of the clock on the church in the middle of the lake, echoed discreetly by a chorus of more distant clocks in the town of Bled.

Villa Bled, where we're staying, is a beautiful, tranquil spot, the sort of place that monks or dictators might choose as a hideaway from the distractions of the world. In this case it was dictators, for this vast pile was built, in 1947, as a getaway for Josip Broz Tito, a.k.a. Marshal Tito, one of the giants of post-war communism.

The hotel manager tells me Tito loved Slovenia because it was as far away as he could get from Russia and as close as he could get to Great Britain. Did I know that Elizabeth II had received and decorated him?

The manager shakes his head. 'Unheard of in a communist leader.'

What's more, she gave him a Rolls-Royce, adding to the already impressive stash of cars given him every Christmas by each grateful country of the Yugoslav Federation. Yugoslavia, generally reckoned to have been one of the more successful creations of post-war communism, never stood much of a chance after the charismatic Tito died in 1980. Slovenia was the first to challenge the system. The walk-out by Slovenian delegates in January 1990 made sure that the 14th Congress of the Yugoslav League of Communists would be the last. Two years and a short war later Slovenian independence was officially recognised.

Walking out this morning I have no sense of Slovenia's communist past. A banner slung across the road announces, in English, that this is the 'Month of Asparagus'. History and religion, two of communism's great enemies, are celebrated everywhere, from the impossibly picturesque Church of the Assumption that sits on an island in the middle of the lake like a carnival float, to the soaring ramparts of the seventeenth-century castle high above the northern shore. The language sounds Germanic, lots of 'Ja Ja's, and the boatmen waiting for tourists are decked out in Tyrolean costume. Houses are of the Alpine style, with overhanging roofs, carved shutters and piles of fresh-cut wood neatly stacked by the doorways. It's not just any sniff of communism that's missing here, it's any sniff of the twentieth century. Bled is in Austro-Hapsburg costume.

I take a ride on the lake with an unsentimental, left-leaning theatre director from the capital, Ljubljana (pronounced Loob-li-Ana). Our *pletna*, a stouter version of a gondola, is punted about by a man called Robert dressed in velvet jacket and pantaloons, with a pole in one hand and a mobile phone in the other. He's clearly more interested in what's happening on the end of the phone.

My companion, Zjelko, whilst not exactly nostalgic, misses the artistic contacts which were so easy during the Yugoslav times. People tend to forget that Slovenia is the most westerly Slav nation in Europe. With a population just short of two million, they, perhaps more than anyone, appreciated the cultural kinship of Slav federation.

'Is there anything in the old Yugoslav way of doing things that might have been better than now?'

He replies with feeling.

'In those times families spent weekends going walking in the mountains or going out. You know how they spend them now? In the commercial centres, all the Saturdays and Sundays, shopping and kids playing in the kindergarten of the commercial centres. That's how Slovenians now spend weekends.'

The medical care system was better then too. Now it's all to do with money.

'You can get a cataract operation in a week if you have money. If you don't it's a year and a half.'

By the time he's got onto the resurgence of the Catholic Church, which is trying to revive ancient Austrian laws to claw back property and raise taxes, I feel we're in danger of getting into a What Have The Yugoslavs Ever Done For Us situation, but Zjelko concedes that on the whole people live much better than before, and he adds that Slovenians feel proud to have moved seamlessly into the European Union and even prouder that next year they'll be in the Eurozone. I suggest that for the Slovenes this is exchanging one federal system for another, that Europe is 'the bigger country' that Yugoslavia once was before it all went wrong.

Zjelko considers this.

'There's a stereotype saying that Slovenians are always eager for someone outside to rule, like before it was Vienna, then it was Belgrade and now it's Brussels. So,' he smiles, 'they need someone to listen to.'

At the hotel tonight I meet someone who can put a little more flesh and blood on the man for whom the Villa Bled was built. Lado Leskovar is in his sixties, and in a colourful life has been Richard Burton's stand-in, sung the Yugoslav entry in the Eurovision Song Contest of 1967 (Britain's Sandie Shaw won, Lado came ninth) and danced with Tito's wife.

He remembers Tito as 'a very charming man' who liked cars, ladies, movies, food, and the good life generally. Politically he gained great respect for standing up to Stalin in 1948, developing his own mix of socialism and capitalism and for pursuing a foreign policy of non-alignment.

'We used to call him the walking credit card,' Lado remembers. 'He arranged credits for Yugoslavia from West and East.'

Tito was always keen to know what was going on in the world and liked to drink with journalists, cartoonists and writers and hear what they felt about him and what they were saying about him.

On such occasions Tito might play the piano and often, here in the Villa, Lado was called upon to sing for him.

So there's a frisson of nostalgia about tonight, as Lado sings a song for me in the bar, with Marshal Tito's portrait on the wall behind him, and Lado's effusive Serbian wife looking on as if it were the first time she'd heard it.

The song is called 'The Sad Death of a Vagabond'.

It seems somehow appropriate. Tito has been dead for twenty-six years, but for Lado, and I suspect many of his age, the mourning still goes on.

Day Three: *Slovenia to Croatia*

Our journey out of Slovenia begins at the run-down station of Jesenice. It's late afternoon and the three-coach local is full of adolescent schoolgirls, with the outnumbered boys looking wary. This line, built in 1906 when Slovenia was part of the Austro-Hungarian empire, linked Vienna with the port of Trieste and it was opened with great ceremony by Archduke Franz Ferdinand, whose portrait was hung in every station and whose assassination in Sarajevo eight years later precipitated the First World War. I don't think he'd be impressed by what has become of his great dream. As the shabby little train rattles through thickly forested slopes there's loud argument, mock fights and smoking in the toilet.

The infant River Sava tumbles alongside. Flowing out of the Julian Alps, it will grow to become one of the significant rivers of Central Europe, forming the northern border of Croatia and Bosnia and swelling to join the Danube in Belgrade. But all that lies ahead.

I get talking to one of the few non-schoolgirl passengers, a man called Boris. He points out a long block amongst the trees. It was a barracks, occupied by the Yugoslav army who tried unsuccessfully to keep Slovenia from leaving the Federation in 1990.

'They were helped to leave,' he says, modestly. 'But our army is not very big now. Most of them go home at weekends.'

I tell him I'm heading for Istria, a peninsula on the Croatian coast. It was part of Italy between the wars but handed over to Yugoslavia by the Allies in return for keeping nearby Trieste a free port. After the break-up of Yugoslavia the Croatians took most of it, allowing Slovenia a minuscule share of coastline. Boris admits there are tensions over access and fishing rights but he feels the politicians make too much of it and basically they are brothers and sisters.

He taps Istria on the map.

'They are smart people. They didn't get involved in the war. Fabulous blue waters. It's a rare combination, normally you get beautiful waters and barracks.'

A few hours later, I'm on the Slovenian border and it's quite a shock to realise that as we cross it we'll be leaving the European Union behind. For all her diminutive size little Slovenia is the only one of the countries of former Yugoslavia to be admitted to EU membership. I reach for my passport and Nigel reaches for the carnet – a list of all the equipment that must be declared at the frontier of any country outside the European Union, and that, for the foreseeable future, includes Croatia.

Croatia

Day Four: *Istria*

Istria is famous for its truffles. The truffle is an unprepossessing, misshapen off-white tuber which grows in the soil around tree roots and which is considered so good to eat that men risk imprisonment to smuggle it across national borders. My guidebook describes the taste so many desire above all other as 'part nutty, part mushroomy, part sweaty sock'. And Istria is famous for them. Truffles, that is, not socks.

We drive through a sedate and timeless rural landscape that reminds me of Tuscany, with crops growing from deep-red earth and small towns growing from the tops of the hills.

In the Mirna valley is a stretch of thick oak and birch wood where we are to go truffle-hunting with Damir, a tall, rangy old hippy with a goatee beard, Guinness baseball cap, ex-army jacket and baggy trousers, and his eighty-six-year-old uncle Zdravko. Zdravko, who has a ruddy, outdoor complexion, wears an old forage-cap and carries a small stainless-steel spade slung across his shoulder like a rifle. Damir laughs when I worry about his octogenarian uncle.

'He's up every morning at four and in the forest until nine!'

But the two most important members of the expedition are Betty and Dick (a bit of a shock here as they're the names of my aunt and uncle), a four-year-old Labrador and a seven-year-old Retriever respectively.

Lovely, lively dogs that they are, I can't disguise my disappointment that they're not using pigs to nose out the truffles as depicted on the folkloric postcards they sell in France.

Apparently pigs tend to eat the truffles as soon as they find them, which cuts down profits. So off we go into the forest. Betty, Dick, Damir, Zdravko and me. (And, of course, Nigel, Pete, John, J-P, Uncle Tom Cobley and all.)

It has taken two years to train Dick and Betty. They can now sniff out a truffle at 50 yards, even one buried an arm's length below ground.

Dick and Betty hare around among the silver birch saplings like children just let out of school.

Damir's honestly not expecting much. For the last two years it has not been obligatory to have a licence and there are various cowboys who come in, buy up what they can't find themselves and smuggle the truffles (*tartufi* in Italian) across the border into Italy where they have plenty of black truffles but few of the highly prized Istrian whites. Their other concern is for the delicate ecosystem of this part of Istria. Truffles thrive in unspoilt forest and they need the minerals from unpolluted rivers, but Croatia is on a building spree, with twenty-three golf courses seeking planning permission in Istria alone. Just then Zdravko calls across. Dick has dropped down beside a beech tree and is nuzzling into the earth, using his nose and his paws to uncover something. Damir kneels beside him and together they pull out what looks like a soil-covered stone. He rubs the soil away and holds it up to the dappled sunlight.

Dick, duly rewarded, races after a ball. 'That's about, well, 15 grammes.' Worth around 14 euros he reckons. The biggest he's ever found was over 300 grammes.

The largest truffle ever recorded was found by a local man, Giancarlo Zigante, though there are muttered reservations about the claim, and rumours that Zigante took the credit for someone else's discovery.

At the village of Livade, a few miles away, a replica of the truffle, looking like an inflated brain, stands proudly on a plinth at the entrance to Zigante's restaurant, together with the citation from the *Guinness Book of Records*. 'A White Truffle (Eutuberaceae Tuber) weighing a world record 1.31kg was found by Giancarlo Zigante of Pototoska on 2nd November 1999.'

Giancarlo, an ordinary-looking middle-aged man with black hair brushed forward and a belly pushing at shirt and belt, has prepared us a special menu. Truffle cheese and ham is followed by home-made truffle pasta, which in turn is followed by truffle ice-cream. I personally feel that each dish would have been better without the truffles, but many, including Marilyn Monroe and Winston Churchill, would think me an unsophisticated lout.

I wish I liked them more, if only because there's no escaping them. Tonight, at a town nearby, Giancarlo Zigante will try to claim another place in the *Guinness Book of Records* as he personally supervises the making of the world's largest omelette.

A truffle omelette, of course.

In the centre of the small town of Buzet, a circular tent has been constructed to house the omelette pan, which measures 20 feet in circumference, 7 feet across, with a 6-foot handle sticking out from one side and getting in everyone's way. It rests on a mesh of radiating gas jets and an earnest young man I talk to says that the hardest problem of all was providing consistent heat over such a wide surface area. It was a problem he personally solved and he's now Mayor of Buzet – further evidence, were it needed, of the truffle effect.

The evening's ceremony is quite surreal. Crowds gather as night falls. Zigante, brow shining in the harsh strip light, fusses about, nervous in a suit and tie, whilst his team, in matching white T-shirts, fans out around the pan like Formula One mechanics at a pit stop, each clutching a large bottle of cooking oil. When the signal is given, they upend these into the pan, to be followed by blocks of butter which they move around with long metal rods like those croupiers use in a casino. Then, with TV cameras whirring, the signal is given and three large milk churns filled with the contents of 2,006 eggs, broken earlier, are tipped into the pan, to be followed by 10 kilos of white truffles.

Croatian TV and film stars step modestly forward to help stir the mix, and just when you thought it couldn't get any sillier, four musicians and a singer, in blue and white striped T-shirts and red-bobbled nightcaps, leap into the ring to play jolly omelette-making music.

The mayor offers me a glass of wine, Giancarlo's son offers me a glass of wine, and to cap a day of dizzy madness I am called forward by the Truffle King himself to be a stirrer.

The mayor winks as I step forward into the limelight.

'You are a big star in Croatia.'

Day Five: *Rijeka*

Spend the night at Opatija, at the north-eastern end of the Istrian peninsula. Once a favourite watering hole for the rich and successful of the Austro-Hungarian empire, it has the languorous, stuffy air of a place that will change only reluctantly. My guidebook damns it with faint praise. 'Attracts an elderly clientele of middle-class Europeans.'

The next working city down the Croatian coast is Rijeka (in Italian Fiume – both words meaning 'river') and I have a special reason for stopping here. When I was making *Around the World in Eighty Days* I remember a slow and rather magical voyage across the Bay of Bengal aboard a Yugoslav freighter called *Susak*, captained by a man of infinite, if lugubrious patience. He, like the rest of the crew, viewed the Madras-Calcutta-Singapore run as some sort of punishment and the only time I saw him cheerful was when he talked of his home and family, back in Rijeka. The name didn't mean much to me then but now I'm looking at it on the road signs ahead, and Captain Sablic has agreed to meet me again, eighteen years on.

With some difficulty we find a place to park in the busy port area, and as we're a little early I walk around a nearby fish market. It's like a small cathedral. Built by an Italian the year the First World War broke out, it has an apse, a gallery and a fine timber roof through which the sun filters onto glistening slabs of tuna steaks, nine inches thick, squid, shrimp, mackerel, sardines and mountains of conger eels. Business is done in traditional fashion. No computerised cash tills here. The fish are weighed in standard-size brass buckets and measured with brass weights.

Round the corner from this piscatorial palace, I find Captain Sablic at one of the outdoor cafés. Any worry that I might not recognise him is quickly allayed for, even without the uniform and with a few more pounds on him, the face and the posture are unmistakable. The captain had a way of occupying a chair that suggested he might be in it for ever, and his face betrays the same grave world-weariness that I knew from nights in the mess-room on the *Susak*.

We walk into the Old Town, along the Korzo and through the Gradski Toranj, the gateway that is one of the few relics of the medieval town. Captain Sablic has long since given up working for Bengal Tiger Lines and now captains the Ramsgate-Ostend Ferry. When I last saw him he was a Yugoslav. Now he's Croatian. I ask him about the war of the early 1990s that followed the break-up of Yugoslavia.

He tells me that he took part in it. When the predominantly Serb-controlled rump of Yugoslavia forbad Croatia to import arms, he brought a ship packed with smuggled weapons and ammunition from Constanta in Romania to Rijeka.

I'm surprised by his matter-of-factness. He never struck me as a man who'd take risks.

'What would have happened if you'd been caught?'

He shrugs. 'Maybe I will go in prison. Who knows? It was my duty to help the country.'

He takes me to his house, which has a stunning view down the Adriatic, and I meet his vivacious wife and his daughter who's a doctor; and I understand now why he missed his family so much on those long, anonymous days at sea.

We eat at their neighbourhood restaurant, where lamb is being roasted on the spit in the car park. I opt for scorpion fish with *blitva*, or mangelwurzel, which complements it perfectly. Captain Sablic insists I call him Miloje and we talk over marine matters like the outrageous price of tugs at Ramsgate (£600 a manoeuvre), which led him to take a pilot's course so he could do it himself.

It was worth meeting up again, if only to see another side of the captain. Miloje Sablic is, I can see now, neither quiet nor resigned.

We leave Rijeka on the night ferry to Split. It's called the *Marko Polo*, which sounds like a good omen at the start of a very long journey.

Day Six: *Split*

Two of our four engines have been switched off during the night, reducing a hammering thump to a low throb, as we thread our way through the chain of over a thousand islands that runs the length of Croatia's coastline.

Up on deck at five o'clock. A brisk wind blowing. Visibility clear. The sun still only a glow behind the low mountains of the mainland. What I'm looking out on now is Dalmatia, and I'm not the only one to be excited by it.

Matthew Arnold wrote a poem about it, Shakespeare set part of *Twelfth Night* here. Dalmatia, homeland of the Illyrians, was settled for 5,000 years even before the Greeks and Romans arrived. This is not new Europe, this is very old Europe. I feel positively Homeric.

Although Split is only 200 miles south-east of Rijeka, everything about it feels very different. The buildings along the waterfront are lower, less crowded, with white walls, red-tiled roofs and shuttered windows. The buildings reflect colour and light and an avenue of palm trees confirms that, in the course of a night's journey, we have exchanged Mitteleuropean gravitas for Mediterranean repose. The skyline has its quota of concrete housing blocks but it's the bell-tower of the old cathedral that still dominates the view.

I'm introduced to Split by Goran Golovko, a tall, youngish man with short-cut dark hair who works in children's theatre. I'm struck by how much Split resembles Nice, and a walk through the arcades of the long, stone-flagged Republic Square, known as the Prokurative, only increases this sense of neo-classical with a light touch. Goran puts this down to the city's pedigree. It became part of the Venetian empire in the fifteenth and sixteenth centuries and went through a period of French occupation at the time of Napoleon's conquest of Dalmatia.

Though the corrosive Balkan wars of the 1990s did not affect Split as much as the northern and eastern parts of the country, the fighting that led to the creation of an independent Croatia for the first time in 500 years was brutal, with Croats and Serbs inflicting appalling casualties on each other. Nor has the aftermath of war been easy. Organised criminal gangs have stepped into the vacuum left by the rapid change from benign socialism to a capitalist free market. A lot of girls from further east, from Ukraine, Romania and Moldova, are trafficked through here, says Goran. They're kept as virtual slaves, accompanied everywhere, never allowed time of their own. There's a growing problem of drug addiction.

I ask Goran how the children he works with feel about the war. They only remember it vaguely, he says.

'They're interested in MTV and what happens in Hollywood with Brad Pitt and Angelina Jolie.'

The day is warming up and we take lunch at a small, friendly place a little way up the hill from the seafront. Zdravko, the owner, is gregarious and chatty. He introduces me to his son and grandson, both of whom are wearing Arsenal T-shirts.

Fish is the speciality here.

'We always say in Croatia that fish has to swim three times. Sea water, wine and olive oil!' Zdravko enthuses, and a plate of anchovies, sardines and whitebait washed down with a pale pink Croatian rosé is just about faultless.

We talk, inevitably, about the new Croatia.

'I'm very critical, of course,' says Zdravko, 'but imagine living through the fall of communism. It's a fantastic feeling... very emotional.' He doesn't think, however, that Yugoslavia was necessarily doomed and is unusually critical of Marshal Tito.

'You know, the Serbian influence was too strong...especially in his older age. As for your personal human rights there were no limitations, but political expression was cut, harshly. There was no democracy in Yugoslavia and that's why everything fell apart.'

He won't, however, hear any criticism of Croatia's hardline nationalist President Tudjman, who took the country to war in the 1990s and who some think could have stood trial as a war criminal if he'd lived.

'Our President is criticised much more abroad than here...I consider him a real statesman...the father of our country.'

After another bottle of chilled rosé the talk veers towards present-day rivalries. Like the Eurovision Song Contest, taking place tonight. It's already been a small Balkan war of its own, with

Serbia and Montenegro withdrawing from the contest because
the Serbs accused the Montenegrins of unfairly swinging the vote
for their own song. Croatia's hopes lie with Severina, a local girl
and a national star. Unfortunately they are not the only things to
have lain with Severina. She recently featured in a pornographic
video that was broadcast across the country on the internet. Goran
shakes his head.

'The day the video was released, nobody worked in Croatia.
In the police, in the ministries, in the government, universities,
banks, schools.'

'Really?'

'Well, of course there are rare people who say they didn't see it,
but I don't trust them at all.'

Later that evening, in a bar by the sea we watch the Eurovision
final from Athens. Severina's song, 'Moja Stikla' ('High Heels'), is
loud and bouncy and frenetic and her red skirt, slit to the crotch,
is whipped off fairly early in the song. She comes thirteenth.

Croatian pride must have taken a pasting. Not just because she
was thirteenth, but because she was soundly beaten by the only
two other ex-Yugoslav entrants, Macedonia and Bosnia.

And the bar was half-empty. Perhaps they knew what was
going to happen.

Day Seven: *Split*

The chief glory of Split is Diocletian's Palace. Not because it is a
perfectly preserved and restored example of Roman architecture,
but because it's neither of these things. It is a rich, complex,
stimulating mess of human settlement, a massive statement of
imperial power onto which has been grafted the flotsam and
jetsam of centuries of activity and occupation. A city within a city
within a city. Lines of washing hang out to dry from the windows
of apartments built into the old Roman walls.

Flowers sprout from the top of Corinthian columns, cash tills
are embedded in the white limestone walls.

Gaius Aurelius Valerius Diocletianus was a Dalmatian of
humble origins who rose through the ranks to become Emperor of

Rome for twenty-one years. He acknowledged a division between western and eastern Europe as far back as AD 286 when he divided control of the Roman empire between himself in the east and his friend Maximian in the west, with subordinate 'Caesars' being given control of two other areas. He's had an unfavourable press, partly because in later life he had delusions of divinity, but mostly for his persecution of the Christians. He had, however, an insatiable appetite for new buildings, of which the palace at Split was the most ambitious.

It's a massive structure, part living quarters, part military garrison, measuring 700 by 600 feet with walls 6 feet thick and 25 feet high.

Four great gates give access on each side and it is before the *Mjedna Vrata*, the Bronze Gate, that Goran and I stand this morning. In Diocletian's time ships would have sailed in through here, but access now is from a wide promenade called the Riva.

Inside, in the high-vaulted undercroft where helmets, shields, armour and weapons would once have been unloaded, there is now a busy tourist market selling postcards, candles, carvings and religious icons (which, considering Diocletian ordered the beheading of Domnius, the patron saint of Split, is a nice irony).

The original layout of the palace, by which all streets lead to the peristyle, the central courtyard, hasn't changed and the square itself is powerful testimony to the skill of Diocletian's masons and builders.

The reign of Diocletian marked the high point of imperial power and the air of invincibility he wanted his mighty palace to project was increasingly tried by Goths, Huns, Avars and others spilling over the eastern borders of the empire. With the Romans gone, the local population used the palace as a refuge and began to build permanent homes inside it. And so it went on. It was too big and strong to demolish, so successive occupants merely adapted the space, turning it into one of the world's most thriving ruins.

There is a compact horseshoe-shaped bay just below the hotel called Bačvice, its sheltered waters and strip of well-worn sand packed with people on this hot weekend. In the shallows a group of men of a certain age are, literally, throwing themselves into a game I've never seen anywhere else. It's called *Picigin*, pronounced Pixigin, and is so local that none of the contestants in the World Championships last year lived anywhere apart from Split. The aim is simple, to keep a tennis ball in the air using any part of the human body, and it's best played in water just above ankle deep, allowing the maximum foot movement and a minimum cushion for the falls. There is only one rule: to keep the ball in the air. Beyond that the game is less about what you do, than how you do it. Execution is all.

Aerial leaps, back-foot flips, skimming headers, scissor-kicks and wildly reckless full-length falls are all encouraged. Improbably, it was first developed here in the 1920s by a group of academics, journalists, professors and others who were looking for a new form of exercise they could do in the middle of the day. It was very much an anti-club game and one of the first stipulations was that it should be played only on public beaches. Now a group is as likely to include truck drivers as it is night editors. They fling themselves about with enormous good humour, while paddling children scarcely bat an eyelid as middle-aged men come flying through the air. Watching *Picigin* in full flow, I understand better why Yugoslavia was the first non-English-speaking country ever to buy *Monty Python*.

I leave Split on the ferry to the island of Hvar. It's Sunday night and all seats on the deck are taken by a combination of tourists and Hvar-ians returning from a weekend in Split. Cans of beer are ripped open and long-suffering waitresses chatted up. We find some space below in a cabin thick with an old-fashioned fug of cigarette smoke and the sound of gruff voices getting louder by the beer. A game-show plays to nobody on a TV screen in the corner.

Maybe she's just trying to cheer me up, but a bright, intelligent girl, educated on the mainland, but now living back on the island, can't stop raving about the attractions to come. Hvar, she says, is, quite simply, paradise.

Day Nine: *Hvar*

I find that what catches my fancy most is the smell of the place. Like a slice of Provence cut loose and floated down the Mediterranean, Hvar is famous for its lavender fields. This is not even the lavender season and yet the aromas around me are powerful. The scent of pine mingles with those of broom, dill and oregano, wafting up to me as I stand amongst the stout stone walls of a sixteenth-century hilltop village. Vines are everywhere and each of the courtyards has its own delicately carved winepress.

But the village is deserted and its inhabitants have moved away, to cities like Split or Zagreb or even as far as Australia. My companion and guide Igor Zivanovic loves the island with a vengeance and yet sees that the rural life, however picturesque it might be for visitors like us, offered only hard work and low rewards. Hvar's beauty has never helped its inhabitants. Malta, another Mediterranean island of similar size, sustains a population of 400,000. There are 10,000 living on Hvar.

Igor is what is called in the business a 'character'. He's fifty-one, born in Istria and has lived here since 1961. He wears his long, greying hair in a stumpy ponytail which he is constantly adjusting. Sometimes it's at the back of his head and sometimes perched on top of it like a Mandarin emperor. He wears worn jeans and a shirt which pops open rather frequently to reveal a round, bulging stomach.

He has found some donkeys to take us around the deserted village, but even that hasn't been easy. Once the staple form of transport on the island, they have been comprehensively superseded by the motor car and the pick-up truck. Of the two he was able to find, one is lame.

Igor points out the details of the deserted buildings, the carved lintels, decorated keystones on the arches, and the funnel in the millstone on which the wine was pressed.

'They made wine right here. Dark wine. They call it black wine. Very strong.'

Igor dispenses information and opinions with impulsive finality. He doesn't do musing.

In the sleepy little port of Starigrad, on the east side of the island, behind a modest doorway off a winding lane paved with polished slabs of creamy Dalmatian stone, Igor has a *konoba*, a bar/restaurant, which seems to embody his highly individual lifestyle. Marenko, Igor's business partner, is a short, solid Croat with a lined and lived-in face. On his T-shirt is a picture of the Taj Mahal, and underneath it the tortuous slogan 'Via Agra – Man's Greatest Erection for a Woman'.

In the dark cluttered interior Igor is already at work hunting down a bottle of wine. From the ceiling hangs a mobile sculpture on which computer chips are balanced by two books. Plastic hands stick out of an old-fashioned meat grinder. A mannequin's leg is stretched out in a cooler cabinet and there are clocks everywhere, all stopped at 3.04.

'The time Tito died!' shouts Igor from the kitchen. 'He was the greatest hedonist of all time,' he adds, approvingly. 'Me, I have to go to the cinema to see Gina Lollobrigida. Tito, he just ring her up.'

The bottle empties quickly and as Igor grabs a corkscrew to open another, Marenko insists I come next door to see something wonderful. It turns out to be a 1904 Swedish-made wall telephone.

Marenko winds it up proudly. 'The oldest telephone set in Croatia.' He hands me the receiver. 'And it still works.'

Sure enough, there is a clear greeting on the end of the line. I reply in English. Much laughter. It obviously happens all the time.

Back at Igor's there seems little sign of the meal, or even a table. Glass in hand, the patron lights another cigarette. 'I hate smoking, but I love cigarettes.' He takes me across to a wall of photos. One shows an emaciated old man apparently being shaved in a public street.

He explains, with unusual warmth of feeling, that this is a man who had been given a day to live and was being given his last shave surrounded by all his friends and neighbours.

Our director looks at his watch and mutters something about lunch. Igor makes for the kitchen.

'Come and help me cook,' he shouts behind him, pausing only to point out a bumper sticker from Alaska that reads 'If It's Tourist Season, Why Can't We Shoot Them?'

An hour or so later we are treated to an excellent meal, served on red table mats with hammers and sickles in the corner.

Artichoke risotto and polenta, made palatably creamy with butter and oil, freshly caught sardines and a peppery hot lamb stew with *blitva.*

'This is the food of my grandfather and my grandmother,' Igor announces with deep satisfaction, before a familiar theme refuels his anger.

'Tourists! They breed unscrupulous people. People who give them food and take their money without any local people involved at all.' He tips another glass down.

'When McDonald's open here…' He stops, grabs at an imaginary rope round his throat and yanks it upwards.

Back at the villa we're renting I take a dip in the clear, warm waters of a nearby bay. Only when I'm in the water do I become aware that almost every rock below me is covered with sea-urchins.

I swim carefully around and with some skill, though I say it myself, reach a jetty without once having to put a foot down. Am climbing out with a bit of a swagger when a gentle wave propels me forwards and my knee makes contact with a black pincushion. It takes Basil and a razor blade almost half an hour to extract every single quill.

Day Eleven: *Hvar to Međugorje, Bosnia & Herzegovina*

At the compact little port of Sućuraj, on the south-eastern tip of Hvar, I leave for the mainland on an equally compact fishing boat. Nets, with their black marker buoys attached to them, lie along the deck like giant jellyfish as we sail out of the harbour beyond the outstretched hand of St Nikolai, patron saint of fishermen, whose statue on the sea wall is, in both senses, the last image of Hvar.

As he rolls the nets out the captain tells me that, contrary to much of the rest of Europe, Croatia's waters are still plentiful. He can bring in 200 kilos a day, but they're mainly scampi, for which the price is low.

'Too many Croatians eat meat,' he grumbles.

The Dalmatian coast, where fish is taken seriously, is eclipsed by Zagreb, the capital, around which half of Croatia's four million people live. And all paid-up carnivores, apparently.

The nets out, our captain produces fresh bread and a dish of anchovies in his own olive oil. He delves around in a locker and brings out a bottle of local wine called Vinka, in a bag of ice. We bob around in the sunshine. The food is simple and satisfying. Ahead of us is the narrow coastal plain and behind it the tall grey limestone wall beyond which are all the troubles of Europe.

By late afternoon we're crossing the Neretva River and turning north through the rich market gardens of its swampy delta into the ancient land of Herzegovina, which, with Bosnia to the north and the Republika Srpska (pronounced Serbska) to the north and east, is one of the components of the fragile state of Bosnia & Herzegovina, or BiH, created and tended by the United Nations.

We pass pillboxes by the railway and further on the minaret of the first mosque I've seen since we set out.

At a border crossing which would not have been here in Yugoslavian days the flag of Croatia with its red chequerboard shield flies alongside Bosnia & Herzegovina's diagonal of stars on a blue and yellow background.

The town that all signs point to is the old Ottoman stronghold of Mostar. The second name on the signs is Medugorje, a village which has become a boom town since six local teenagers had repeated visions of the Virgin Mary. This is to be our stopping place for the night.

Next to our guest house, in the long main street, is an establishment called 'Pilgrimage Specialists' which overflows with candles, crucifixes, rosaries, Virgin Mary baseball hats and mobile phone straps bearing her likeness. Others sell religious art works, like 3D pictures on which the face of Christ changes into the face of the Virgin as you pass by. There are bottles of holy water piled high and statuettes with sparkling lights and lots of walking sticks (whose significance will only become clear later) and establishments called 'Kathy's Irish Kitchen' and 'Paddy Travel'. The main street leads to the twin-towered, cream-painted façade of St James Church, around which are gardens and a fountain and terraces full of people. On this balmy evening they sit or stand, many in groups, quite a lot in wheelchairs. Some are talking quietly, others, hands clasped together, are kneeling in prayer. Others are limping painfully towards the church for mass.

There is such an overwhelming feeling of devotion that writing in my notebook makes me feel like some sort of spy, observing humanity when they are here to observe God.

But I needn't have worried. They're all preoccupied. So rapt that no-one gives me a second glance.

Bosnia & Herzegovina

Day Twelve: *Međugorje*

IN THE evening of 24 June 1981, on a rocky hillside above a village of some thousand people in a poor and predominantly Catholic region of Yugoslavia, six young boys and girls encountered a woman with a child in her arms. The next day, four of them, drawn back to the spot, saw the woman again and recognised her as the Virgin Mary. The visitations became a regular, almost daily event for some of the children. Since then, despite no-one else having seen them and even though the Pope has refused to endorse the apparition, twenty-five million pilgrims have visited Međugorje. What was a village has grown into a town of 5,000 inhabitants, with another 20,000 in the area employed in the pilgrimage business. And new hotels are still going up.

Such has been the impact on the local economy that a cynic might think there's a conspiracy to keep a good story going, and when we're suddenly told that one of the original visionaries is happy to meet and talk I wonder if we're using them or they're using us.

Mirjana, a teenager in 1981, is now married to a builder and has two daughters, both of whom are playing table-tennis in the driveway of a comfortable detached house. She is attractive and friendly and as we sit in her eminently sensible garden and she answers my questions eminently sensibly I feel my scepticism, if not destroyed, certainly neutralised. She describes the first vision she had when she was fourteen, apologising only for her English, which is excellent.

'I saw the woman in the grey, long dress and she was carrying the baby, like this, in the hand.'

The next day, accompanied by members of her family, who saw nothing, she once again found herself before the Virgin, who this time spoke to them.

'We come close to the Blessed Mary and she tells us "My dear children, you don't be afraid of me. I am Queen of Peace."'

I press on, with questions I never ever thought I'd hear myself asking.

'Do you still see the Blessed Mary?'

'Yes, every 18th of March. And she also said I will have the apparition every second day of each month.'

'When do you see her?'

'Always about nine o'clock in the morning. But it is not exactly nine o'clock.' She smiles rather apologetically. 'It can sometimes be before or later.'

'D'you have to be somewhere special?'

'I'm always in Cenacolo.' She points up the road to a drug rehabilitation centre we'd passed on the way here, built by her husband's company and run by a well-funded order of nuns.

The fact that Mirjana, someone whose visions have spawned an industry, appears to be no hysteric or wild-eyed prophetess but an ordinary housewife, leaves me feeling somehow cheated.

Later in the afternoon, back in Međugorje, I hear Ivan, the only one of the visionaries to whom Mary still appears on a daily basis, talking to an enormous crowd in one of the great purpose-built pavilions behind the church. He speaks softly into the microphone, like a comfortable Californian businessman, in a pale blue polo shirt and jeans, his long hair brushed neatly back. It's as if these extraordinary people have worked hard to look and sound as ordinary as possible.

This being the Balkans, there is, of course, a political dimension. The message of Međugorje is for Catholics only, and the power of this whole operation reflects what has happened to the Balkans since the break-up of Yugoslavia. Catholics have always been the majority here in Herzegovina, but at the time of the Ottoman empire they lived alongside Muslims. Now nationalism is in the air and new countries like Croatia and Serbia define themselves not by what they have in common with their neighbours but what makes them different. Thousands of Catholics have moved down here from elsewhere in Bosnia to avoid living with Muslims, making Međugorje, which offers such comfort to pilgrims from all over the world and which preaches the Virgin's message of peace, into another symbol of the new polarisation.

Whilst we're filming in the main street an old car drives up aggressively in our shot and two heavy-set men get out, slamming the doors. I notice a tag hanging from the mirror. It says 'Heroes' on one side, and on the other is the name and likeness of Ante Gotovina, a Croatian general now under indictment at The Hague for war crimes. The EU had made his capture a condition of talks on Croatian membership.

At sunset we follow a long line of pilgrims up to Apparition Hill where Mirjana, Ivan and their friends first saw the Virgin. It's not an easy walk and many have to negotiate the rugged path with the help of sticks. The spot where she first appeared is marked by a white statue with fencing around, set in a rough stony area dotted with pomegranate trees and thorn-bush scrub. Some sit or kneel in quiet contemplation around this sacred place but as I draw close to the statue I hear a broad Irish accent whispering in my ear.

'Which way for the crosses, now Michael?' and mistaking my wide-eyed amazement for confusion, the voice adds, helpfully,

'*Life of Brian*, my favourite film!'

Day Thirteen: *Mostar*

Most means a bridge, and though four or five bridges cross the Neretva River in Mostar, there is only one that really matters. It's the *Stari Most*, the Old Bridge. Though it connected the east and west banks of the river for 400 years it was destroyed by Bosnian-Croat artillery in November 1993, in an act of deliberate and provocative vandalism, targeted because it was a beautiful, graceful symbol of a proud city. A local man tells me that when it was blown apart, it was for Mostarians 'like they have lost their child. Everything that Mostar represents was represented by the bridge.'

What Mostar represented, and had done for several centuries, was an economically and culturally thriving town in which Muslims and Christians, both Orthodox and Catholic, lived side by side, firstly under the Ottoman empire, afterwards under the Austro-Hapsburgs and then as part of Yugoslavia. History was turned on its head in the 1990s as score-settling nationalism asserted itself throughout the Balkans. Mostar was attacked by the JNA, the Yugoslav People's Army (largely Serb and Montenegrin) and defended by a combination of Bosniak (Bosnian Muslims) and Bosnian-Croat forces. In 1993 the Bosnian Croats turned on their former allies and Mostar's agony intensified. Under ceaseless and systematic bombardment, bridges were destroyed and the eastern bank, populated largely by Bosniaks, was besieged for eleven months.

Kamel, a twenty-eight-year-old Mostarian, was a teenager during the siege.

'As a fourteen-year-old you get old pretty fast, because you don't think about normal things that you should be thinking about, like having fun, playing football, chasing girls. You're thinking how to stay alive, how to bring fresh water to your family, or where to find wood to burn for heating. People ate grass, which we boiled and cooked.'

Ironically it took the destruction of the bridge, relayed on television across the globe, to force the outside world into taking notice and the Washington Agreement of March 1994 brought an end to the fighting. UNESCO put money into rebuilding the devastated Old Town and in 2004 their efforts were crowned when a meticulously re-created *Stari Most* rose once again.

I first see it from down on a rubbish-strewn terrace of the river bank, its single stone span a creamy-white stripe dividing the clear blue sky above from the shimmering green waters below. When the original was first built by the Turkish architect Mimar Hajrudin in the 1560s, it was such an unprecedented piece of engineering that a sceptical Sultan threatened to execute the architect if it fell down on the day the wooden frame was removed. It stayed up for 427 years.

Already this morning there is some commotion on the bridge. A young man in a swimming costume has mounted the narrow parapet, and seems about to dive in. A half-scream, half-cheer goes up from a party of schoolchildren on the sandy beach 70 feet below, as he poses, Tarzan-like, flexing his muscles theatrically and peering down from his precarious perch. But then, as we are all willing him to leap, he nonchalantly steps back onto the bridge and walks away.

The diving tradition began centuries ago, and it's maintained, and strictly controlled, by the 100-member-strong Mostari Divers' Club.

Their President is Emir, a trim, barrel-chested, silver-haired seventy-year-old who first dived from the bridge when he was sixteen, since which time he's represented Yugoslavia at the Olympics, been a film double for Richard Burton (who hasn't round here?) and been depicted on a postage stamp. We talk outside the clubhouse, in one of the handsome, rebuilt stone towers at the side of the bridge.

In the approximately three seconds between leaving the bridge and hitting the water 'the diver must feel he is flying,' says Emir. 'It's not long but for a diver it feels like a century.'

The most important things for a diver doing the *lasta* (the swallow dive) are to break the water with his hands and never his head, and to enter the water at an angle of no more than 35 degrees.

Emir explains rather starkly, 'In Olympic swimming pool, the depth of the water is 10 metres. Down there', he peers over at the swirling green waters of the Neretva, 'the depth is around 5 metres.'

Whilst someone else collects contributions from the crowd of tourists now swelling the bridge (150 euros a dive, 40 euros a jump), three young men strip down, and one by one terrify and thrill the onlookers by mounting the unprotected 12-inch-wide parapet and, focusing their gaze straight ahead, pushing themselves outwards and down towards the river. There's just time to catch your breath before they slice into the water and reappear to howls of applause.

Emir is justly proud of their skills.

'This is extreme sport. Only other place in the world where you see this is the cliff divers in Acapulco.'

Though he can remember only one fatality from diving, twenty-three members of the club died in the war of 1993.

The area around the bridge has been well restored, with the inevitable cobbled streets and orderly tidied-up markets, but you only have to climb up into the back streets to see the extent of the war damage. Burnt-out hulks of buildings pitted with shrapnel, the windows of the Union Bank building smashed and the gouges of pre-stressed concrete still hanging down the walls. A richly decorated Hapsburg-style building that used to be Mostar's best hotel is roofless and empty.

Kamel, who lived through the siege, who ran for water for his family at the risk of his life, refused to be bowed. He taught himself English and worked as a runner for the UN force that saved the city. Now they've gone he's retrained into computers.

He thinks it will be a long time before Mostar can once again become the prosperous, tolerant, lively city it once was. Many people who could be helping to rebuild it have left and gone abroad, and the tripartite Croat, Muslim and Serb administration of Bosnia & Herzegovina, with its colonial-style, EU-appointed High Representative is a reminder that of all the countries of the Balkans, this is perhaps the most serious casualty of war.

Day Fourteen: *Mostar to Sarajevo*

Mostar railway station, from which we hope to travel to Sarajevo, is a sad, neglected place. The platforms are functional and bare. The 'M' of Mostar is missing from the only sign and wild flowers sprout from the track.

There are so few people waiting that my belief in the existence of the eight o'clock to Sarajevo is diminishing by the minute. But, bang on time, I see a headlamp beaming out of the tunnel and the metallic green diesel locomotive and three coaches that comprise the Ploče to Zagreb express squeal to a halt beside us.

The compartments are comfortable enough but give off the dusty, sweaty smell of stock that is often used but rarely cleaned. Once we're on the move north what we lack in creature comforts is more than made up for by some fine scenery as we follow the

Neretva into a narrow gorge with dramatic walls of twisted, folded rock.

A Bosnian-Croat army officer is travelling up to Sarajevo. His face is like one of the Easter Island statues, long, with protruding eyebrows and a big, firm jaw. His eyes and his hair are both deep black and he learnt his English whilst training in Texas. He's another who talks admiringly of Marshal Tito and the skill with which he played off West and East.

'Technology from US and Europe, arms from Russia.'

He regards him as a visionary, a man who genuinely tried to create a third force in politics by allying himself with people like Nehru of India.

'I cried when he died,' he says. 'Nowadays everyone says, "I didn't cry. He was a butcher." But I cried.'

Alongside us, as the valley widens, trout farms and ageing hydroelectric plants make use of the river. My soldier friend shakes his head at their condition.

'But what can you do. Over fifty per cent of our qualified people have gone abroad.'

'Do they come back?'

He laughs. 'In the summer!'

I can see why you might want to come back in the summer. As we run deeper into the heart of the Dinaric Alps the scenery is magnificently wild and romantic, sometimes tight and confined by rock stacks and perilous buttresses, then suddenly opening out into a vista of lakes with houses by the water and gardens of beehives and orchards.

As the Romans used roads, the Austrians used railways to cement their empire. They were impressive engineers. Of the 80 miles of line between Mostar and Sarajevo, forty per cent is in tunnels and ten per cent on bridges or viaducts.

The Ivan Tunnel, cutting through 3,000-foot-high mountains, was so difficult to drill that the Emperor Franz Josef, rather rashly, urged on the workforce with the promise of 'one kilo of gold for one kilo of stone'. It marks the end of Herzegovina and the beginning of Bosnia. The weather has completely changed from one end of the tunnel to the other and the sunny skies that we've been blessed with since setting out from Slovenia have been replaced by dark and scowling clouds.

Not the best conditions for a first glimpse of Sarajevo, which presents a grimly bleak aspect as we trundle through an industrial wasteland bordered by tall concrete blocks broken up by scrapyards and factories that look derelict until you see people moving about. This, I later learn, is what they call New Sarajevo.

We walk from the station to the Holiday Inn, a squat concrete core from which hangs a skin of yellow and brown tiles. It was built for the Winter Olympics of 1984 and still bears the Olympic symbol on its side. The nearby shell of the multi-storey Parliament building is a reminder of more recent history, the nightmare of the 1990s, when Sarajevo lived under bombardment for almost four years.

I can feel the first flecks of rain.

In a comfortable, elegantly appointed restaurant off a dusty street I meet a group of Sarajevans who all work in films, television or journalism: Ademir, a film director and producer, Glava, a bearded heavily built Serb who's just written a comedy screenplay, and Srdjan (imagine 'Sir John' in an American accent), also a writer and director. They're full of plans for future projects, but, as a newcomer in town, I can't help asking about the past.

Srdjan sighs. Sarajevans today don't want to talk about the war. But once they start they can't stop. Ademir, tall, thin, with a strong, ascetic face, is the oldest of the men and Bosnia's most respected film maker. He was one of the few who managed to get in and out of the city during the siege.

'The only way was on a plane. They were operated by Germans, Americans and French. We called them Maybe Airlines. Maybe the plane would take off, maybe not.'

Boarding call was a shout or a gesture followed by a sprint out to the aircraft, carrying all your own bags and wearing an improvised UN flak jacket.

The next thing he knew he was in Cannes or San Francisco. 'It was hard to get out, but so much harder to come back. To come from the world like that to a city without electricity, telephone, running water.' He shakes his head as though he still can't comprehend it.

He's bitter about the siege, but reserves his anger equally for Serbia's President Milosevic and the system that allowed him to do what he did and the countries of the West that ignored the plight of Sarajevo for so long.

Then I make the mistake of trying to make instant sense of all this.

'But there's still a Serbian republic within Bosnia & Herzegovina,' I ask with innocent surprise.

Looks are exchanged. Glava explains.

'What do you mean "still"? There has been and always will be a Serb part of Bosnia. It's like asking the Protestants in Belfast why there's still a place called Northern Ireland.'

On the streets of Sarajevo, there's a lively, comfortable bustle, the feel of a city going about its business. It was always the focal point of the Balkans, a place where travellers and traders on their way between Central Europe and the Mediterranean and Western Europe and the East met and mingled, and it remained cosmopolitan and tolerant during the Ottoman occupation. Srdjan reminds me that there was a thriving Jewish community here, with much greater freedom from persecution than almost anywhere else in Europe. A walk through the centre of Sarajevo, he says, is a walk through time, from the old Turkish quarter, through the imperious Art Nouveau façades of the Austro-Hapsburg centre to the Tito-era communist blocks in the west.

As in Mostar, mosques and churches seem to have been restored as a matter of priority and in one square, within a hundred yards of each other, can be found a synagogue, a Catholic church, an Orthodox church, a mosque and a Seventh Day Adventists' meeting hall.

I take a tram back to the hotel. The tramline runs along what was known in the war as Sniper Alley, a place you crossed at your peril. As I step down I look up towards the hills from which the snipers operated with such impunity. They look green, inviting, almost idyllic, dotted with red-roofed villas and bungalows. Only a dozen years ago they were dangerous, malignant places from which the Serb artillery looked down on the city like an audience at a theatre.

Over 11,000 died in the siege of Sarajevo. Ademir says that it took a long time after the war before he could look up at these beautiful mountains without flinching.

Day Fifteen: *Sarajevo*

In the suburb of Butmir, at the house of the Kolar family, is a display headed 'Sarajevo Olympic City 1984, Surrounded City 1992–1995'. It's not absolutely accurate. The fact that Sarajevo survived the siege at all was because it was never quite surrounded. There was one way in and out, and it was through the Kolar house.

In June 1992 the UN struck an agreement with the Bosnian Serb leader Ratko Mladic to keep Sarajevo airport open for humanitarian aid. This in theory offered a break in the chain of encirclement, except that the UN had also agreed with Mladic that no Bosnians should be allowed in the airport perimeter. After some 800 people had died trying to get across, the poorly armed Bosnian army defending the city turned in desperation to a tunnel beneath the airport.

It was cramped, the average width and height throughout its 880-yard length being no more than four and a half feet. It was frequently under water and twice flooded to the ceiling, but it enabled supplies of food, medicine, ammunition and human reinforcements to be moved in and out. A small railway was constructed and eventually telephone cables and a rudimentary oil pipeline were also fed through. It's estimated that this tiny artery beneath the airport saved 300,000 lives.

The house, still bearing the scars of bombardment, is now open as a museum, presided over by Bajro and Edis Kolar. Edis can't be far off thirty but like others I've met in Sarajevo he has the world-weary air of a much older man. His lightly tinted spectacles, soft voice and matter-of-fact delivery give him the abstracted air of a put-upon teacher, but during the war, when in his teens, he was part of a crack military unit whose job it was to select and take out Serbian artillery posts.

'I was a war veteran at the age of twenty-one.' He laughs ruefully.

He remembers walk-ins of over fourteen hours, with full equipment and often in darkness.

'I saw many things that most people will never see in their whole life.'

At the back of the Kolar house is a scene of rural serenity. Rows of beans, spring onions and potatoes, groves of walnut trees and apple orchards grow where the tunnel used to run. Beyond them, almost up against the perimeter fence, I can see a woman in a headscarf, tilling the soil by hand whilst behind her a red airport radar scanner circles the skies. She doesn't look up as one of the only two flights of the morning roars up and away from Sarajevo.

Only about 100 feet of tunnel remains, but small parties of tourists are constantly calling. There are hardly any visitors from Bosnia.

'They don't want to remember,' says Edis. 'But they always will.'

Anywhere with a Hapsburg and Ottoman pedigree will have its fair share of cafés but in central Sarajevo you are never more than 20 yards away from a cup of coffee. Nor do you have to go far to find delightful buildings, like the restful, soothing, wood-scented, sensitively restored Serbian Orthodox church in Mula Mustafa Bašeskija. Despite being Serbian it was the first church to be shelled, and once the Serbs retreated it was the first to be rebuilt. In the Turkish quarter there are stone-built minarets and domes which remind me how graceful Islamic architecture can be. In narrow Sarači Street near the old Turkish market eight elegant stone chimneys with conical lead coverings rise above an old library.

Just outside the Old Town the streets open onto a wide esplanade, built by the Austrians and lining either side of the Miljacka River. The flow moves sluggishly through, its thin stream dribbling over a series of low weirs, in each of which a bobbing jetsam of plastic bottles and beer cans collects, turning and tumbling ceaselessly.

Beside a bridge above this modest stream is, both literally and figuratively, one of the great turning points of history. On an easily missed stone plaque set low in an anonymous wall are the words (in

Bosnian and English) 'From this place on 28th June 1914 Gavrilo Princip assassinated the heir to the Austro-Hungarian throne Franz Ferdinand and his wife Sofia.' Had Franz Ferdinand's coach not stopped here that day and presented Princip with a sitting target, because of the coachman's confusion as to whether to turn into the town or continue along the embankment, the First World War might never have begun. Well, might never have begun just here.

We eat tonight with Ademir, his wife Selma and friends at a traditional restaurant hung with antiques which overlooks the city. An enormous spread of Bosnian goodies including a light and subtle ravioli with yoghurt, intensely tasty little lamb and beef sausages called *ćevapi*, pitta bread and fresh onions, potato pie, spinach pie and spit-roasted lamb. We talk of many things and there is much laughter. Bosnians pride themselves on their sense of humour. For many, jokes were an essential way of dealing with the pain of war.

Unlike the Croatians.

'In Zagreb', I'm assured, 'they don't like to laugh.'

Then two guitarists and an eighty-one-year-old accordionist serenade us, which would be a bit of an intrusion were it not for the accompanying voice of a dark-haired forty-year-old called Almira, who sings in what they call *sevdalinka* style, gliding softly into their rhythms, her voice poised delicately on the edge of sadness and elation.

It's beautiful and haunting. I ask her if she trained as a singer. 'No, I trained as an accountant.'

Recovering from this blow to my romantic imagination I ask Almira if she can describe the Bosnian character. Her dark eyes narrow and she replies without a pause. 'We are stubborn, passionate, impulsive. That's always our problem. But we enjoy our life.'

Whatever has happened here before, I feel very much at ease in Sarajevo.

Day Sixteen: *Sarajevo*

'We have found four anti-tank mines and one anti-personnel just in the bush area over there, so it's a live minefield. Stay within the marked area. Do not go through the tapes. Keep your helmet on at all times.'

We're less than a mile to the west of Vrelo Bosne, one of Sarajevo's most popular picnic spots, where tables are set beneath overhanging willow trees and horse-drawn carriages can be hired by the hour.

There are no horse-drawn carriages where we are. There are pick-up trucks and four-wheel drives, an ambulance, men with helmets and visors and sniffer dogs. The woods and meadows are ringed with red and white police tape and marked with skull and crossbone signs. This is poisoned country, one of Bosnia's many minefields. If you picnic here you could be killed.

'If something happens, do not run, just stay put. There is medical support in place. If something happens they will help you out of the minefield still alive.'

With a disarming grin, Damir, a strong, stocky ex-soldier who's in charge of this clearance operation, brings our briefing to an end, jabs his head towards the fields and beckons us to follow. I'm wearing a flak jacket and helmet, but somehow that just makes me feel more vulnerable, as if something really could go wrong out there. All of us have had to sign disclaimer forms and fill in our blood groups.

We set off along an avenue of blue and white plastic tape. On one side, up the slope, the field has been shaved almost down to the bare earth; on the other side, the uncut grass of the valley floor is threaded with a profusion of blue, red and yellow wild flowers – buttercups, gentian, daisies.

Further up the hill, and half-hidden in the undergrowth, are the shells of good-sized suburban houses destroyed in the war, with stalks of cow parsley nodding through the holes where the windows used to be.

Damir tells me that there are limited funds available for mine-clearance and open countryside, however beautiful, comes way down the list of priorities. His work is paid for by the Norwegian government, and there are many other international donors they depend on.

'But the Balkans is off the TV now. There is Iraq and Darfur and…well, Bosnia is not such a big thing any more.'

I ask Damir about the sort of mines he has to deal with. The Prom-1, 'the bounding one', he says, is particularly nasty.

It turns out to be a device, activated by either tripwires or foot pressure, which, on detonation, jumps out of the ground, and a second charge explodes in the air.

'It's the most dangerous mine you can find in the field, and both my colleagues got killed by that type.'

'You've lost two colleagues?'

He nods. 'Just a moment's lapse in concentration.'

I flinch at the sound of a distant roar as we round the side of the hill. It comes from an adjacent patch to the one we're working on. A remote-controlled vehicle with flailing chains in front of it is doing the primary clearance, ripping out saplings and bushes to prepare the ground for the second stage, the 'gardening work', as Damir calls it. This involves meticulous scrutiny, using metal detectors first then painstakingly slow hands-and-knees examination to search for tell-tale signs like tripwires or antennae. 'And all the landmines are green. Makes things really difficult.'

Only after this work is done are the dogs brought in. They can detect explosive which might have been missed deep beneath the surface (my mind can't help going back to truffle-hunting in Istria).

We watch the dogs work, leading their handlers slowly up the hill alongside a strip of marker tape. The best dogs for mine detection, says Damir, are Belgian Shepherds, though some use German Shepherds or Labradors. Fortunately the stretch is clear, but to show us how the dogs react Damir plants a tiny amount of TNT a few inches down. When the dog encounters it, she actually points down at it with her nose, then sits back on her haunches, gazing proudly up at the handler who marks the spot.

Damir tells me that most of the de-mining teams are made up of ex-military. In many cases those doing clearing are the ones who planted the mines in the first place.

He defends them. Mine-laying was a military tactic, used in war to defend positions and kill enemy infantry who might otherwise kill you. He fought for the Bosnian government army in the war and laid mines himself.

'And at that time you do not think about consequences for civilians. At that time you think about your own life and how to protect yourself. During the conflict we did not think what would happen in Bosnia afterwards.'

Now they're paying a big price. Some of the devices, especially the Yugoslav-made 'bounding' mines are particularly well made and won't deteriorate.

'They don't get old, they just sit and wait.'

We walk back through some of the most beautiful unspoilt natural meadowland I've seen anywhere in Europe. In England this would be a nature reserve. In Bosnia it's a lethal problem.

Day Seventeen: *Sarajevo to Dubrovnik*

I linger at the window of my hotel room one last time, trying to collect together my memories of this extraordinary place. More than in any other city I find it hard to take in Sarajevo without my imagination running the past and present in parallel. I can't look at the road without seeing people racing for dear life across it, I can't look to the broad green mountain slopes without seeing lines of gun barrels pointing back at me. I can't see the shell of the Parliament building opposite without thinking I can hear the whizz and thump of rockets and mortars.

I'm shocked at how the city suffered only a dozen years ago and inspired by how they've come out of it. I also know now that most Sarajevans I've talked to would feel uncomfortable at any suggestion of saintly suffering. They feel they shouldn't have got into the mess they did but they also feel irritated by the crocodile tears of foreigners whose governments let one of Europe's great cities be slowly strangled. Life goes on, is about all one can say as we pack our vehicles up, dodging the stream of taxis and minibuses delivering new guests. Life goes on. Cities heal quickly.

It's very different in the countryside. As the road winds south-east, the aftermath of war is much less easy to disguise. Blasted and blackened shells of buildings can be glimpsed between the trees.

A half-hour outside Sarajevo, signs by the roadside remind us of new enmities. Written now in Cyrillic as well as Roman script, they advise us that we are entering the Republika Srpska, a self-governing entity within the Republic of Bosnia & Herzegovina, which represents the country's 1.36 million Serbs (along with some two million Muslims and 750,000 Croats).

The comparative harmony that's been restored in Sarajevo seems markedly absent here. This is a hardline heartland. Ratko Mladic, leader of the army that squeezed the life out of Sarajevo for three years and hero of the Bosnian Serbs, is from this pretty valley. Local police, in ill-fitting uniforms, with caps pushed back on their heads, wave us down and check our driver's licence. Then, just as I'm beginning to simplify all this into a clear case of heroes and villains, we meet up with a Serbian group of actors and entertainers who believe so strongly in a multi-ethnic Bosnia that they spend their time touring schools in confrontational areas like this.

They call themselves Genesis and they come from Banja Luka, the capital of Republika Srpska, 200 miles away to the north-west. Diana, the driving force behind the group, is a big, dynamic girl with spiky blond hair and tightly stretched pink pants. We follow her to a school in Trnovo (pronounced Turnovo) where today, helped and encouraged by UNICEF, the United Nations Children's Fund, she and her team are to present their 45-minute puppet show, teaching the children co-existence, tolerance and how not to be killed by landmines.

The school is in pretty bad shape. It's barely recovered from being hit by NATO planes, which after three years' vacillation finally began their attack on Serb positions in 1995. It was built for 600 children, but now only 120 attend. Many young families couldn't wait for the firing to stop before moving away from Trnovo, leaving behind a ghost town whose population is predominantly over sixty-five.

For Diana and Genesis this is the sort of challenge they relish. They've bussed in thirty Bosniak children from a nearby school to swell the audience and to mix the communities. They all get on fine, the way children do.

And the show is terrific. It takes the form of a trial and the judge asks the children to be the jury. Up pops a landmine, a green puppet with mad-staring eyeballs, sharp teeth and a long yellow neck. This is followed by a grenade, which arrives with a very realistic whizz and explosion. A fat friendly Bumble Bee is especially popular with the children. He tells them that landmines can be moved by water, relevant in a country that has so many rivers and streams. Cat has brought Mouse before the court because he has a gun in his house. The children are encouraged to tell Mouse all the things that are wrong with playing with a pistol.

It's all done with noise and energy, and for a grim subject, a great deal of humour. The children sit entranced.

The good news from Diana is that the rate of accidents from mines is falling each year. In 2005 there were nineteen victims throughout BiH, so far in 2006 eight people have been killed and four seriously wounded. The bad news is she reckons it will be seventy years before they can safely till every field and pick herbs in every forest again.

As we drive south and east we enter the increasingly wild and desolate landscape of the Trebišnjica valley. The rain pours down from a big, black threatening sky and the settlements become increasingly few and far between. At a roadside restaurant surrounded by low gnarled pine scrub our arrival stirs a big dog, as black as the sky, to a fury of barking and clanging as it twists and turns in its chains.

The weather and the scenery become even more apocalyptic as the mountains rise around us and the cloud and rain thicken. It's night by the time we reach the Republika Srpska border and a few hundred yards further on the red chequer flag announces our return to Croatia.

Croatia

Day Nineteen: *Dubrovnik*

As THE crow flies, Sarajevo and Dubrovnik are less than 90 miles apart, but their outward and visible appearances could hardly be more different. In Sarajevo the scars of war are plain to see, whereas her southern neighbour gleams and glitters as if freshly polished. Yet one of the first things that confronts you as you walk through Ploče Gate into the immaculate Old Town is a large map showing that even 'the jewel of the Adriatic' was not spared the violence that convulsed the Balkans.

Beneath the heading 'City Map of Damages Caused by the Aggression on Dubrovnik by the Yugoslav Army – Serbs and Montenegrins – 1991–1992' is a pattern of coloured dots and triangles analysing the bombardment in minute detail. 'Roofs damaged by direct impact', 'Houses burned', 'Roofs damaged by shrapnels' and even 'Direct impact on pavement'. You would probably need a map the size of a football pitch to record the damage sustained by Sarajevo, but the fact remains that, in the eyes of the West, the two great outrages of the war were the destruction of the bridge at Mostar and the shelling of Dubrovnik.

Dubrovnik, or Ragusa as it was known until 1918, was always a magnet for visitors. The stout sixteenth-century walls were designed by Italian architects to protect merchants and traders and to rival the power and glory of Venice, their aggressive competitor to the north. So when the mortar shells, specifically targeting the historic Old Town, began falling in November 1991, it was not only an affront to her dignity, it was a major threat to her livelihood.

Branka Franicevic, now a tour guide, was in her thirties when it all happened and we talk together outside a *kavana* (café) in the *Stradun*, the long, paved street that runs the length of the Old City.

She remembers the morning of the very first hit. 'I believed that nobody normal, at the end of the twentieth century, could shell a town like Dubrovnik,' she recalls. 'Then I heard a very strange sound. I thought maybe I had turned in my dream, but my mother came and forced me to go to the cellar of the house, and the first thing that happened was my neighbour who came with a glass of cognac and a cigarette.'

From then on it was not the shells falling that was the worst thing, but the cutting of the water and electricity supplies. 'For five months we were permitted only five litres of water per family per day.' Six centuries after they were built the great stone fortresses guarding the city became sanctuaries once again.

'In the Revelin fortress at the east gate, 2,000 people moved in and spent nine months with only one toilet. And, interesting, no diseases, nothing like that.'

One thing of which there was no shortage was *rakija*, a potent herb brandy.

'It added to the spirits of the locals,' recalls Branka, with a trace of an apologetic smile. They had big meals, sang and danced a lot, enjoyed discussing what they might do if the Serbs tried to enter the city – boiling olive oil was considered – and generally had such a good time that when the war ended with the tourist business in terminal decline, Branka felt a perverse relief.

'I felt I had been given my city back.'

Frightening though it must have been to have 2,000 shells lobbed, with fiendish arbitrariness, into such a confined area, nothing here came close to the suffering inflicted on Sarajevo. Within months of the siege being lifted, seventy per cent of the roofs were relaid, the stonework was patched up and Dubrovnik was back in business.

As if to illustrate the point, a tidal wave of tourists pours through the Pile Gate, the western entrance to the Old Town, and within minutes the *Stradun* is filled with wall-to-wall sightseers.

Branka and many other locals feel that it is the cruise ships that are overwhelming the Old Town. From one vessel alone, up to 2,500 visitors can spill into the narrow streets, spending, as she points out, an average of only 13 euros each, whereas those staying in hotels and pensions on land spend over 100 each. There is pressure from many who love the Old City to limit the size of the ships in order to preserve its character. This may be one of the very few instances of a city legislating against its own appeal, but Dubrovnik/Ragusa has an honourable and progressive tradition of civic pride. The writer Dervla Murphy notes that the city introduced Europe's first rubbish collection, a drinking water system with fines for pollution, abolished torture in the seventeenth century, the slave trade in the fifteenth century and never allowed the Inquisition within its walls. They have had pedestrianisation for hundreds of years. Rationing tourists shouldn't be beyond this redoubtable city.

A torrential downpour clears the streets more effectively than any legislation, leaving the *Stradun*'s shiny smooth paving – limestone from the island of Korčula, a dozen miles away to the north-west – glistening in fresh sunshine.

Later I swim in a cool Adriatic with smells of grilling fish wafting out from the shore and a hazy lemon sunset replacing the baleful clouds of yesterday.

Day Twenty: *Dubrovnik*

'Those who seek Paradise on earth should come to Dubrovnik', wrote George Bernard Shaw, in one of his comparatively rare tourist endorsements. I think of this today as, on my way to the hotel breakfast room, I hear a plaintive Yorkshire voice drifting up from the back stairs.

'I'm lost.'

Another, equally Yorkshire voice, only male this time, shouts down.

'Which floor are you after, love?'

'Minus One.'

Nowhere is far from anywhere else in the old walled city and, only a few yards away from cruiseliner land, complete peace and tranquillity can be enjoyed in the cloister of the Franciscan priory, where we gather to listen to a Bosnian-born lute player called Edin, so expert at his craft that he has just come from working with Sting on a recording of the work of the English lutenist and contemporary of Shakespeare, John Dowland.

The courtyard is intimate and attractive, criss-crossed with aromatic box hedge, oleander, bougainvillaea and palm and fruit trees. The arches of the cloister are simple and elegant, of pale stone in slender double columns, but it's the elaborate, well-restored capitals that catch the eye, including one which they say depicts the architect himself, Mihoje Brajkov, his jaw swollen with the toothache he was suffering at the time. The man clearly had a sense of humour as it is grotesque creatures, human caricatures and wild beasties that dominate rather than angels and disciples. He died in 1348, of the plague they called the Black Death, which raged through Europe, killing one-third of the population.

Edin could be a latter-day Brajkov. He's extraordinarily skilful and has a deadpan humour. His big face is dominated by wide, eloquent eyes and he's constantly worrying away at an undisciplined fringe of floppy black hair.

'I have to have it cut,' he says apologetically. 'I look like a Bosnian bus driver.'

I learn from him that the lute was first mentioned in the seventh century, in Syria, where the instrument was called *al oud*, which came to Europe through Spain, became *la oud* and eventually 'lute'. The one he's playing today has fourteen strings and dates from 1600. Wanting to avoid any Golden Hits syndrome, Edin tests himself with an adaptation of Bach's *Toccata and Fugue*, originally written for the organ.

He frowns as he adjusts his fingers.

'It's difficult. They have two hands and two feet.'

The result is lovely and technically dazzling, and even when one of the strings snaps it seems to snap in time with the music.

'Is there anything you can play without the string?'

Edin frowns, nods and goes into a perfect rendition of 'Over the Rainbow'.

His star is in the ascendant now as people discover an instrument whose popularity seemed to have been on the wane since the days of Mozart.

'I play in concert halls, but there is no place like here, where I can play outside. In Dubrovnik you can do anything. In Venice police is everywhere, everything is controlled. Here you can do anything you want.'

To mark our last night in Dubrovnik we end up at a jazz bar down by the old port. The band is augmented every now and then by a Gérard Depardieu lookalike who rolls out of the bar behind them, launches into thunderous versions of the jazz classics and disappears back in for a top-up.

I'm told I'll get to know him well over the next couple of days. He's the captain of our boat to Albania.

Day Twenty-one: *Dubrovnik to Durrës*

Our boat may be called *Adriatic Paradise* but Captain Neven (I never find out his surname) admits that there are problems. One is that he's never been to Albania before.

'Perhaps only fifty Croatians ever have gone there.'

The other is that he doesn't want to go and can't really understand why anyone else would.

Having established that, he's friendly enough and points out various interesting features along the way. As we leave the harbour we pass an elegant suspension bridge supported by a fan of grey steel cables. There had, apparently, been much political controversy over the naming of the bridge. The left wanted to call it the Dubrovnik Bridge, the right wanted to call it, after their nationalist President, the Franjo Tudjman Bridge. After long and bitter argument a compromise was reached and it is now called the Dubrovnik Bridge of Franjo Tudjman. Captain Neven, wild of hair and round of stomach, chuckles loudly as he tells me this.

We have a fine last view of the ramparts of old Dubrovnik on one side and on the other the offshore island of Lokrum. The Hapsburg Archduke Maximilian decided to turn the monastery on the island into a summer residence for himself and his wife. The locals knew that no good would come of this and they were right. Maximilian later accepted the title of Emperor of Mexico, where he was shot by firing squad in 1867. His wife went mad. Crown Prince Rudolf ignored local superstition and chose the island for his honeymoon. A few years later he committed suicide after shooting dead his mistress.

But it does have a nudist beach.

The crew of the *Adriatic Paradise* is an odd bunch, consisting of two slightly surly men in their late thirties, and a mysterious and glamorous woman in a low-cut dress, high heels and a black straw hat who we assume is the waitress/hostess we were promised.

'She is Nada,' says the captain, which seems a bit hard, until we realise that this is her name.

At lunchtime she fixes some beers, but totally ignores us after that and spends the afternoon out on deck taking more and more clothes off until she's wearing only her black straw hat. None of us dares ask her for a cup of coffee.

Captain Neven sits behind the wheel, usually on his mobile phone. He's from Zagreb, the Croatian capital, and spends the summer running a boat charter company with his brother and the winter singing in musicals and light opera. Last year he was Judas in the Zagreb production of *Jesus Christ Superstar*, which had a fifteen-day run. This is apparently quite good for a foreign musical sung in Croatian. In the former Yugoslavia there were much better prospects for shows like this, he says, when five countries shared a language and there was five times the potential audience.

In the afternoon a rubber dinghy, which doubles as the ship's lifeboat, is commandeered for Nigel to take some shots of the *Adriatic Paradise* in full sail. Unfortunately the dinghy is half-full of stagnant seawater, which, as it's dragged over the side, spills through an open porthole and onto a suitcase of fresh, clean clothes, which an hour later I discover are mine.

Meanwhile the task of raising the sails proves impossible and the shot is abandoned.

The captain glowers at the crew and takes it out on Albania.

'Albania is for us like some kind of black hole,' he scowls. 'There is no need to go there and for them I think the same.'

I try to tell him it's the secrecy and isolation that attract me to the country, but he isn't impressed by such romantic nonsense.

It's clear, even at this late stage, that the captain will try anything to avoid going to Albania. He suggests at one point that we should put into Montenegro to see their independence celebrations. (On Thursday last week they voted in a referendum to secede from Serbia, making them Europe's newest country, despite a population little bigger than that of Sheffield.) There should be a good party, he says, the Montenegrins being famously lazy.

He recovers his natural ebullience over a glass or two and as the sun quietly sets, cooks us a superb mussel risotto with Turkish spices – 'Croatians don't like to use spices' – and becomes very jolly and relaxed.

Later I lie down below deck in my hot little cabin with both ports open and the only sound I can hear above the hammer-blow thudding of the engine is the captain, singing at the top of his voice.

Day Twenty-two: *Dubrovnik to Durrës*

When I wake up the dawn has barely broken. The coastline, indistinct in detail at this early hour, is lower and gentler than the tall grey cliffs of Croatia.

There's nothing Homeric about the *Adriatic Paradise* this morning. Nada and the other two crew members are nowhere to be seen. Captain Neven is strapped to the wheel, fast asleep, rolling gently to and fro with the swell. I look anxiously ahead and wonder whether to wake him up as we're heading straight for a small island.

Two hours later, we've made ourselves some breakfast and the captain is now awake, standing at the wheel and talking animatedly into his mobile while casting anxious looks at the coast ahead.

The city of Durrës, Albania's chief port, slides into view to the south-east, between green hills covered with vines, golden-flowered broom and communications masts. Missing are the red-roofed whitewashed houses which helped make the towns and villages of the Croatian coast look attractive, but Durrës looks busy, with big modern blocks and builders' cranes dominating the skyline.

Captain Neven gazes out at it.

'All new. None of this building here in communistic times. All new. Italian money.'

He shakes his head. He remains resolutely unimpressed. 'In Croatia, nobody would let them to build such buildings. Not on the coast.'

But not totally pessimistic.

'I think they have good food, a bit like Turkey. Albania is eighty per cent Muslim country. We all have this five hundred years' influence of Turkey. In food and in mentality. In blood as well.'

'More so here than in Croatia?'

He nods and peers towards the shore.

'More here, yes.'

The radio crackles insistently. Someone is anxious to get in touch with us. Captain Neven ignores them. Three steep-prowed fishing boats cut across our bows heading out to sea.

The captain prevaricates until it's clear that the voices on the radio are ordering us to come into port and identify ourselves. It occurs to me as he reluctantly swings the wheel that, given his fatalistic suspicion of all things Albanian, Captain Neven thinks that once in he may never get out again.

We pull in past the sea wall to a compact, well-kept, not overcrowded port. There are two big ferry boats, in from Italy, only 70 miles away on the other side of the Strait of Otranto. Moored up against the long harbour wall are half a dozen battle-grey patrol vessels, apparently operated by the Italians, Albania's near-neighbours, and, since the demise of the isolationist dictator Enver Hoxha in 1985, once again their main trading partners.

At the dockside we're met by smartly dressed port officials who give our captain a dressing-down, in English, for not flying the Albanian national flag when in her waters. The captain, it transpires, doesn't have an Albanian national flag, but one is found for him.

We haven't been here long when a Mercedes pulls up beside the boat, and two thin men with short dark hair, swarthy complexions and unsmiling faces get out.

'We are press,' they announce with a certain flourish, fingering accreditation tags the size of breastplates. 'What do you think of our country?'

We reply that as none of us has yet set foot in it, it's hard to say.

They rapidly lose interest and are gone as swiftly as they arrived.

The next voice I hear in Albania has a broad Scots accent. It belongs to a short, sunburnt, hairy-legged man who, with a group of colleagues, is driving aid trucks from the Hebrides to Kosovo. He warns us that the roads are dire.

Eventually, all papers checked, we're allowed onto Albanian soil. Within minutes Captain Neven has turned around and is heading for dear life back to Croatia, the double-headed black eagle of Albania flapping from the rigging as he picks up the breeze.

Albania

Day Twenty-three: *Durrës*

THUNDERCLAPS AND the sound of rain lashing at the window punctuate an unsettled sleep.

The dawn view from the Hotel Adriatik is of a storm-ravaged sky, dark clouds massing on the western horizon, a pale sun fighting for survival.

The beach is lined with row after row of empty deckchairs.

Last night's meal here was pretty good, but breakfast is peculiarly depressing. Tinned fruit, slightly out-of-date butter and meagre strips of white bread in a dauntingly tall columned dining room with painted panels of Albanians in folk costume.

Among the few other guests are a couple, he Namibian, she Swedish, with a small child called Felipe. He's almost the same age as our first grandchild, Archie, born two months before we set out. Alert and quite devastating when he smiles, Felipe makes me suddenly and quite poignantly homesick.

Go for a walk along the shore. Unlike the rocky coast of Croatia, Durrës has a long and sandy beach, but it's hardly golden and already men are out working to clear the scum of marine matter swept in by last night's storm. Judging by the ranks of freshly built hotels and apartments Albanian tourism must be flourishing. Neon flashing signs reading 'Fast Food!' are everywhere. A lot of Kosovans come here for their holidays, I'm told.

At intervals along the beach is a chain of circular concrete bunkers ranging from 4 or 5 feet to 20 feet in height. Some lie half-collapsed in the breaking waves, others are sound enough to have been painted bright colours and turned into makeshift bars. There are 400,000 of these dotted all over Albania, which works out at one for every eight members of the population.

They are the legacy of Enver Hoxha (pronounced 'Hodger'), who led Albania into hardline Stalinist communism after the Second World War. When Stalin was discredited and the Soviet Union began to split with China over the future of communism, Hoxha took China's side, identifying with Chairman Mao's Cultural Revolution and declaring tiny Albania the first atheist state in Europe.

Paranoid about invasion, he not only ordered the construction of the bunkers, but made it illegal for Albanians to own maps of the country, or to listen to the BBC World Service, a crime punishable by eight years in jail.

This had a cryogenic effect on Albania. Past and future didn't exist, and for forty years or so it was left in self-imposed isolation.

One effect of the rehabilitation of Albania since the hardliners left is that its history has been rediscovered, and found to be long and rich. A city called Epidamnus was founded here seven centuries before Christ. Changing its name to Dyrrachium, and later Durrës, it became one of the main supply ports for the Romans' eastern empire, and, interestingly, a hotbed of Venus worship.

There's little evidence of any hotbeds but Durrës does have the remains of Roman baths and an amphitheatre, which is the largest of its kind in the Balkans. It's not far up the hill from the harbour and though one side has had houses grafted onto it, enough is preserved to help the imagination fill the terraces with a 15,000 full house baying for blood. The tunnel from which the gladiators emerged is still there and my guidebook tells me that during excavation they unearthed forty skeletons with their necks broken.

Today the area around the floor of the amphitheatre is green and swampy and all that emerges from the tunnel is the sound of hundreds of frogs croaking.

Outside the amphitheatre is another layer of history, a city wall 6 feet thick and 25 feet high, built of brick and rubble with antique capitals embedded in it. It dates from roughly 1,500 years ago, when the Roman empire had split and this area was ruled from Constantinople. From this time onwards Albania was effectively a part of Eastern Europe and remains even now one of those countries least influenced by Western thought and ideas.

Then I met Ardi Pilaj. With his constantly demanding mobile, white trainers with red laces, black velvet jacket, ear studs, and Germany 2006 rubber wristband, he's no different from any young man on the streets of the West, and his attitudes are fresh and well informed, as befits a journalist working for, among others, the BBC.

He's accompanying us on the train to Tirana, and as we've time to spare we go for a coffee near the station. An apologetic waiter is about to serve us when the electrical supply cuts out. He suggests somewhere across the square but just as we get there their supply goes off as well. Ardi says the problem is not the availability of electricity, it's down to a distribution system that hasn't changed since Hoxha's time. Albania has not, like some, made a smooth transition from the days of communism. In 1996 their economy was shattered by the simultaneous collapse of a number of pyramid-selling schemes followed by near-anarchy in the streets.

A small group of children follows us from the café to the station, rubbing their stomachs and putting hands up to their mouths. They can't be more than ten or eleven, but they have the creased, prematurely aged faces of fifty-year-olds. Inside the station itself, a bare, functional slab of a place, people move slowly, dully. A world at half-speed.

The sparrows, darting and wheeling above our heads, are the only creatures with any energy.

A Czech-built diesel locomotive brings in the train from Tirana and we climb aboard. Though most of the windows are cracked or shattered – children with stones, says Ardi – a team of lady sweepers moves methodically through, brushing up every speck of dust.

Tirana is no more than 25 miles from Durrës and the journey takes a little over an hour. The flat plain rises to low hills crowned with billboards on which the names of Albania's new friends are writ large. 'Vodafone', 'Heineken', 'DHL'.

Ardi talks about his country. He's weary about its image abroad as a haven for criminals, sex-traffickers and the like.

'You haven't seen many criminals, have you?'

I smile and shake my head.

Ardi spreads his arms. 'I would feel safer in Tirana walking at night, than in Amsterdam or Paris or London, you know.'

For him the bigger problem is not criminal gangs but the exodus of skilled Albanians, the brain drain that has seen so many intellectuals and qualified people leaving to work abroad, in Greece, Italy and the United States. Until they come back Albania will always lag behind the rest of Europe.

We reach the outskirts of the capital. Homes are built right up against the line, and the train horn is in constant use. The old-fashioned houses, packed tight together with small gardens smothered in vines, could be in the countryside. Men play chess reclining on a grassy verge inches from the train.

In the Stygian gloom of Tirana Central the few passengers dismount. I watch an elderly man in a black suit shuffle slowly across the track to relieve himself by a fence, whilst his wife, equally smartly dressed and holding an umbrella, stands on the railway line and waits for him.

With its pervasive smell of rotting rubbish, and complete absence of any facilities whatsoever, Tirana Central is not a place to linger. Even the station approach is a gentle upward slope of mud, which we pick our way through with some care only to find ourselves, quite abruptly, in the middle of big city noise, light and bustle.

We walk the length of Zog One Boulevard, named after the king who led Albania into the Second World War, on Hitler's side, but spent most of it in a private suite at the Ritz in London. By the time we've reached the wide and rather grand space of Skanderbeg Square, in which every other car is a Mercedes, memories of Albania's dark, neglected railway are beginning to blur.

Day Twenty-four: *Tirana*

Skanderbeg (real name Gjergj Kastriot) is Albania's national
hero. He won fame for rallying his country's resistance against
the Ottoman Turks in the fifteenth century and in the square
that bears his name he is commemorated by a handsomely fierce
equestrian statue set atop a chunky stone plinth. The fact that all
his courage and tenacity was ultimately wasted is gently rubbed in
by the building next door to him, the small but perfectly formed
mosque of Et'hem Bey, one of the Ottoman Turks who, after the
death of Skanderbeg, ruled here for 434 years, until Albania was
finally granted independence in 1913.

The rest of the square is a mixture of communist and fascist,
from the wide triumphal boulevards built by Mussolini's architects
in the 1930s, to the National Museum with a fine Social Realist
mural above the entrance and the mighty columned Palace of
Culture, currently home to a touring version of *Madam Butterfly*
by Opera Macedonia.

Tirana appears much less dysfunctional than I'd expected.
There are cafés where a cup of good espresso can set you back a
lek or two and a street named after Lord Byron. (He spent time
in Albania in the early 1800s meeting, among others, Ali Pasha,
according to Robert Carver's book *The Accursed Mountains* 'an
enthusiastic lifelong pederast and paedophile' who boasted of
personally killing 30,000 people. Byron found him very charming,
with a beautiful singing voice.)

What impresses me most is the way in which the post-war
concrete housing blocks have been quite strikingly painted, not
just in one colour but with a real artistic touch, mosaics of primary
colours, chequerboards, diamonds, stripes and triangles picked
out in washes of red, yellow and green. Little bays have been built
onto the façades to break down the monotony of the outline.

The man most responsible for this grooming of Tirana is the
socialist mayor, Edi (pronounced 'Eddie') Rama. Recognising that
he can't afford to demolish all the dull and soulless housing of
the communist era, he came up with a policy he has called art in
building. In consultation with the occupants he has put a team of
artists to work on decorating whole neighbourhoods.

In 2004 Rama was voted World Mayor of the Year.

A famously busy man, and an artist himself, he's agreed to meet me at his office, in one of the ochre and claret-painted Italianate terraces overlooking the southern end of Skanderbeg Square. We walk down corridors that are anything but institutional, painted with carefully chosen rich, dark colours and lined with quirky art.

Rama is in his forties I should think, grave, taciturn and very tall with a shaved head. He wears baggy black trousers and a big black collarless shirt with a fine red stripe. He looks like a man of the night. His eyes are dark and hooded and this world of crepuscular colours creates an ambience that is more Dracula's bedroom than council chamber.

His office is equally idiosyncratic. Irregular, almost diamond-shaped, it's painted a restful maroon with dark-red wood panelling. Scrolled out across the wall behind the long desk is a huge computerised enlargement of a photo of the city seventy years ago.

I take some comfort from a quick glance at his desk. A bowl of colouring pens sits next to a pile of business papers and his screensaver is a picture of himself and his young daughter.

As soon as we start talking about Tirana and his plans for the city he becomes a changed man, from monosyllabic to polysyllabic.

'It was a different city when I came in. It was basically without hope any more. After communism we passed from nightmarish collectivism to wild individualism, which was not democracy, it was more an anarchy. People built everywhere. Public space disappeared, physically and mentally.'

His administration began by demolishing 2,000 speculative buildings.

I ask him about the bowl of pens.

He gives a smile, bleak but encouraging.

'This is my box of medicines. Just to escape mentally from boring meetings.' He reaches for some sheets of paper which are covered with meticulous doodles.

'The minutes of last week's meeting?' I ask.

He nods. 'Yes. The therapeutic diary, you know.'

Boring meetings seem to have been his inspiration. From the

colouring-in of these elaborate doodles came the idea for the painted buildings.

'Colours are part of our life and it's really a pity that cities are not reflecting this.' He gestures to the window.

'Tirana has a big potential...because we don't have a really strong tradition of architecture, we don't have buildings of which we should be really proud...so the only way to keep them updated with the contemporary world is to colour them. If every building would be painted, every corner would be painted, it'll be amazing you know.'

For him this is not just an aesthetic thing. He calls it 'politics with colours'. A way of supporting democratic change at street level. I've never understood why cities have to be so grey and I'm rather fired by his enthusiasm.

'This is a first, isn't it?'

'Many things are. We were first in Albania for blowing up all the churches and the mosques and becoming the only country in the world without any religious practice. It was a very bitter first. I hope this can be a sweet first.'

We walk out together into Youth Park, an area where a mass of concrete has been cleared and replaced with fountains and cafés. Just across the river is 'The Block', a square mile or so which was once reserved for the villas of the communist elite and off-limits to ordinary Albanians. Hoxha's rather interesting modernist house remains, part of it now, by a supreme irony, given over to an English-language school.

Edi remembers the Hoxha years.

'The whole country had maybe 200 cars...Private cars were not allowed, private life was totally controlled. Cafés didn't exist. We were isolated from West and East. It was like a concentration camp.'

He reaches out and shakes my hand.

'But, of course, freedom has also its own difficulties you know, so...'

He smiles, turns and with long, slow strides heads back through the trees towards his office. Two middle-aged women on a park bench rise in unison as he passes. An older man salutes him and they stop and talk. The charismatic Edi clearly has friends, but he also has powerful enemies, from the top of the national government downwards. His vision of Tirana as the world's first art city is a brave one, which would help put Albania back on the international stage and hasten the climb out of isolation and paranoia. But I fear that many of Edi's natural supporters are living abroad. He, more than anyone, needs to reverse the diaspora.

Tonight, just about ready for bed, when a cacophony of thumps, whooshes and screams splits the silence. Rush to the window expecting to see some gang shoot-out on the streets below. Instead I see a salvo of rockets and an arc of red, blue and silver starbursts rising high above the city. Where are they coming from? The gardens of the mayor's office. Where else?

Day Twenty-five: *Tirana to Krujë*

Today we get to see for ourselves the fabled pot-holes of Albania, for we're driving out of Tirana to the hill town of Krujë. After some mild rattling through the streets of Tirana, the really good vibrations begin about a mile from the hotel at a notorious interchange called the Blackbird Roundabout, so named after a brothel of the same name which used to stand on the site. It's an ambitious mess, more half-started than half-finished, caught in a deadlock between mayor and Prime Minister. Whilst they argue, the roundabout resembles a slowly moving car park. A section of motorway, unconnected to anything else, lies stranded in the middle of this chaos, like some ancient dolmen.

Once past this stretch of urban no-man's-land things improve. A narrow highway lined with an unfeasibly large number of furniture warehouses, petrol stations and good old-fashioned ads with cowboys pulling hard on Marlboros takes us out along the flat plain to the north-west of Tirana.

This neither country nor city road is a touch depressing, and not helped by the appearance of the word 'Shitet', on many of the buildings, though this, I'm later assured, means 'For Rent'.

Krujë is dominated by a terrific battlemented castle set on a rocky crag with a fine view across the plain and out over a hazy

Adriatic. In the same year as Henry V was inspiring English soldiers on the battlefield of Agincourt, the Turks swept into Albania and captured this mighty fortress. Enter national hero Skanderbeg (who had learnt his fighting from the Turks) to retake Krujë and hold it against not one but three Turkish sieges.

His success is the reason for all the bazaars, museums, guest houses, restaurants and lines of schoolchildren filling the cobbled streets and pathways. The defence of Krujë, though ultimately unsuccessful, is seen as the golden age of a country without a lot to celebrate. Krujë is a national shrine.

Illir Mati, my guide, is a cheerful, chatty, middle-aged Albanian, much given to smacking one hand with the palm of the other to reinforce his, many, opinions. His father was an admiral and he himself spent twenty years as a submarine engineer. When Albania was part of the Warsaw Pact they had twelve Soviet submarines but after Hoxha split with Russia this was reduced to four. Three of these were, as he put it, 'for show'. Only one was maintained, and that saw little action. Ordered to keep an eye on 'enemy activity', they patrolled the Otranto Channel and used their periscope to scan topless sunbathers on Italian beaches.

We walk up to the castle through a bazaar selling peasant furniture, wooden cradles, butter churns, cow bells, water jugs and Albanian flags and scarves. Vehicles aren't allowed up here so heavily laden donkeys push their way through. Illir pithily sums up Albania's transport revolution.

'From donkeys to Mercedes in twenty years. With nothing in between!'

Like everyone else I've asked, Illir seems unable to account for why, in a country of straitened circumstances, there should be so many Mercedes.

He shrugs, as though the answer's obvious. They're smuggled.

'People working very, very hard in the communist period, and all working for the State. Today, everyone work for himself. He don't believe in the work in Albania. Albania is a rich country, rich with oil, minerals like chrome, but what is main export now?'

'Tell me.'

'Prostitutation.'

He counts off on his fingers.

'All we have to export now is prostitutation, drugs, weapons.'

In the castle I fall into conversation with a rather serious boy from a school group. They see very few foreign tourists and are interested in trying out their English.

'This is a beautiful country,' he says. 'But the government...'

He puckers up his nose.

'You know...'

'What don't you like about the government?'

'Well,' he says, and points to a corner of the castle. 'You see the tower there?'

'Yes.'

'It smells.'

'Ah.'

'They should keep it clean.'

We both nod and I move the conversation onto the safer ground of the World Cup, which begins in Germany today.

'Next time Albania will be there I hope.'

He smiles politely, but I have a sense that the smelly tower worries him more.

In the afternoon Illir and I scramble up the mountain to a monastery of the Bektashi religion, one of the offshoots of the Sufi order of Islam. Brought from Turkey by *babas* (fathers) or dervishes, it was never an institutional, organised religion, relying instead on personal communication with God through mystical folk beliefs, often close to paganism.

We are accompanying a young pilgrim from the village below who is taking a sheep to be sacrificed by the *baba*. His mother had a dream in which members of the family working abroad appeared to her and the sacrifice is the best way to stave off any harm the dream may have intimated.

After a slow climb through scrub and scree and dramatic limestone overhangs we reach the complex of buildings on the top of the mountain and are led into the presence of the *baba*. He is dressed in a thin white robe with a long green jacket over it and a multicoloured band around his waist. On his head is a green fez-like cap. He's clearly a prodigious smoker, his white beard stained almost mahogany around the mouth.

He sits, looking vaguely impatient, on a bed of cushions in front of a carpet with a large stag pictured on it. On the walls are framed pictures of holy men, the largest of which depicts an illustrious convert to Bektashism, Pasha Tepelena, builder, statesman, friend of Lord Byron and one of the most enlightened of Albania's Ottoman rulers.

When we are all introduced and seated on our cushions an assistant, in clothes as drab as the *baba*'s are bright, brings a succession of offerings. First, a bowl of wrapped boiled sweets, then, after an appropriate period of appreciation, a bowl of wrapped chocolates (which look suspiciously as if they've been gathered from the world's hotel pillows), followed by glasses of thick peach juice, cigarettes and, finally, glasses of *raki*. The *raki* and the cigarettes seem to break up an awkward atmosphere, but what really cheers the *baba* up is when I make the awful gaffe of raising my left (unclean) hand to my heart during one of the toasts.

From here on we get on like a house on fire and he insists that I come down the steps with him to watch the sacrifice from close range. Try as I might I can't move further than 3 feet away, as the *baba*, surprisingly deftly, upends the sheep and swiftly draws the knife across its throat. Blood pumps out and the sheep writhes and shudders. With one of the last jerks of its back leg it catches the knife with which it's just been despatched, sending it spinning across the floor towards me. Then there is silence.

The pilgrim, immensely cheered by the sacrificial visit, invites us to have a drink and some food with him down in the village. He's one of four brothers of a handsome family whose business is coopering. Festivities take place beneath the cherry trees in a little garden outside a house his father has just bought. Bulbs dangle from exposed wires, tangles of pre-stressed rods poke out of the concrete and garlands of electric cabling hang down from the windows. An abundance of food and drink is brought round by the women and children whilst the brothers gather round to make music, the sheep-sacrificer on the mandolin, three others on clarinet, accordion and tambourine, and father on the fiddle, as they say. One of the granddaughters, in a fine white dress and an embroidered black waistcoat, dances a nimble variation on what could just as well have been a sword dance or a Highland reel or a sailor's hornpipe.

The light slowly fades, along with any Anglo-Albanian inhibitions. I can't think of a better way to spend the last night of my brief visit to this secretive country than up here in the hills in the back garden of someone I don't know, singing songs in a language I can't understand. Tonight, in our various ways, we're all celebrating. *Gezuar*!

Macedonia

Day Twenty-seven: *Ohrid*

THE PLODDING Balkan highway, the E852, that enters Macedonia from the Albanian frontier, was once the illustrious Via Egnatia, a hugely important trade route, carrying goods from Italy to Constantinople. It was laid down by the Romans to join their empire with another they'd just conquered, the empire of Alexander the Great. Or as he's remembered here in his homeland, Alexander III of Macedon.

Today there's nothing left of the Via Egnatia or the trade that once must have flowed along it. The E852 connects the poorest country in Europe with the poorest country of the former Yugoslavia. Yet there is something about this first view of Macedonia that has power and presence, that makes you feel that whatever has befallen the country is a temporary aberration. This is a corner of Europe where history is made, not merely suffered.

It's all to do with the charismatic presence of Lake Ohrid. Overlooked in the west by the steep frowning mountains of Albania and by broad forested slopes to the east, it demands respect. Measuring almost 20 miles long and 10 wide, it plunges to a depth just short of 1,000 feet.

There has been a lake here for at least three million years, making it one of the oldest in the world, comparable with Titicaca and Baikal. It's perhaps no surprise that there are believed to be 350 religious establishments around its shores.

Tonight its waters are dark and agitated, sending explosive walls of water bursting against the promenade. Clouds of spray fly over the 'You Are Here' tourist map which, a little sad and damp now, helpfully points out not just the local churches but also where to go for body piercing. On a plinth nearby the sculpted figures of the tenth-century saints Clement and Naum stare out at the troubled waters. They are credited with inventing the Slavic language and Clement, a disciple of Saint Cyril, is thought to have devised a new alphabet, called Cyrillic, which is still in use across Russia as well as here in Macedonia. It's a sign that we're moving away from Central European influences and into the Slav Orthodox countries and the Russian sphere of influence.

There are few people about and the only two who come over to talk to us turn out to be Serbians who complain that the Macedonians won't change their currency. We help out by exchanging euros for the Serbian dinars which they're almost inexpressibly grateful to get rid of.

We find a waterfront restaurant called Dalga in the cobbled Old Town which serves the famous Lake Ohrid trout, but in portions as big as the lake itself, and this after an abundant *ordever* (hors d'oeuvres) of red peppers, feta, Parmesan cheese, salami and Croatian prosciutto. The walls are covered with photographs of the patron with various high-profile visitors. Mostly in black and white and degraded by time and the weather, they look as if they're all out of FBI files.

Filled to the brim with food and good Macedonian wine, we run the gauntlet of crashing waves along the promenade, coat collars tucked up.

Day Twenty-eight: *Ohrid*

Slight feeling of déjà-vu this morning when I discover that our hotel is located on Quay Marshal Tito. The great man clearly had a thing about lakes for he had a palatial summer home here, to match the one at Bled in Slovenia, Ohrid and Bled virtually marking the eastern and western limits of his Yugoslavia.

For good measure, there's a formidable fortress overlooking the lake here too. Its sandy-brown walls girdle nearly 2 miles of hilltop. It was built by Samoil, a Bulgarian who, after his armies wrested his country away from Byzantine control, was crowned king of Macedonia with Ohrid as his capital and borders that stretched over most of the Balkans. It proved to be one of the world's least resilient empires, lasting a mere twenty years before the armies of Byzantium won their land back. After their defeat in battle, Samoil's army was systematically blinded on the orders of the Emperor Vasilius, leaving one eye for every hundred men, to enable them to find their way back home.

I meet up with Kaliopi Bukle, an Ohrid-born singing star of the former Yugoslavia now married to an elfin-slim, and much younger, actor called Vasil.

She's sensible and down-to-earth as big stars go, mid-thirties, attractive in a homely sort of way, but concerned enough about her looks to have a make-up artist in tow. When I ask her if there are things she misses about Yugoslavia, her brow furrows in concentration then clears almost instantly.

'Smells!'

She doesn't immediately elaborate so I'm left wondering if this is literally what she misses or some kind of metaphor.

'I'm missing the smell of the old time in Yugoslavia. When I think about the things I love in my life, everything has his smell.'

She laughs rather sweetly and apologises for her English. (Why should she? I know only one word of Macedonian: *zdravo*, hello.) When she goes on she's thankfully off the smells and onto more pragmatic ground.

'It was a different thing singing for twenty million people then, and two million people today.'

This is the same nostalgic refrain I'd heard from Lado in Slovenia and the Croatian captain on the boat from Dubrovnik to Durrës. And I don't think it was just about making money, but more an assertion that whatever might have been wrong with Yugoslavia, it was artistically and culturally a better place then than now.

We walk around the *Mesokastro*, the Old Town, beginning at a gnarled and stooped old plane tree which has supposedly been hanging in there for 900 years. They know it as the Cinar tree and it's the symbol of the city of Ohrid. Up the hill, past a few well-restored old houses with storeys attractively cantilevered out one above the other, is the amphitheatre, not as big as the one in

Durrës, but impressive enough to show how important Ohrid was to the Romans. Once we've done very old things there isn't a lot to see. Modern Ohrid is undistinguished and scarcely does justice to the beauty of its situation.

We end up at a taverna by the waterfront.

My eye is drawn irresistibly to the lake. It's magnetically attractive, especially today when fast-scudding clouds and wind-rumpled water combine to create a shimmering, constantly changing play of light and shade.

I ask how they get on with their neighbours across the water. Vasil says they have good relations with the Albanians, though there are issues about dumping waste in the famously pristine waters of the lake.

Other neighbours are more problematical. After the break-up of Yugoslavia the Greeks insisted that if Macedonia were to be given independence it should be called the Former Yugoslav Republic of Macedonia (Fyrm), to distinguish it from the Macedonian region of northern Greece. It was only in 2003 that, for the first time since the end of the Second World War, the Greek government issued visas for Macedonians to visit relatives on the Greek side.

There's even been a long-running dispute over ownership of Alexander the Great, who was born in what is now Greece, but spoke Macedonian.

Kaliopi spreads her hands, helplessly.

'I don't understand what is "Fyrm", it's nothing to me.'

But the Greeks take it very seriously. Vasil was at a recent arts festival in the Ukraine from which the Greek contingent walked out after the organisers referred to him as being from the Republic of Macedonia.

Kaliopi's love for her country seems unequivocal, like their love for her. She struggles to find the words to best express the relationship.

'I am like paprika for the Macedonian people!' she declares, which takes me a bit by surprise.

'Paprika?'

She nods eagerly.

'Because the Macedonian cannot live without paprika, and maybe that is the best compliment for me.'

Paprika or otherwise, it's significant that when she goes on to talk about the many new projects she has with Vasil the one that enthuses her most is a musical of the life of Marshal Tito.

Macedonian she may be on her passport, but Yugoslavia still exerts a powerful spell.

Day Twenty-nine: *Ohrid to Prilep*

East from Ohrid the road swoops up and over a landscape of high passes and thickly forested slopes which broadens into a wider rolling plain. A town appears, dominated by weirdly eroded rocks, the white scar of a marble quarry and a monumental, derelict fortress built by King Marko, a Serbian who became Macedonia's last king before the Ottoman invasions.

This is Prilep, a modest town, currently in the throes of a beer festival and preparing itself for tomorrow's Festival of Saint Mary, or as she translates rather spectacularly in Macedonian, Saint Bogorodica. The centrepiece of the religious celebrations is not in the town itself but in a monastery 6 miles away, tucked so snugly into the smoothed and sculpted rocks that you have to get right up close before you believe in it.

There is a dirt road, but on holy days ninety per cent of the worshippers take the old cobbled path and a two-hour walk from the road below.

We're met at the fine, frescoed gatehouse of Treskavec monastery by the only monk in residence here, Brother Kalist, a tall, straight-backed, gentle man in a black robe, circular black velvet cap and with a long, curly beard streaked with grey. Once an economist in Macedonia's capital Skopje, he's now training for the priesthood.

The grounds of the monastery are already filling up with people who will spend the night here before tomorrow's festival, but Brother Kalist, despite being continually buttonholed about this and that, takes time to show us around.

There have been establishments of various kinds up here in the shelter of the mountain since pre-Roman times. Recent archaeological work has uncovered remains of a temple to Apollo and fragments of sculpted toga-wearing figures can be seen, incorporated into much later walls.

The compact basilica at the centre of the monastery has a pair of elaborately patterned doors, each one carved from a single piece of wood and depicting not only scenes of the life of Christ, but also a Buddha. They're supreme examples of the work of the Prilep School of Flat Wood Carving, Brother Kalist tells me proudly. In the narthex, where people are lighting votive candles, there are paintings from the fourteenth century and the decorations in the main body of the church are fifteenth century but look distinctly modern in their treatment of flowers and animals.

Brother Kalist points upwards. 'Have you seen our Gaudí ceiling?'

I peer up obligingly. It's a moment before I notice the twinkle in his eye.

'I tell my Spanish visitors it's by Gaudí.' He looks rather pleased with himself. 'Just for a joke.'

My favourite building in the complex is the sternly functional 650-year-old vaulted refectory, with its table made from one long stone block with niches cut around the base into which the monks could fit their feet. A long, finely carved gully runs down the centre along which bones and other left-overs could be sluiced away.

Brother Kalist regrets that he will have to leave us now, as the mayor of Prilep has arrived for the evening mass. I have the feeling that his visit is a rare event, less to do with devotion and more with appearances.

Day Thirty: *Prilep*

Sunrise on Saint Bogorodica's day and I'm being hauled slowly and noisily up the damp clay track to the monastery in a thirty-five-year-old, ex-Yugoslav army, Fiat jeep.

'Alfa Romeo engine!' shouts my driver above the screaming roar, as he revs us round another steep and slippery bend.

I'm put to shame by the column of people already making their way up on foot: old, young, male and female, families with children, many carrying gifts and money for the monastery.

We also pass quite a few groups of spiky-haired teenagers. In England you'd be pushed to find them out of bed at this time, let alone walking to church.

When we reach the top and are welcomed once again by the ever-attentive Brother Kalist, I ask him about them. He tells me they always have a lot of students at this particular festival day, as it's just before the schools and colleges go back and they're here to get the Virgin Mary's blessing for the next school year. He gestures approvingly at the groups already staking out their places on the grass, even though the sun's barely risen.

'We are a young church.'

It points to the remarkable resurgence of religion in Macedonia after the Tito years when priests were not allowed to practise. Brother Kalist won't be drawn on politics, but he speaks with great admiration of the people of Prilep who made sure their monastery was kept open and looked after during those difficult times. I suggest to him that the church may appear to be above politics but it's surely a much sought-after political ally.

He concedes the point. 'Oh yes. That was why the mayor was here last night.'

A middle-aged man appears up the last steep slope of the path. He's clearly run up the hill and his T-shirt is sodden with sweat. He stops, rocking on his legs, takes huge gulps of air, crosses himself at the threshold of the monastery and walks respectfully inside. He's followed by groups of young men, sprinting then sauntering up the hill and pausing to hurl schoolyard abuse at their friends below. But no matter how laddish they are, they too cross themselves before entering the monastery complex, and three times if they're going inside the church.

After a two-hour morning mass has been sung, specially prepared bread and cake is set out on a platform in the grounds. Preceded by a black-robed nun swinging a censer, the prodigiously bearded and ponytailed bishop, in an embroidered cope and bejewelled mitre, blesses the food, water and wine. He's accompanied by three young men who sing lovely, mellow chants. Afterwards they tell me, with some pride, that these are recently rediscovered eighth- and ninth-century Byzantine Macedonian works.

Another symptom of resurgent Balkan nationalism you might think, but these singers are not little Macedonians. They speak excellent English, are huge fans of Pink Floyd and very excited at the visit of the Pet Shop Boys to Skopje in two weeks' time.

Today's celebrations are by no means solemn. This is as much a community as a religious event and the meal that is now served up is prepared and paid for by a local family. I'm invited to sit at the top table with the bishop, the deacon and 'Kalist', as they all call him. A homely atmosphere as fathers, mothers, uncles, aunts and lots of children wait on some 250 of us at a single long table.

We're served a thick bean soup, with coleslaw salad, cold fried fish, freshly blessed bread and sweet cake. The bishop offers me red wine, made in the monastery. A huge glass is poured, Kalist looking on rather apologetically. 'Not quite up to standard yet,' he mutters, and he's right.

Next to me is a burly tank of a man, who's the head of a construction company which has done a lot of work in the rebuilding of the monastery and he and his family will be next year's sponsors. He's an Alexander the Great fan, and talks of his frustration at the richness of the archaeology in Macedonia and the difficulty in raising money to preserve it.

Treskavec is packed tight as the time comes for us to leave and yet in a couple of months it will be the start of winter. St Mary's Day will have come and gone, the children will be hard at work and the only occupant of this mountain-top eyrie will be Brother Kalist. I wish him luck and ask him when he will become a fully qualified monk.

He looks bashful. 'It's not up to me. The bishop is deciding that.'

'I'm sure you're wishing he'll make up his mind soon.'

'The monks don't have wishes,' he smiles and looks around him and out over the great sweeping plain beyond. 'But if I had some wish, my wish would be to die here in the mountains.'

It's a three-hour drive to the Bulgarian border, through lakeland scenery, green meadows and wooded steep hills. The human scenery is less attractive. Towns are small, run-down and dominated by shoddy apartment blocks. I have the feeling, admittedly on very short acquaintance, that Macedonia may have suffered most from the break-up of the Yugoslav Federation. Within Yugoslavia it had the strength and support to survive. Without, it is fragile and vulnerable. Average earnings, I'm told, are around 250 euros a month. Their security depends on old Russian fighters and Bulgarian tanks and Mafia influence is widespread. Even their national flag, an eye-catching gold-on-red rising sun, which we see for the last time fluttering above the border post beyond Delčevo, had to be changed after complaints from the Greeks that it incorporated the star of Vergina, the symbol of the ancient Macedonian kingdom to which the Greeks lay sole claim.

Unlike comfortable Croatia or even ignored Albania, Macedonia is a country trying to convince the world that it should be taken seriously.

We walk up the hill into Bulgaria. The first, and indeed only building beyond customs and immigration doesn't look promising. It bears the faded name 'Snek Bar', and it looks as if it closed down years ago. Then I notice signs of life. A donkey is grazing in the long grass beside it and from within I hear a dog bark. A man with a wild look in his eyes and an axe over his shoulder appears from nowhere and heads inside. I follow him, a little cautiously, thinking a cup of coffee might not go amiss. A fetid smell, a combination of bad food and unwashed dogs, makes me move smartly away, but not before I catch a nightmarish glimpse of an old woman, and a dog, dressed up like a child, sitting in a chair.

Bulgaria

Day Thirty-one: *The Rila Mountains*

I'M WOKEN at half past five this morning, but I didn't need to be. I've been mentally marking off the minutes for almost an hour. It may be summer in the Balkans but in my tent, beneath clear skies and on a mountainside 7,500 feet up, the cold comes as an unwelcome shock.

There are some thousand people camped around me and I'm already worrying about how we're all going to fit into five toilets. Struggle to dress and clamber out of the tent. And there are all my neighbours of the night, huddled beside calor gas lamps or heading down the hill by torchlight towards what's laughingly called the bathroom block. It was dark when we arrived here yesterday evening, by four-wheel drive along the near-vertical course of a dried-up stream and then by horseback, so I've little idea of quite where we are. All I know is that it's a place special enough to be chosen for the annual coming-together of the White Brotherhood, a non-drinking, non-smoking community of vegetarians who follow the teachings of one Peter Deunov, whom they call The Master, and on whom the Spirit of God descended on 7 March 1897.

I try to find out a little more but it isn't easy. A tall, long-haired rangy figure in the tent next to me is a doctor, who gives off the irritating air of someone who knows more than I ever will, however hard I try.

Are you all members of the Brotherhood, I ask. He reproves me quite sharply. Of course not. They're not members of anything. More tentatively I ask if their choice of this place is an expression of their religion. Wrong again. They are not a religion.

'Our Master said,' and here he fixes me with ominously clear eyes, 'with paneurythmy I give you a weapon, it is for you to use it right.'

There is no time for me to ask what the hell paneurythmy is as everyone is getting up and heading up the mountain to greet the sunrise.

Sartorially, the White Brotherhood is a bit of a let-down. Most of my fellow sun-greeters are in anoraks and windcheaters of every shade but white. We congregate on the edge of a rocky bluff. Hundreds of us clinging to whatever foothold we can find. As J-P, our director, observes, it's like a human puffin sanctuary.

Unlike in the tents last night, there is almost total silence. A reverent hush. Light slowly fills the sky to reveal a dramatic landscape. Directly below us a rocky slope falls away to a lake. Beyond that a panorama of interlocking mountain spurs stretches as far as the eye can see. A thin mist rises as if the whole land has been freshly baked.

Looking up at the faces around me I'm reminded of the Easter Island statues. Grave and passionless faces all turned to the horizon. Then, slowly, right hands are raised, palms open, directed at the new light. When the sun is fully risen the hands are lowered and for the first time there are sounds from the multitude: prayers, low chants, people reading from texts, some thin music.

I'm as glad to see the sun as they are, and my mood is transformed as it illuminates the full glory of the place they call Sedemte Ezera, Seven Lakes, the spectacular heart of the Rila Mountains.

At breakfast I'm introduced to a young man of regular good looks, wearing sandals, white linen trousers and a sensible sweater who could be, and it turns out is, an IT programmer on his day off. His name is Dimitar and I gather he is quite high up in the hierarchy of the White Brotherhood – if indeed they have a hierarchy, which they don't.

Perhaps he can at least tell me what paneurythmy means.

'It's a spiritual dance.'

'Ah.'

I ask him why the Brotherhood should come to dance in such an inaccessible place.

'It's because of the spiritual nature of the energies here.'

It turns out that The Master, Peter Deunov, an impressive figure who, in photos, looks like a cross between Abraham Lincoln and Rasputin, was the one who first identified the Seven Lakes as having special qualities.

'High energy, high vibrations,' Dimitar explains.

I'm quite relieved when, in mid-morning, the campers set out, en masse, for the upper slopes for the aforementioned paneurythmic dancing. The theory may be nebulous but the practice promises to be quite spectacular.

I'm not disappointed. Climbing a steeply winding mountain path up from the campsite, I emerge onto a broad saddle of grassland and there ahead of me, framed by grey rock walls, dabbed with patches of unmelted snow, over a thousand people dressed in white are moving slowly round in huge concentric circles.

It looks less like dancing and more like one of those mass PT displays the Chinese are so fond of. Breathing deeply and regularly, and emitting a low cosmic hum, the participants raise and lower their arms (in what I'm later told are variations of the thirty-seven movements laid down by The Master), point their bare feet at an angle to the ground and stare beatifically off into the middle distance.

After half an hour or so there's a welcome change of tempo, from the near-funereal to the almost jaunty. The choreography becomes gradually more ambitious. Circles stop and face the centre, turn and move the opposite way, break up and reform in a series of kaleidoscopic patterns, and all in near-silence.

Gone are the anoraks and fleeces of the sunrise ceremony. The all-white dress code has been largely observed and with the sun, the mountains and the clear glacial lakes all being in the right place at the right time, the White Brotherhood and their paneurythmic dancing make an inspiring sight.

This being a national park, and a weekend, curious spectators appear. Walkers dressed in shell-suits or shorts that look like underpants stop and stare, or blast away with their cameras before waddling on and I find myself admiring the Brotherhood for their poise and stillness and, yes, style.

When it's all over I join Dimitar and his family for a picnic. They're good people, bright and generous with their time. But as Dimitar explains once again about love, harmony, circles, symbols and the prayer of movement and dance I realise that they are the converted. Their Master's voice has a relevance for them that cannot easily be shared with outsiders. They're more interested in protecting their purity than selling a watered-down version to the rest of the world. As we begin our long descent from this beautiful place I reflect, a little wistfully, that perhaps the White Brotherhood is not the place for a meat-eating, wine-loving comedian.

Day Thirty-two: *Godech*

Stefan Kitov, known to all as 'Kita', works in the film business in Sofia, and is a great fan of *Monty Python*, but an even bigger fan of *rakiya*, the powerful local brandy which has seen Bulgarians through many troubled times. He is most concerned that I should not pass through his country without tasting the real thing, as made by his father.

So it is that I find myself, an hour's drive from the capital, passing through deserted swathes of agricultural land on my way to the small town of Godech.

Kita confirms that Bulgarians are not only moving off the land but their birth-rate is falling too. With a national population the same size as London this is not good news, but Bulgaria has never had a lot to celebrate. One of the many tribes emanating from Central Asia, the Bulgars were first noted by the Emperor Constantine as 'a race of new and vulgar people' from the north Balkans. Even when they did get their act together, as they did under King Samoil in the tenth century, they were quickly slapped down by the army-blinding Byzantine Emperor Vasilius (later immortalised for bloodthirsty schoolboys as Basil the Bulgar Slayer).

Following the fall of Constantinople, Byzantine occupation gave way to Turkish, and another 400 years passed until, in the Treaty of San Stefano of 1878, Bulgaria became independent again.

A series of self-inflicted blows followed, and after ending up on the losing side in two world wars Bulgaria survived, like Hungary, as a classic example of a small country that had been much bigger.

Unlike Tito's Yugoslavia, which did comfortably well by playing off East against West, Bulgaria threw in its lot firmly with Stalin and the Soviets. In the 1980s it alienated its substantial Turkish minority with an extreme policy which required them all to change their names into Bulgarian.

Only recently, with accession to NATO in 2004, did the course of history begin to turn to their advantage and the possibility of EU membership in 2007 would seal a triumphant turnaround.

Kita shrugs off the vagaries of their history. What can you expect, he says, of a people who nod for no and shake their heads for yes.

'We always do things the other way round.'

In Godech, on the gentle slopes of a broad valley, police have pulled over a motorcyclist, whilst a man walks past them on the pavement, leading his cow. Kita's father bought a plot here thirty years ago and built his attractive little house himself. He was deputy director of a sports goods business.

'Deputy director was the highest he could get without joining the Party,' Kita explains wryly.

A house like this, modelled on the Russian dacha, served an important purpose for people at that time, not just as a place to grow one's own food but as a political safety valve, an escape from the rules, restrictions and supervision of the socialist State.

'Socialism was a system of limits,' says Kita. 'On a plot like this you could set your own limits.'

His father, a straight-backed, sharp-eyed, restless man, takes me on a tour of the garden, showing off tomatoes, peppers, cauliflower, spring onions, cucumber and pumpkins of considerable girth, all grown, he is at pains to point out, without the aid of any chemicals. He also shows off his rabbits, an outdoor shower made from old bits of sheet metal, and his new extension.

But it's the trees he's most proud of. Apple, pear, wild plum. There's only one rule. He won't plant a tree that can't produce *rakiya*. In vain does his wife suggest a nice walnut or a decorative maple. If it doesn't bear fruit, he's not interested. Which is the cue for us to follow this indefatigable old man down to the house of two equally old and indefatigable neighbours, Lubo and Tzeta, in whose back garden the best *rakiya* in Bulgaria is made. So they say.

It's in many ways an idyllic place, a repository of unreformed village life, with a donkey grazing at one end and coal-black chickens at the other. The donkey is completely placid until the camera turns to film my entrance, whereupon it becomes almost frantically active, rolling on its back and emitting a salvo of well aimed farts.

Beneath an apple tree, a table has been set with glasses, bottles of water and a plate of grilled sausage, already being attended to by a cat which darts out from behind an upturned wheelbarrow when it thinks you're not looking.

Lubo and Tzeta, solid and silver-haired seventy-year-olds, show me the shed in which they've been distilling *rakiya* for the past twenty years. The fruit mix is heated by a wood fire and rises into a copper still called the *kazan*, before cooling down and running out, rather prosaically, into a brown plastic bucket. The process is then repeated to strengthen the alcohol content. Tzeta dips a thermometer into a cracked glass test tube and pronounces that what's in the bucket today is fifty-two per cent proof.

When I ask how long they leave it to mature there's general laughter. Laying it down is a luxury. Or as Lubo puts it: 'There's no bad *rakiya*, only little *rakiya*.'

I ask if bootleg *rakiya* like this will be outlawed if Bulgaria joins the EU.

Kita nods a little gloomily. 'You know it's the same with the size of the cucumber. When we go to the European Union they'll want us to make exactly the same size of cucumber and they will want to stop this sort of breweries. But,' he warns, 'I think there will be a real revolution in Bulgaria!'

The meal that follows is a triumph of unbureaucratic self-sufficiency. Starting, in the traditional Bulgarian way, with *rakiya*, both of plum and prune, we have peppers in batter, aubergines stuffed with cheese, a plate of Bulgarian white and yellow cheeses, a red wine called No Man's Land, and, to finish off, cold beers.

As we all join the cat in tucking into the *meze* Kita raises a glass for two toasts. The first is to his favourite film. 'When I saw *The Life of Brian* the first time I fell twice from a chair.'

The other toast is to the donkey.

Day Thirty-three: *Sofia*

I'm in the garden café of a smart hotel in the intimate, walkable centre of Sofia. A quartet of soberly but elegantly dressed conservatoire girls are tuning their violins and cellos. As they raise their bows and I raise my cappuccino, I take quiet satisfaction in having discovered this little oasis of civilisation.

So lulled am I by the pleasantness of it all that it's almost half a minute before I realise they're playing 'Tulips from Amsterdam'.

I leave with the strains of 'My Way' fading behind me and wander through the City Garden past a group of elderly and oddly disputatious chess players and an accordionist leaning up against a tree, counting the coins in an upturned cap. At the far end of the park are some gardens, laid out a few years ago on the site of what was once one of the most venerated places in Sofia, the mausoleum of Georgi Dimitrov, the father of Bulgarian communism, and Prime Minister from 1946 to 1949. By all accounts he was a very nasty piece of work who attended to the bourgeoisie with a pragmatic brutality that Stalin might have envied. On his orders thousands were killed or sent to forced labour camps, robbing his country of a generation of talent.

In 1990, following the abrupt collapse of the Soviet empire, his remains were removed, but the mausoleum proved so solidly built that it was not successfully demolished for another ten years.

Dimitrov and his friends have left their mark on the city. The wide plaza called the Largo was laid out by the communists after the Allied bombers destroyed much of central Sofia at the end of the Second World War. It's still dominated by the Party Headquarters building, but tucked in amongst the monumental stucco façades is a less boastful architectural gem, the Buyuk Djami, a mosque built in 1496. It now houses an archaeological museum. I've never been easily seduced by such places but this is a revelation. The collection is of incomparable quality, for Bulgaria sits on one of the greatest resources of ancient artefacts in the world. Even before the Greeks and Romans were here, and a thousand years ahead of the Bulgars, the land was home to Thracian tribes, rich enough to produce exquisitely detailed work in gold and silver and precious stones. Much of this was produced for the elaborate graves of the rich and powerful, who would be buried with their treasure all around them, to accompany their souls into immortality.

Their tombs are scattered across Bulgaria, many still sealed. What has already been unearthed is often extraordinary work, as graceful and intricate as anything that might be designed nowadays. For me the highlight of this dazzling collection was a Thracian gold-leaf death mask, made some two and a half thousand years ago. Powerful and delicately fine at the same time.

More modern workmanship can be found at the flea-market outside the exuberant explosion of domes and towers that is the Alexander Nevski church, which was built as a memorial to the 200,000 Russians who died fighting the Turks in the cause of pan-Slavism in the 1870s. Here, amongst stalls full of Nazi and Soviet memorabilia, I find whole regiments of Russian dolls painted to suit all tastes. Yasser Arafat, Saddam Hussein, Osama Bin Laden and George Bush stand shoulder to shoulder with the Queen, Tony Blair and Stalin. It was a toss-up, but in the end I did my patriotic duty and bought the Queen.

Sofia is not a spectacular city. The Bulgarians don't seem to do excess. Many of the city-centre streets are narrow and tree-lined, more like those of a laid-back provincial capital. Few official cars race through, there is little triumphalism, and men in suits and ties are rare enough to be noticeable. The clothes look neither downtrodden nor particularly chic, the shops are up-to-date but lack flair, the people content but not demonstrative.

Which is why I'm rather looking forward to meeting a man described in my *Rough Guide* as 'Bulgaria's most controversial gender-bending phenomenon'.

Azis is portrayed by some as the devil incarnate, by others as a very naughty boy but when we meet, in the modest, slightly shabby suite of rooms that passes for his office, I find myself shaking hands with a plump young man with peroxide blond hair and the shrewd smile of a wary attention-seeker. His skin is dark and a swirl of tattoos runs across his neck and shoulders and down beneath a black T-shirt. Not quite a choirboy, but very different from the huge posters of him on the wall in crutch-hugging glitter and full make-up. He's a delight to talk to, not just because he's nice and droll but because he so clearly relishes being different. He's Gypsy, one of an estimated 380,000 in a country of seven and a half million people, and he's gay, with plans to marry a man later in the year and adopt children 'from all over the world'.

None of which should endear him to the Bulgarian people, who seem quite old-fashioned in these matters. What makes it all work is the success of the *chalga* (Romany) music he performs so powerfully and the attraction of the flashy, loud, nouveau-riche lifestyle that goes with it. And he does love his mother.

When he was still a child she had what he calls 'sick ambitions' for him to be a mega-star like Elizabeth Taylor, but because he was Gypsy all the doors were closed. When I ask him who his audience is he says the underground world, prostitutes and gays.

'The free people,' he adds.

'And the Gypsies. Could there be others, inspired by his example?'

He shrugs his wide shoulders.

'They're still as dirty and miserable as they were. It'll never change.'

He's stubborn and patient and these are not Gypsy values.

'The problem with them is that they want something and on the next day something completely different.'

We talk about what it was like growing up in socialist Bulgaria. Did he have to join organisations like the Young Pioneers?

He grins less warily now. Yes, he was a Young Pioneer, but always wanted to wear the girls' uniform.

'I wanted to be the majorette rather than the football player!'

So what of the future?

Though he says he's a patriot and whenever he hears a Bulgarian song he's moved to shed a tear, he feels the country is now too small for him. Once his wild and raunchy transsexual persona shocked people here. Now they're only shocked when they see him in normal clothes. So he's contemplating leaving home to find fame and fortune elsewhere.

In America perhaps?

He shakes his head firmly. In America, he says, they'd probably throw stones at him. No, he'd like to work in London where, he reckons, you're free to do what you want and be who you want.

A bodyguard moves position at the door and I realise that this candid and engaging man is also a big star and we've outrun our allotted time. Patient to the end, he finds time to pose for a few snaps beside the rudest poster we can find.

Day Thirty-five: *Plovdiv*

Moving deeper now into the south-east corner of Europe, along the fast four-lane autoroute that connects Sofia and Bulgaria's second city, Plovdiv, across the Plain of Thrace. The landscape of heathland and low bare hills is undistinguished, and remarkably empty. In Western Europe a major highway like this would be a development magnet, studded with warehouses, distribution centres and business parks.

The present and the future may look a little subdued but the past is thriving in Bulgaria. Plovdiv is one of the oldest cities in Europe, first settled by the Thracians 7,000 years ago, then rebuilt in the fourth century BC by Alexander the Great's father Philip of Macedon, who modestly renamed it Philippopolis.

The Maritsa valley, in which the city lies, was a natural conduit for trade through the Balkans and the commercial importance of Plovdiv/Philippopolis is marked, as in Durrës in Albania, and Ohrid in Macedonia, by the remains of a large Roman amphitheatre, set on a hill with a perilously balanced wall of columns and pediments creating a dramatic frame for the city beyond.

I meet up here with Mira Staleva, a young woman born and brought up in Plovdiv. Record temperatures, above 40° Celsius, are expected later today and already the white marble terracing of the outdoor theatre is like a hot iron, so Mira and I take refuge at a café nearby. A mindless drum and bass sample thuds out, hugely over-amplified. No-one is listening, but no-one seems to want to turn it off.

Plovdiv, says Mira, was a good place to grow up. It was a cultured city, tolerant and laid-back. 'It's very Mediterranean. I mean when you go for a coffee you go for at least two hours.'

There were Jewish, Romanian, Greek, Turkish and Gypsy quarters, and the only bad time she can remember was the ill-fated name-changing policy of the 1980s when those of the minorities who refused to change their name to a Bulgarian equivalent were victimised, being refused work and all benefits. She had many Turkish friends in school who were forced, temporarily, out of the country.

'I was sixteen or seventeen years old, but nobody reacted. It was really sad. The communist system can make you really passive, you know.'

Like Azis, Mira was a Young Pioneer, and she remembers learning how to strip down Kalashnikovs whilst still at school.

'You go in the classroom with thirty Kalashnikovs on the desk and everybody starts. We check the time. It was like a competition, who would be first.'

'Who was the enemy?'

'It was an abstract enemy. But in the Pioneers' organisation you were "always ready".'

At sixteen she was attending military camp, wearing uniform and getting up at five in the morning.

'But it was the best time of my life, actually. When someone is trying to press you to do something, you find different ways to escape.'

Close by the Roman theatre is a network of cobbled streets, often huddled against remains of the old Byzantine city walls. Built along these steep slopes are houses as strikingly attractive as any I've seen on the journey so far. They date from the late eighteenth and early nineteenth centuries, and were built by merchants who had made money from trade with the Ottoman empire. With solid stone-walled bases and half-timbered upper storeys cantilevered out over the street, they also have distinctive wooden balconies, oriel windows, decorative plasterwork and louvred shutters. They create a sort of Alpine-Turkish feel and could well be the backdrop to those Orientalist paintings that nineteenth-century travellers to the Balkans were producing for an increasingly fascinated audience back home.

One of those responsible for awakening this interest in all things Ottoman was the French poet Lamartine and his house, now open to the public, is one of the grandest in this picturesque little enclave.

Many of these houses were commandeered by the State after World War Two, but since the demise of communism a restitution policy has been under way and many of the original owners, or their families, have been given back their properties and are sympathetically restoring them.

Looking back at the city from the shallow, sandy river you can glimpse the hill where the amphitheatre stands, through a forest of eight-storey blocks made of prefabricated concrete. They are now mainly occupied by Gypsy families (also called Roma, or *Tsigani* in Bulgarian). Originating in India, the Gypsies made their way into Eastern Europe some 600 years ago, but have never really integrated with the local people. They're seen as outsiders who reject the social system, whilst enjoying its financial benefits. Mira doesn't see much hope. There are foundations and welfare groups who are trying to build a bridge between Gypsies and the rest of society but she can't see how it will work. Current figures bear out her pessimism. Around eighty-five per cent of Gypsies in Bulgaria are unemployed and only ten per cent of children are in secondary school education.

Today, with the help of the city council, we're trying to do our bit for Plovdiv's Gypsy community by providing pin money for a horse and cart racing event. A dozen contestants have come forward, some behind old nags shackled to rickety wooden carts, others perched on stripped-down frames of steel on rubber wheels. The racetrack is a section of dual carriageway which has been blocked off for the afternoon.

The organisers, Gypsies themselves, are taking it very seriously. Pieces of paper are waved about. Children, half-naked in the heat of the day, crowd around us, curious, but not aggressive.

But there is aggression elsewhere. There seem to be two kinds of

Slovenia Starting out: on the top of the Julian Alps, with Italy behind me and Slovenia ahead.

Slovenia Lake Bled and the 1,000-year-old town around it. The church in the middle looks as if it's a ferry crossing the water.

ABOVE RIGHT: *Rijeka, Croatia* The market at Rijeka. A cathedral of fish.
BELOW RIGHT: *Split, Croatia* Diocletian's Palace, Split. The peristyle is the heart of these massive Roman remains. The black granite sphinx is pre-Christian and the white bell-tower, begun in the thirteenth century, wasn't finished until 1908.

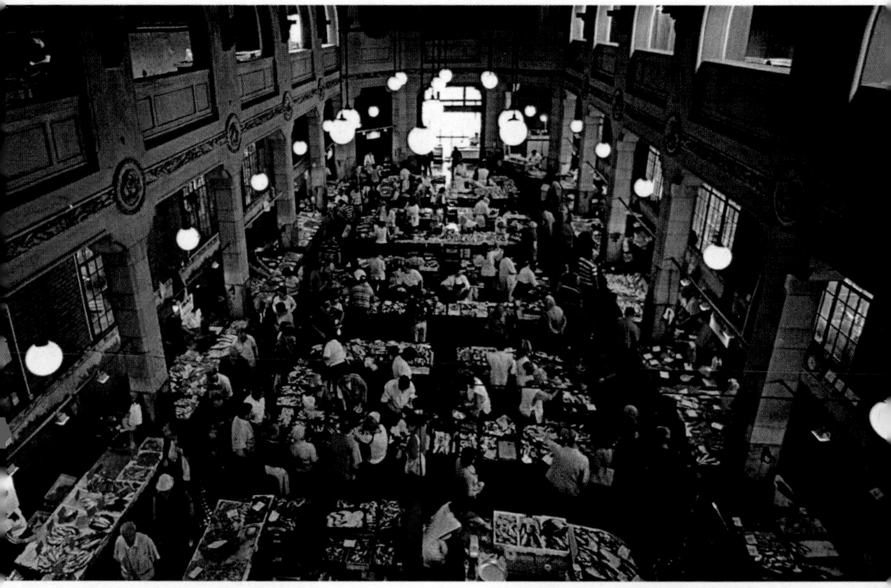

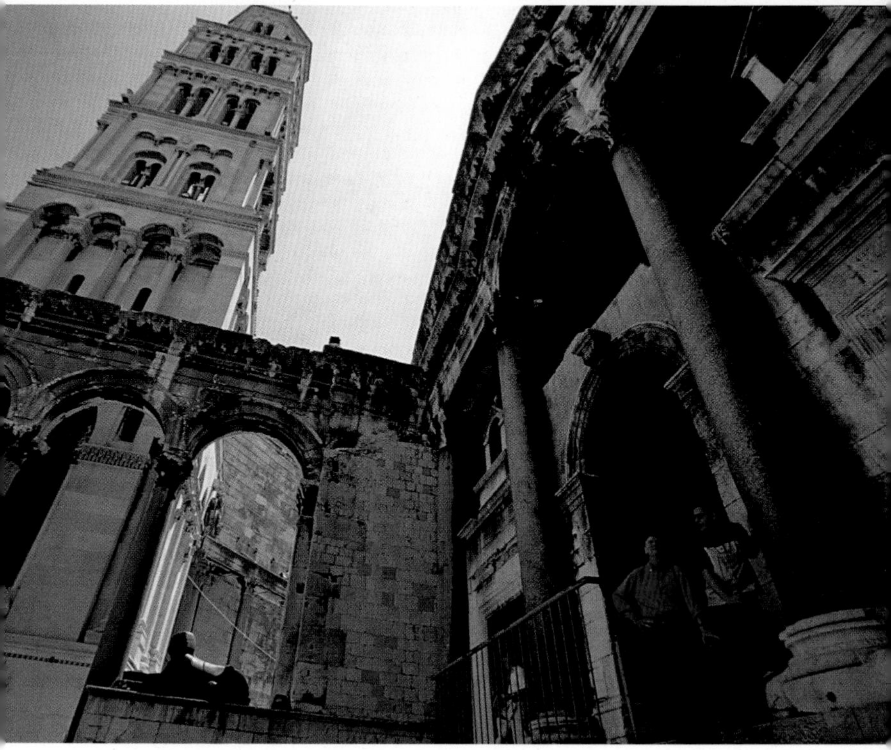

Mostar, Bosnia & Herzegovina Kamel Ratkusic shows me how Mostar, once the cosmopolitan heart of Herzegovina, is recovering from the destructive war of the 1990s.

Sarajevo, Bosnia & Herzegovina Inside a restored section of tunnel. An average of 4,000 people used it each day for over two years.

Dubrovnik, Croatia Stradun. Dubrovnik. The fine limestone paved main street that runs the length of the old city. Always busy when the cruise ships are in.

LEFT: *Durrès, Albania* Looking like giant jellyfish washed ashore, a few of the 400,000 concrete bunkers put up to guard Albania during the Hoxha regime dot the beach at Durrès.

LEFT: *Tirana, Albania* Politics with colours. How to brighten a drab city without spending too much money.

BELOW LEFT: *Tirana, Albania* Edi Rama, artist-mayor of Tirana, shows me his 'therapeutic diary'.

RIGHT: *Macedonia, Prilep* In the Treskavec monastery above Prilep, with Brother Kalist. Behind us is the fourteenth-century church of St Bogorodica. People walk miles to worship here.

The Rila Mountains, Bulgaria Mass paneurythmic dancing, the highlight of the year for the White Brotherhood.

Sofia, Bulgaria This is Orthodox country and icons abound in the streets near the Alexander Nevski Church in Sofia.

vehicle in this community, the horse and cart and the souped-up, flashily customised old banger, always driven to deliver maximum tyre squeal. It's one of these that threatens to completely ruin the first race. Packed with cheering and yelling punters, it drives so close to the lead horse that no-one can overtake it. This results in a protest of such ferocity that the protagonists have to be held apart. Exactly the same thing happens with the next race. The horses, besides being whipped to flared-nostril frenzy, have to put up with the squealing roar of a car and its occupants right beside their heads.

Eventually a winner is chosen and we're invited to join a party in amongst the blocks themselves.

The buildings are stained and the paintwork blistered and peeling. Uncollected rubbish is piled up, and stagnant puddles of sewage overflow the gutters. Between the blocks the occupants are sitting around in groups with waste, blown by the wind, drifting around them. Silhouetted against the strong evening sun they look like survivors of some apocalyptic disaster.

The party is getting under way in a yard between the blocks. A loud and brassy band is playing, massively amplified of course, and the floor is taken by a dozen or so elderly Gypsy women who gyrate rather gently to the cacophonous music. One of them has a gun, which she waves about her as she dances, occasionally taking aim at someone and grinning broadly. No-one seems to bat an eyelid.

The menfolk look on, unimpressed, rolling up their T-shirts to reveal large and rounded bellies which they stroke from time to time as if they were much loved family pets.

Even our friendly organisers don't encourage us to stay on too long. Once darkness falls and the drink takes hold they can't ensure our safety.

For the moment I'm content to be the only man on the floor, with the undivided attention of a swaying harem of Gypsy matrons, some of them armed.

Day Thirty-six: *Perperikon to Zlatograd*

As one does on a Monday morning, I find myself riding a mule up a steep track between oak, ash and hazel woods that leads to an

8,000-year-old city which an archaeologist (on horseback, ahead of me) thinks could be on a par with Troy or Mycenae.

The fact that I'm on a mule and he's on a horse says much about the Quixote-like character of Nikolai Ovcharov, the man who, by sheer force of his own conviction, has persuaded the Bulgarian government to spend good money putting the lost city of Perperikon on the map.

Below us, bulldozers, excavators and graders are clearing and levelling a wide swathe of hillside for an approach road. Generators hum beside the new visitor centre. Minibuses from the surrounding villages are delivering some of the 130-strong workforce, and a line of gleaming new toilets stands amid the dust. This is archaeology as big business. And archaeologist as celebrity.

Nikolai Ovcharov clearly loves the attention. Well built, with a carefully trimmed grey-flecked beard, he has a strong, commanding voice and a touch of a swagger. Some call him the Bulgarian Indiana Jones, and with his safari hat clipped up at the sides and a knife sheathed on his belt, he seems quite happy to invite the comparison.

At the top of the hill my reluctant mule delivers me into a shady glade where a couple of hammocks are slung and a rough table with wooden bench seats is set beneath a makeshift canopy of leaves. Smoke rises from a fire. This is command headquarters for the dig, but we don't linger as Nikolai strides off to inspect progress.

We're in the Eastern Rhodopi Mountains, in the land of classical legends, two hours south of Plovdiv and just 21 miles from the Greek border. Orpheus, the man whose music could charm wild beasts and make rocks and trees move, is said to have been buried here after being torn to death by women on his return from the underworld, and Spartacus raised his army against the Romans here.

The side of the hill is ringed with massive white rock faces, so spectacularly sculpted by the combined effects of rain, sun and earthquakes that it's hard to tell what is naturally shaped and what is humanly carved. Nikolai has no doubt that he has stumbled upon evidence of what he calls 'the culture of the Rock People', and points out a huge throne, holes in the rock where timbers were secured, fortified gates to the citadel, a stone-walled grid for fifteen graves, and a slab on which the marks of an ancient fire circle can be seen and where sacrifices would have been made.

For two months of the year a small army of students from Sofia University join local Bulgarian-Turkish labourers in Ovcharov's kingdom, mapping the site, marking the rocks, digging trenches and generally strengthening the case for Perperikon as not only a sanctuary, fortress and sometime acropolis, but also one of the great religious sites of antiquity.

Whatever they find, Ovcharov's work is already done. By convincing himself and the Bulgarian government that it is everything he says it is, he has transformed a lifeless local economy, given tourists a more urgent reason to visit the beautiful Rhodopi Mountains and made an international name for himself. Though to be honest, Napoleon suits him better than Indiana Jones.

Within a few months Bulgaria will be given some of the most momentous news in its recent history, when a decision on their European Union application is made. From what I see down here they have decided it'll go their way and that the border crossings into nearby Greece will be reopened. Considerable amounts have been spent upgrading the roads and local amenities (with signs not just in Cyrillic but in the Latin alphabet as well). A town with the unpromising name of Zlatograd turns out to have a wonderful collection of 200-year-old Bulgarian-Alpine houses, restored and brought to life in an Ethnographic Museum. The houses have pantiled roofs, tall white chimneys and deep wooden balconies on one of which we're treated to a last intense shot of Bulgarian cuisine. After a week and a half of the ever-present *salata shopska*, a mound of salad shrouded in grated cheese, these local delicacies are a revelation. Fragrantly spiced meat stew, cabbage leaves stuffed with rice yet light as a feather and a spicy bean soup called *bob*.

Afterwards we're served dense Turkish coffee, made in little copper pots and heated in the sand whilst three singers and musicians treat us to unique local music. The songs are delivered in a style I've heard nowhere else, a deep, resonant throaty flow of great, if controlled, power. They're accompanied by the equally unfamiliar strains of the *gaida*, a sheepskin bagpipe, with three tubes, one to keep the bag inflated, another to play the melody and a third the drone. On paper it reads like a formula for the most difficult way to produce a sound, yet they manage to make these old songs of love and longing intensely poignant. They tell me that an example of this remarkable way of singing is aboard the Voyager 2 spacecraft.

Which is as it should be. After all, Orpheus, the greatest musician of them all, was a local Rhodopi boy.

Turkey

Day Thirty-seven: *Plovdiv to Edirne*

THERE IS nothing very beautiful about the E80 interchange east of Plovdiv, but there is an excellent truckers' café, the Motel Merita, with an engagingly ebullient patron, fine kofta kebabs, succulent meat rolls and an irresistible speciality of metre-long loaves of bread, crisped in the oven and sprinkled with sesame seeds.

I manage to cadge a lift in the direction of Turkey with a big, full-bellied man with a remarkable head. Almost exactly pyramidal in shape, it tapers from a bull-like neck to a small square crown. He hauls himself up into the cab and surprises me by getting out a very neat pair of horn-rimmed glasses, as if we were in a library instead of a 40-foot truck.

He's a friendly man and his few words of English are mostly destinations. I learn that one of his recent journeys took him all the way to Uzbekistan. Two weeks there and back doing 430 miles a day.

We pull out of the parking lot, a sudden halt to let another vehicle pass sending a row of hanging icons swinging above the windscreen.

After a mile or two we come to a sign that sets the pulses racing. Well, mine anyway. 'Istanbul'. Two hundred and eighty-five miles down the road.

Late afternoon. Crossing into Turkey at a village called Kapikule. The Greek, Bulgarian and Turkish borders all meet here as Europe funnels down towards Asia. A large mosque is marooned in no-man's-land, but apart from that there's nothing remotely attractive about this place. Blighted by the frontier, Kapikule seems to consist of little more than a lot of concrete tarmac, a lot of steel fencing, a huge gantry with the badge of Turkish customs at its centre, a filling station, a railway line, a truck park and ploughed fields, strewn with paper bags, stretching away on either side.

I take a taxi the few miles into the nearby city of Edirne. Flanking the four-lane autoroute are a scattering of functional buildings, small hotels and modest houses flying big red flags bearing the star and crescent moon of Turkey, an oddly Islamic symbol for a secular republic with no official religion.

Going the other way, a long line of trucks moves slowly westward. Whatever the outcome of their government's bid to join the European Union, Turkey's businessmen seem to be there already.

A first and quite thrilling glimpse of the skyline of Edirne, dominated by the massive domes and soaring minarets of one of the finest mosques in the world.

Closer up the city is less dramatic. The streets are busy, the lights are coming on and shoppers are out in force. There are supermarkets in the main street and in the side streets people sell fruit and vegetables off the back of pick-up trucks. Our hotel is tucked away amongst a cluster of low buildings of varying ages and states of repair. Inside it's like a small museum. Big, comfortable, old-fashioned armchairs and sofas are surrounded by all sorts of period bric-à-brac. Adding machines, sewing machines, an old steam iron, a reel-to-reel tape recorder, a trumpet. It's a time-capsule of the 1930s.

An open fire rounds off the distinct impression of not being in Turkey at all, but a thousand miles away. In England.

Day Thirty-eight: *Edirne*

My bedroom at the idiosyncratic Hotel Efe continues the cosy, but culturally confusing, Agatha Christie theme with some bakelite fittings, dodgy wiring and lovely old glass lampshades. I leave it early, and rather reluctantly, to explore the city with Selen Korkut, our translator, whose family comes from this most westerly part of Turkey.

We're drawn first, and quite naturally, to the crowning glory of the city, the Selimiye Cami mosque, designed by Mimar Sinan when he was in his eighties. It is considered to be the finest work of the finest architect the Ottoman empire ever produced.

Built like a small mountain range, it has eighteen subsidiary domes clustering around a single spectacular cupola with the whole complex marked at each corner by graceful sandstone minarets, which at 232 feet are the tallest outside Mecca.

There is a chain low across the arched gate of the mosque, designed to make sure that one enters with bowed head, but once inside the central prayer hall our heads go up again, in sheer wonder at the immense scale of the place. Eight sturdy supporting columns raise a dome 103 feet across and 144 feet high, with no central support at all. The genius of the architect is to make this colossal weight of stone look light and airy, hovering above us as if suspended from the heavens, rather than raised above the earth. It's by no means an exclusively Islamic statement. In shape and style it owes much to the great Byzantine church of Aya Sofya in Istanbul, built almost ten centuries earlier, and though the Ottomans came originally from Anatolia in the east, Sinan was a military architect who had travelled all over Europe and must have seen Renaissance masterpieces like Brunelleschi's dome in Florence.

Nevertheless prayer here, with two thousand others around you, must be a powerful experience for a Muslim worshipper. I ask Selen, very much a modern Turkish woman, if she goes regularly to the mosque. She shakes her head. Prayers can only be spoken in Arabic, never in any other language, so if she wants to pray she would have to learn the Koran. And there was me assuming, stupidly, that Arabic and Turkish were somehow the same thing.

The reason the city is so richly endowed with fine buildings is that for forty-five years before the fall of Constantinople, Edirne was the capital of the Ottoman empire.

It has three other great Ottoman mosques, down the hill and less dominant than the Selimiye Cami. Eski Cami, the Old Mosque, is square in shape with nine domes, and on one of its outer walls the words 'Allah' and 'Mohammed' are spelled out in giant calligraphics. It was built between 1403 and 1414 as the Islamic armies of Sultan Mehmet II were beginning to encircle Constantinople, slowly squeezing the life out of the Christian empire that had lasted there for over a thousand years. Across the road is the Üç Şerefeli Cami, the Mosque of Three Balconies, whose minarets are all different. One is plain fluted, and the others all decorated with red sandstone patterns, one in chevrons, another in diamonds, and one with red spirals, like a maypole, a marvellously fluent feat of masonry.

The architectural treasures of Edirne exude the confidence of conquerors.

Selen takes me a little way out of the city to see one of her favourite buildings, a multi-domed mosque complex of austere beauty apparently stranded amongst ploughed fields.

The Beyazit Kulesi, built in 1485, just over thirty years after Constantinople finally fell to the Ottoman Turks, was intended by its founder to be much more than a mosque. It was also a school, guest house, mill, bakery, public bath, soup kitchen, and most intriguingly of all, a psychiatric hospital, which has been restored and opened as a Health Museum.

Entering a walled enclosure, we pass a row of domed consulting rooms giving onto a small garden and sheltered by an arcade. At the end of this two arches lead into the *darüş-şifa*, the healing house, where for nearly four hundred years those with mental illness could be treated with the most enlightened methods like music, odours and the sound of flowing water.

Each room has life-size figures illustrating various aspects of the therapy.

In one there is a melancholic, someone suffering from what Selen calls 'black love' or what we might call a 'broken heart'. Another is labelled 'Room for Treatment by Keeping Busy', what we might call 'occupational therapy'.

The *darüş-şifa*, supported entirely by charitable donations, is all the more remarkable when you think that right up to the nineteenth century the only place for the insane throughout most of Europe was the madhouse.

Ironically the asylum here, having operated under the Turks for almost four centuries, closed its doors in 1878 when the

Russians occupied the area and the Congress of Berlin confirmed the beginning of the end of the Ottoman empire.

As surprising to me as the existence of a 400-year-old psychiatric hospital is the news that Selen, a small, serious, Istanbul liberal, went out for two years with a man who made a living from wrestling, while covered from head to foot in olive oil.

Not only that but she's taking me down to the banks of the River Meriç, which forms the border between Greece and Turkey, to watch this bizarre sport in action.

'Why oil wrestling?' I ask her.

Selen smiles. 'Turkish men are very macho,' she explains, 'and they have to do something about it. When my father was young he was always with oil wrestlers. Even before he went to school he was pouring for them.'

'Pouring?'

'You'll see.'

What I see as we arrive at a woodland glade beside the river is a number of bulbous men wearing only tight, black, buffalo-skin pantaloons (called *kisbet*), being doused in diluted olive oil which they rub all over their bodies, with no particular sense of urgency, as if they were in a shower. Two of the wrestlers are young boys, no more than eleven or twelve I would think, who look like cheerful ragamuffins from an *Oliver* chorus line. Selen says it's common for the up-and-coming to learn alongside their elders.

On the back of their pants is a name, which Selen tells me is that of their sponsor. This may be a small warm-up event, but these men are all professionals, and at the big summer festival their fights can be watched by thousands of people.

'It's a very traditional Turkish sport,' Selen assures me. 'It has 640 years of history.'

Whilst the wrestlers (known as *pehlivani*) oil themselves up, a band of musicians, another vital ingredient in the sport, are also gathering. They wear loose blue waistcoats and baggy trousers with black-embroidered patterns and their instruments consist mainly of drums, *davul*, and oboes, *zurna*.

At last an announcer, the *cazgir*, brings them all together. Before the bouts begin, and some of them can last up to ninety minutes each, the *cazgir* introduces the competitors in his own inimitable fashion, often with a poem or a few jokes.

'The crowd love these people,' whispers Selen.

When the grappling eventually begins, all the pairs fight at the same time, supervised by a referee for each of them. Victory is achieved only when you can get your opponent flat on his back. Punching is not allowed, nor poking in the eye, but otherwise the rules of contact seem quite liberal. As it's almost impossible to get a grip on the lavishly oiled bodies they are allowed, nay encouraged, to slip a hand down the trousers of their opponent and use the buttocks as leverage, whilst the other hand grabs at the leather hem of the trouser just below the knee.

Intense concentration is required, and very often two slippery men will just lean upon one another, breathing in great heaves and waiting, sometimes for several minutes, for the moment to surprise their opponents. The band plays its part too, dictating the tempo of a bout by slowing down or speeding up the rhythm.

There is no danger of the physical effort becoming any easier once the oil is rubbed off, for attendants are prowling with fresh supplies and reanointing glistening bodies whenever possible. Now I know what 'pouring' is all about.

At the end of each bout, victor and vanquished have to hoist each other off the ground in a manly hug.

It sounds absurd, grown men covered in olive oil, hands down each other's trousers, but there is a curious dignity to the whole procedure. Nothing is arbitrary, moves are carefully worked out and sanctified by a history and tradition that goes right back to the Greeks and Romans. But it has been refined into something wholly Turkish, something that strikes a deep and patriotic chord in the country people.

Day Thirty-nine: *Istanbul*

The train from Edirne pulls into Sirkeci Station. Not the largest station in Istanbul but the most famous, linked for ever with the Orient Express, the train that, in various shapes and forms, has connected Turkey with the rest of Europe since 1883.

It's a delightful small station with an original roof supported by three graceful rows of cast-iron columns that follow the curve of the platform.

Our Zagreb-built locomotive squeals to a halt, face to face with the man who created modern Turkey, Kemal Atatürk, whose gold-painted head protrudes from a stone plinth beside the buffers. With his long straight nose and beetle-browed stare he looks vaguely sinister, like a magician. Which, in a sense, he was.

In little more than ten years he created the Turkish Republic, separated religion and state, introduced the Latin alphabet, and gave women full voting rights. It's particularly appropriate that his likeness should be here at Sirkeci for he did more than anyone to turn Turkey's mindset westward, towards Europe.

I leave the station, down a flight of marble steps and into Istanbul. The city doesn't work its magic straightaway. There's a filling station and some ugly concrete blocks to negotiate before you reach the waterfront. And there you are, quite suddenly, at one of the crossroads of the world.

Nowhere do history and geography merge as spectacularly as they do here, at the end of Europe and the beginning of Asia, where the Mediterranean meets the Black Sea. The great north–south, east–west corridors converge here and the city built on these low hills, by its various names of Byzantium, Constantinople and Istanbul, has been at the centre of world affairs longer than any other.

The location seems to heighten ordinary experience. Views seem more dramatic, departures and arrivals more significant, encounters more promising, awareness sharper. Istanbul always strikes me as a city with a foot in two distinct worlds and I can't imagine it ever jumping completely onto one side or the other.

As Orhan Pamuk says in his book on the city, 'Istanbul's greatest virtue is its people's ability to see the city through both Western and Eastern eyes.'

I set out across the Galata Bridge, my back to the great Ottoman and Byzantine monuments, heading up to Pera, once a colony of Genoese merchants. Fishermen line the bridge and flat-topped water taxis slide beneath it with inches to spare. On the piers are huge posters quoting Atatürk, 'Our most sacred duty is to keep the Republic alive'. These strident reiterations of republican ideals suggest that people need reminding of them, which in turn suggests that they're under threat.

Opposite Galatasaray School, at a fashionable, very Westernized café named after him, I meet Ara Güler, one of the most experienced documentary photographers in the world. He looks and sounds wise, with a big strong grizzled head, bald at the top and heavily bearded at the bottom. He is still digesting the news that has rocked the country of the assassination, two days ago, of the Armenian Hrant Dink, a liberal writer and publisher. Güler knew him well, had played poker with him a few days before.

'I took rather a lot of money off him,' he says, with a rueful grin, as if he was saying what his friend would have expected him to say in the circumstances.

The news coming through is that his killer was a young man from Trabzon, on the Black Sea, an extreme nationalist who regarded people like Dink and Nobel Prize-winning author Orhan Pamuk as bringing the country into disrepute by, among other things, daring to mention Turkish genocide of the Armenians ninety years earlier. Before dismissing the assassin as a madman, it's worth remembering that this same attitude is enshrined in law here. Article 301 of the Turkish Penal Code makes 'denigrating Turkishness' an offence.

Ara, a Jew and also an Armenian, is shocked but not altogether surprised. He lived through the trauma of a few years ago when four bombs went off near here, two one day, two the next, aimed at synagogues and British interests in the city. Two years before that sixty-four people were killed when a local synagogue was bombed.

There are threats to the Republic from both sides, from religious extremists and nationalists, and though the authorities are anxious to appear on top of the situation it is having an effect. Visitor numbers from Europe were down by eleven per cent last year though they're now climbing again. But Ara Güler, for all his fame and his international connections, has Istanbul in his blood and would never consider moving. He's just got himself a digital camera and he sets off to show me his favourite part of the city.

'Every day I discover a new Istanbul,' he tells me as we clamber up some steep steps in the Jewish quarter where once fine old buildings now seem old and neglected, unsteady and unloved, leaning on each other for support. He takes pictures of these old neighbourhoods because he fears that much of what he loves about the city will soon be gone for ever.

'We are walking in the dead body of Istanbul,' he declares, adding, 'the smiling dead body.'

'Smiling?' I query.

'No, no! Smelling. The smelling dead body.'

His friend Orhan Pamuk has said that Ara Güler's photographs show an Istanbul 'where there is as much melancholy in the faces of the city's people as in its views'.

Pamuk seems to think that melancholy is the prevailing mood of the city, a mood he clearly approves of, and which he feels is in danger of being threatened by money and materialism. Istanbul has certainly boomed since I was last here on my way from *Pole to Pole* in 1991, with two new bridges over the Bosphorus and a number of dull but unavoidable modern towers muscling in on a skyline that was once dominated by domes and minarets.

To avoid becoming too much affected by others' regrets, I take a ferry into Asia, and up into one of the many suburbs spreading out over the exposed hillsides of the eastern bank of the Bosphorus. This is new Istanbul, without decay but without character, where everything is fresh out of the box.

In one of these security-gated suburban villas I find Tanyeli's Dance Academy, where people can learn to belly-dance like Turkey's greatest star.

Tanyeli is the go-ahead, hard-working face of Turkey's enterprise culture. Not content with being able to move her belly in almost any direction, at any speed, she has built herself into a brand, with a television show and a chain of similar academies as far afield as Florida and Australia. She's bright, sublimely confident, in very good shape and effortlessly in control of the three girls she's teaching today. At the end of a session with them she has a brief pit-stop when make-up checks her hair, wardrobe checks her clothes and as she takes a call on her mobile, someone else towels down her armpits.

When I ask her when she started to belly-dance, she spreads her arms wide, 'I think it started in my mother's tummy.'

She certainly knows how to sell it to a modern audience.

'It is like a meditation. If you feel the music, and if you know how to move your belly, you lose your negative energies and you don't have to run to the pharmacy to get your little pills.'

I ask her if she can teach belly-dancing to men.

She grimaces.

'It doesn't belong to men. The belly-dancing history started thousands of years ago when a woman wants to give birth and all the girls tell her to push it, breathe in, breathe out. So do you think it belongs to you or it belongs to us?'

Nevertheless she politely inspects my tummy and asks me to roll it for her. The best I can do is a rather obscene pelvic thrust.

'Think about salsa, samba, waltz,' she says sweetly, but firmly. 'Any kind of dance but not belly-dance.'

Day Forty: *Istanbul*

A boat up along the European shore of the Bosphorus. Meeting Ara Güler and reading Pamuk's *Istanbul* have sharpened my senses and I search the coast for signs of the fast-disappearing *yalis*, the elaborately stylish timber houses built as waterfront retreats for the city's prominent families. Few have survived the weather and the insatiable appetite for property by the water, and those that survive remind me of the houseboats in Kashmir, delicately beautiful, made for pleasure not for permanence. What they do show is how Ottoman architects and craftsmen of the nineteenth century were absorbing more and more European influence. It worked both ways and the French, as Lamartine's house in Plovdiv showed, were particularly fascinated by things Oriental. (Pamuk punctures any rosy picture of this relationship by pointing out that the nineteenth-century euphemism for syphilis in Turkey was *frengi* or 'French'.)

We pass the well-preserved ruin of Rumeli Castle, whose walls ride up the hill, almost immediately below a suspension bridge that carries six lanes of cross-Turkey traffic across the Bosphorus. Rumeli, ominously for the Byzantines, was the Ottoman word for 'west', and, completed by Mehmet II in 1452, it was the springboard for his conquest of Constantinople a year later. A victory of the East over the West, Islam over Christianity.

The new conquerors of Istanbul are still to be found beside the Bosphorus and one of them is Sakip Sabanci, once a cotton-picker from the southern city of Adana, now a self-made businessman of such wealth that some say he owns Turkey. He has spent a fortune turning a 1920s villa in Emirgan into a home for his fine art collection.

Here I meet Raffi Portakal, a debonair art dealer who has advised on the collection. He is bemused by the idea of Turkey not being thought a part of Europe. Even leaving aside the 500-year Ottoman presence in Eastern Europe, Constantinople was, for 1,000 years before that, the eastern outpost of Rome. Christianity survived here when Rome was being sacked.

As evidence for his country's continued interest in things Western he tells me of the Picasso exhibition he recently put on. Though entry had to be rationed to 2,000 a day, a quarter of a million people visited. This was not just the Istanbul elite, but people from all over Turkey. Indeed the exhibition will soon be going east to the capital, Ankara. For Raffi, the equation is quite simple.

'The Turkish people like the Western art, because the Turkish people are Western.' Which is why he is so frustrated about European behaviour over his country's membership of the EU. 'We know as a club member you have to accept many rules, but if the club start to create different rules... ' His words are obscured by a crowd of schoolchildren, all in neat private school uniforms, who emerge in a babble from the museum.

The thorny question of whether women in Turkey should wear the veil is addressed in a highly original way by Rabia Yalçin, who designs haute couture for Muslim women from an apartment five floors above the busy streets of Nişantaşi. Since the Republic was set up in 1923, Turkey has prided itself on separating state and religion and, like the French, does not permit women to wear the veil on state premises.

Rabia Yalçin, a small, doughty lady with a great sense of humour, wears a headscarf as she shows me her sensational, defiantly sexy outfits for Muslim women who want to maintain respectability without losing their femininity. Two tall, impassive models from Belarus demonstrate the dresses, one of which plunges down to the hip at the back, but can be easily covered with a whisper-thin veil.

This compromise between religious belief and feminine beauty is a very modern view, and one which I dare say traditionalists, especially men, would have problems with. Does it shock people, I ask her.

'Oh yes,' she says with a flashing smile. 'I like shocks.'

I'm in for another surprise in the evening as we visit one of Istanbul's old taverns, known as *meyhanes*. They are unpretentious neighbourhood places serving an uncomplicated fare of *meze*, *raki* and live music. The oldest *meyhani* in town is the Madame Despina Meyhanesi, which has been in business for 160 years. Its big bear of an owner welcomes us to what he says is 'the oldest entertainment culture in Turkey', beloved of artists, intellectuals and craftsmen. I read somewhere that they were all-male establishments, but that doesn't seem to be the case tonight, and I fall into conversation with a voluble Turkish woman who warns me against jumping to easy conclusions about her country. Istanbul is not all of Turkey, she says, and what Istanbul thinks is not the same as what the sixty million in the rest of the country think.

As far as membership of a wider Europe goes, she believes the question is not how much the EU needs Turkey, but how much Turkey needs the EU. Her agricultural system would almost certainly not survive the European competition.

She urges me to go east and see what people think there.

I'm halfway through a plateful of kidney beans, ratatouille, red peppers, beetroot and a glass of the aniseed-flavoured *raki* when an attractive woman with long earrings and dark hair pulled back introduces herself and sits down beside me. My hopes rise briefly, only to be dashed by the arrival of the house band, a daunting quartet of violin, drums, screechy oboe and a magnificent multi-stringed zither, which clusters around her as she serenades me with a heartstring-tugging number.

She's called Sevval, she sings in ten languages, and has an English boyfriend called Rupert whom she met on a beach. Her songs are part of an old tradition of classical Turkish music peculiar to the *meyhani*.

'Turkish people really love to be sad, you know. The songs make an imitation sadness.' The name *meyhani* is, says Sevval, a combination of two Turkish words, *mey* meaning drink and *hani* meaning house.

'And you start to drink *raki* and listen to this kind of music and you start to open your heart and cure your soul.'

'Rather than wine or beer?'

'Oh yes,' she assures me, 'because with this drink, you are going to wake up better tomorrow.'

With this Holy Grail of all drinkers in mind, I have my glass filled and wait to have my heart unlocked, and my soul cured.

Day Forty-one: *Selçuk*

At the entrance to a natural amphitheatre formed in the lee of a hill beside the deep blue Aegean Sea there hangs the splendid sign, '25th Selçuk-Ephesus Camel-Wrestling Festival'. The names alone are epic, Selçuk being the home of the first Turkic tribe to test the Byzantine hegemony and Ephesus once designated capital of Asia by the Romans.

It's a fine day with clear skies and smoke is drifting from barbecues already cooking sausages and kebabs for the expected 20,000 camel-wrestling fans.

On the curving slope hundreds, if not thousands, of white plastic chairs and tables are laid out and on top of the hill is a steel frame to which has been lashed a huge likeness of Atatürk, looking dapper, as he always did, in an astrakhan hat.

The fact that this event is set out in the open, rather than in a specially built stadium, makes it a very folksy, traditional affair, part county fair, part point-to-point. This is essentially a country sport, a celebration of the camel and all it represents in Turkish culture – the nomadic life and the camel trains that brought goods and prosperity along the Silk Road. No matter that there

are hardly any working camels left in Turkey, no matter that
those who will be wrestling here today are the pampered pets of
those that can afford to keep them, no matter they're more like
racehorses than beasts of burden, there is something reassuring
about the camels. Something that inspires deep affection. Camels
are a good thing.

Having said that, this is clearly a boy's thing. The spectators
filling these slopes have the air of men who've got away from
shopping, or visiting the mother-in-law, for a day. They're doing
what Turkish blokes seem to enjoy doing, lighting fires in their
portable braziers, grilling a few sausages, opening jerrycans of *raki*
and smoking like chimneys.

I'm here with Yusuf Yavas, a local archaeologist. From the top
of the hill we can see, in no particular order, a coach park, filling
rapidly, a big bland estate of holiday homes and a canal built in the
sixth century BC to connect Ephesus with the sea. We're sitting on
top of twenty-seven centuries of continuous human occupation.

'More Roman sites than Italy, more Greek sites than Greece'
is how Yusuf describes this stretch of the Aegean coast, adding
regretfully that his government doesn't attach a high priority to
the work of himself and his colleagues.

He's fifty-two. His grandparents were originally Greek-
speaking Muslims from Crete and Salonika who were forcibly
moved out of their traditional homelands in the exchange of
populations which followed fighting between Greece and Turkey
after the First World War. Enormous hardships and ignominious
loss of property were forced on two million people. Now he wants
to see Turkey closer to the rest of Europe, away from the fanatics
of right and left. I ask him why he thinks some Europeans are
dragging their feet over Turkish admission. He puts it down to
fears over religion and unemployment.

'Turkey is ninety-eight per cent Islamic country. Also
unemployment rates in Turkey are quite high, I think European
people think, OK, all the Turks will come to Europe and take our
jobs.'

For a moment his mild manner slips.

'I think European people are not informed very well. They
have an image in their heads of an Arabic country. Turkey is not

Arabic. It's a secular country. We have democracy for about eighty years. They should learn more about Turkey.'

Then he smiles, a little apologetically.

'Maybe it's our fault too. We must express our feelings better.'

We're interrupted by a cheer from the crowd as the first camels are led into the arena below us. They're much bigger, taller and hairier than the camels I saw in the Sahara. They come from Iran where they breed two-humped with one-humped camels to produce this big single-humped breed. Not that one can see anything of the hump itself for it's obscured by the *hamut*, a sumptuously decorated wooden superstructure covered with silks and brocades, lengths of embroidered felt and carpet, a leather saddle and a bell which rings whenever they move. This edifice is both decorative and very heavy and causes the camel to sashay and sway like some great diva. Yusuf tells me that for the last three or four months they will have had to live from the fat stored in their humps as their trainers deliberately stop feeding them in order to increase their aggression. It's also their rutting season, so the combination of hunger and lust will, they hope, make for some good entertainment.

It may also explain why most of them, the camels not the trainers that is, are foaming at the mouth.

All the camels have names, and their pedigree is studied carefully by those who gamble on the outcome. Apparently a few years ago there was a fashion for calling camels Saddam, Bush and Clinton.

The atmosphere is, almost literally, intoxicating. Smoke, rich with the smell of tobacco and grilling meat, drifts across the hillside, along with the whining, thumping squeal of drum and pipe bands, whose relentless rhythm mingles with a P/A system booming out non-stop commentary from the podium.

Balloon- and candyfloss-sellers work the noisy crowd. The camel owners – men in suits with mobiles at their ears, well-dressed women inscrutable behind dark glasses – take their places in the VIP enclosure. The ring fills as the competing camels, some of whom may have spent eight to ten hours in a truck on the way here, get to stretch their legs, foam a bit and generally get angry. Each one is accompanied by a team of *urganci*, rope men, who follow their camel like dockers around a ship, ready to restrain their beast should things get out of hand.

As the tension rises the camels have their wicker muzzles removed, though their jaws remain restrained by thin string to prevent any serious biting. Then they're divided off into pairs. The unstoppable commentator's voice rises an octave and, finally, the wrestling begins.

Despite the foaming and the starvation and the randiness some of the camels seem remarkably uninterested in starting a scrap, and have to be raced towards their opponents by the *urganci*. Once they get locked together their necks seem to do most of the work, pushing against each other and occasionally entwining so that two heads appear to spring from one neck, a surreal parody of the double-headed Hapsburg eagle.

The camels are divided into three categories, roughly corresponding to small, medium and large, and after some inconclusive early bouts things move up a gear as the more popular heavyweights, roared on by their supporters, face up to each other.

One breaks away from its minders and gallops off across the ring, aiming straight for any other camel it can find. Two more collide so hard that one of them is completely lifted off its front legs and remains inelegantly suspended for quite some time as the other one tries to kick his back legs away. Which is not as easy as it looks, for the back legs, thin and spindly as they may appear, are, once splayed, as tough as steel cables.

There are certain established moves in camel-wrestling, which they call 'tricks'. Biting ankles and forelocks seems a speciality, and the headlock, with the opponent's head trapped between the two front legs, is much appreciated, except of course by the camel whose head it is. Ribbons of saliva fly everywhere as they push, grab, bite and lock before a winner is declared and the rope men rush in to haul the beasts apart.

In early afternoon, a near-perfect bout has the crowd on their feet. Two top-weight camels are, without doubt, wrestling. Leaning, twisting and grappling each other with their long, thickly maned necks. After a long stalemate, one begins to dominate, slowly forcing the neck of his opponent down onto the sand. Then the other flicks his neck away and they start again, until not only the head but the entire trunk of one of the camels flicks over and lies in the dust. What with the shrieks from the crowd, the manic thudding of drums, and the apoplectic ranting of the commentator, I feel I've been knocked out too.

I've had a glimpse of another Turkey, away from metropolitan Istanbul. A glimpse of the strength of old traditions (the 20,000 crowd here was almost entirely Turkish). But even here there has been much change. Selçuk's population has doubled in the last twenty years and the once quiet bays of the Aegean are choked with holiday apartment blocks. But perhaps the most poignant image of change is the vehicle ahead of us as we leave the wrestling arena. It's a pick-up truck, and in the back, wrapped tight in a white canvas sheet, with only its head protruding, is a magnificent Iranian camel. For thousands of years his ancestors carried the trade that made Europe rich, Now he's another commodity.

Day Forty-three: *Göreme, Cappadocia*

We're 300 miles east of Istanbul now, at a city called Kayseri. With a population of over a million, its thriving business parks and gleaming new automobile distribution centres are clear evidence that the commercial boom is not confined to Istanbul and the west. This is the heart of Anatolia, the ninety-five per cent of Turkey which is geographically part of Asia. Its size, both in land and population numbers, would, if accession were to go ahead, make Turkey by far the largest country in the European Union. And this worries a lot of Europeans.

Yet the history of this area links up with the very heart of European culture. In the years after the birth of Christ, Kayseri, then called Caesarea, was where St Paul (born Saul in nearby Tarsus) began to make the first Christian conversions. The province of Cappadocia became the epicentre of the early Christian Church, and core beliefs such as the concept of the Holy Trinity were first formulated here by a group of leading ecclesiastical writers known as the Cappadocian Fathers.

Cappadocia was once a huge area, home to the Hatti and

then the Hittites two to three thousand years before Christ. It was known as far back as the reign of King Darius of Persia as Katpatuka, the 'Land of Beautiful Horses'. Now the name refers only to a small area characterised by the weird and wonderful rock formations, some of which I am riding through, on a good-tempered grey called Bulu, in the company of Hasan Çalci, a local boy from Göreme who studied art and design in Italy and now runs one of the most beautiful of the cave hotels in Cappadocia.

All around us are tall thin pillars of honey-coloured rock which look like giant asparagus spears, or as most people seem to prefer, colossal phalluses. Indeed, so geologically aroused is the scenery that it's popularly known as The Valley of Love.

Millions of years ago a volcano, known to the ancient world as Mount Argaeus and now on my map as Erciyes Daği, erupted, spewing lava across a wide area. The compressed ash solidified into a soft rock called tufa, which was easily eroded by the wind and rain, but of such complex composition that the erosion was never uniform and rather than whole valleys being scooped out and washed away, vertical columns of rock have been left standing, like trees that have survived a forest fire.

Not all resemble giant phalluses; there are tall conical shapes, rectangular slabs and thin columns with precarious, table-like basalt caps, eroding much more slowly, perched on top. And behind the rock faces are elaborate troglodyte networks which often provided refuges for those fleeing religious persecution.

The most interesting of these is a complex near Göreme where thirty rock churches, out of an estimated thousand throughout Cappadocia, are clustered in a comparatively small area, now an open-air museum. These date back to anywhere between the sixth and eleventh centuries and one of them, the Dark Church, has an almost self-contained interior, with a set of mock architectural features, non-supporting columns and faux arched vaulting carved from the rock. The advantage of being the Dark Church, so called because this amazing place was lit by one small window, is that the rich and complex frescoes that cover the walls have been well preserved. The only damage to the robed figures and the biblical characters is that the eyes, and in some cases the mouths, have been scratched out. This is believed to have been done by Muslim Turks who took refuge in these caves after they'd been abandoned by the Christians, and who believed that the eyes carried some sort of curse.

Hasan's hotel in among the rocks is called the Anatolian Houses and every room is carved in a different shape and decorated with carefully chosen local artefacts. It's out of season at the moment and we have the place almost to ourselves. Hasan was born, the son of a carpet-weaver, in these caves he's converted. Starting out with just a donkey and an English dictionary, he began to show tourists around.

I ask him how much physical closeness to the Middle East (Syria is little more than 200 miles to the south) affects this part of Turkey.

'Of course we are believing in the same religion,' and here his brow furrows, 'but the mentality of our life is totally, totally different with Easterns than with Europeans. West has always been more exciting for the Turkish people.'

Day Forty-four: *Göreme*

One of the best ways to see the spectacular Cappadocian landscape is from a balloon, and I'm all prepared to go up at first light this morning when the telephone by my bed rings and I'm given the bad news that our ascent has been cancelled owing to strong winds and the likelihood of snow.

Having sustained mild sunburn on the horseback ride yesterday, this comes as something of a shock, but when I peer out of the window there is no rosy-fingered dawn, but a leaden grey sky and a hissing wind that turn this eccentric landscape of rock stacks and fissured stone columns from friendly to vaguely sinister.

In Göreme the gift shops have their wares out, but few people are buying. Walk up the hill to meet up with a German anthropologist and his wife who keep a guest house called The Fairy Chimney Hotel. It sounds a bit whimsical but there is a sound historical background to the idea of fairy chimneys. The Turks who rediscovered this area after much of it had been abandoned looked with some awe at the rock towers, many of which had small holes in the top where birds nested. They concluded, quite rightly, that no human beings could live up there, but, rather less rightly, that the inhabitants must therefore be fairies.

Andus Emge is a bit of a lone wolf amongst anthropologists. Trained at Heidelberg, his speciality was vernacular architecture, adobe mud dwellings, that sort of thing. He first came here as a student twenty years ago at a time when the Turkish government was encouraging those living in caves, fairy chimneys and the like, to resettle into newly built conventional houses. He returned in the 1990s, when the prevailing wisdom had begun to change. UNESCO had declared this both a World Heritage and Landscape Heritage area (leading, says Andus, to a double dose of bureaucratic confusion) and insisted that the old rock dwellings should be lived in after all, at the same time imposing restrictions on materials and design that put many people off.

In 1997 Andus paid the local council 25 euros rent a year and began work on a property that had been abandoned for so long that it was widely assumed to be haunted. He's done wonders, but there are aspects that would give any health and safety inspector minor heart failure.

Andus' workroom, for instance, is only accessible from a steep and narrow outside staircase with no rail of any kind to hold onto. A small hobbit-like door through which you have to bend double to enter gives onto a warm and womb-like room carved out of the rock. A cave it might be, but it's a cave with ADSL broadband access and the first I see of Andus, he's illuminated by the light from an Apple Mac screen.

Andus concedes that there were good reasons for resettling people. None of the rocks is altogether stable and there had been instances of people being killed by collapse. Degradation is inevitable, and he likens the chimneys to icebergs, slowly depleting all the time.

But the majority have been occupied quite safely for centuries, and his cave complex was once a monastery. They have all the usual advantages of being warm in winter and cool in the heat of summer and because the tufa is so soft, many of the usual home alterations can be done with a chisel or a pickaxe. If he wants a new shelf he just chisels an alcove out of the wall. And what's more, this is no below-ground cave. It's a chimney, a cave with a view. A troglodyte skyscraper.

Outside the rain has turned to snow and the buildings of Göreme, both natural and unnatural, have disappeared into a swirling white mist. We pick our way carefully down the now lethally slippery steps and into the living room, or more accurately, living cave, where Andus' Turkish wife Gülcan has prepared food and some tea.

Gülcan is a round-faced, merry lady some years younger than Andus, with braided black hair, a multi-bangled ethnic necklace, big attractive eyes and a mischievous smile.

When Andus came to live here, she remembers, he was considered to be either mad or possibly a secret agent. Her Turkish friends, especially the younger generation, were not interested in living in caves, seeing them as difficult to keep clean, impractical for all mod cons and quite possibly haunted. She herself is now completely converted to life in a fairy chimney and refers to Andus as 'my good and lovely fairy', which embarrasses him. Rather happily.

After we've eaten, the talk turns to the strength of superstition round here and Gülcan invites me to meet a neighbour of theirs who can read fortunes from coffee grounds.

The three of us sit cross-legged on a divan whilst some strong Turkish coffee is prepared. After I've drained my cup the neighbour, a woman of early middle age with a sharp face framed by a headscarf, instructs me to put my saucer on top of my cup and turn the cup upside down. After allowing a few minutes for the residue to cool she asks me to lay a finger on top of the cup, make a wish, then turn cup and saucer the right way up and pass it over to her.

She studies the grounds on the saucer and on the side of the cup carefully, flicking her eye from one to the other.

While we're waiting, Gülcan talks up her neighbour's skills. She once told her mother that she would have a big fire in her house and, sure enough, two weeks later it happened. She also admits that, as far as the Islamic religion is concerned, reading coffee grounds is a sin.

'But I don't believe,' she says cheerfully.

'What if someone saw really bad news?' I ask her.

Gülcan's expression changes, and she casts a quick glance at the other woman.

'Once she told me she was reading for another neighbour and her brother was lost for some time and...' she lowers her voice to a whisper, 'she says I hope it will not happen, but I have seen a dead body in the coffee.'

However silly my rational self says these things are I can never have my fortune told without a slight drying of the mouth and dampening of the palms, so I'm relieved that there's nothing nasty to be seen. I will travel far. I must be careful of dark places where I will encounter snakes.

'Bad animals,' she confirms, but won't be drawn as to whether the snakes are pythons.

That is apparently the extent of the bad news. The good news provokes a lot of giggling between the two of them.

'You are going to meet with two different ladies. They are very beautiful and one is much richer than you.'

'Does the coffee indicate what my wife might think?'

'Ah,' says Gülcan, 'you have a wife too?'

I nod. More consultation.

'Well, there is a new love for you. In the Cappadocia area.'

They then break off for quite intense speculation around the coffee cup, broken by ever more frequent giggling. Gülcan nods significantly. 'Oh, that's interesting. You are going to meet this rich lady in the internet chat room.'

My impression is that the whole process has less to do with psychic penetration and more to do with a good old gossip. Coffee-reading is, Gülcan told me, very popular but eighty per cent of it is done by and for women. It's probably a good way of winkling out the scandal, talking about what they couldn't talk about just face to face. That's my theory.

Meanwhile I'm thinking of setting up a new website – Richladies.com.

Day Forty-five: *Göreme*

This morning's phone call brings good news. The wind has dropped, the skies are clear and conditions look ideal for our balloon flight. The only trouble is it's not yet six o'clock and it's pitch dark and bitterly cold. Not much talk as we're driven just outside the town to a clearing amongst the cones of rock, where two huge balloons are being prepared.

The pilot of my balloon is a Swede called Lars and his co-pilot is his English wife Kali. They have flown all over the world but are almost as excited about today's flight as we are. The air will be both clear and cool. Visibility should be near-perfect.

We're up in the sky about the same time as the sun, and for a while it is uncomfortably cold. The ride, though, is magnificent. The strange and unique landscape all begins to make sense as we rise above it. The eastern horizon is broken by the 12,848-foot peak of Erciyes Daği, its summit partly ripped away by the eruption that helped shape everything we can see. Long, flat tables of rock mark the height of the plateau created by the vast lake of lava, most of it now cracked, fissured and fashioned into the bluffs, cones and tall pillars that cover the ground like sentinels of some petrified army.

With the hard, bright sun at a low angle and a fresh-fallen blanket of snow on the ground, it's not only the rocks that stand out. We can see the fine detail of fields and orchards and vineyards. Though the volcanic rock makes for fertile soil, the climate has changed over the last few years and, according to Kali, the combination of warmer winters and late frosts has ruined harvests. Vines and apricot trees have been worst affected and certainly the apricot orchards look especially vulnerable under the snow. Many farmers are turning to tourism instead, or leaving the area altogether.

'What used to be farms have now been abandoned,' she says, with the regret of someone who first fell in love with the area sixteen years ago. 'When everybody had a horse and cart and everybody worked the fields. Give it another ten years and I don't think we're going to recognise much.'

Lars seems less interested in what's happening on the ground than what's happening in the air. He reads the air currents with obsessive delight, alert to all the subtle shifts and patterns, such as the emptying of the cold air from the valleys as the land warms up. His greatest wish, he says, would be to be able to colour the air to show us the streams and eddies and waterfalls and rapids all around us, which only he seems to be able to see. He takes us up to 8,000 feet. From here the detail is less distinct. The rock forests of Cappadocia have given way to a wider view. From the Taurus Mountains in the south to the rising Anatolian plateau to the east. Here the Tigris and Euphrates rivers, around which the earliest civilisations in the world were born, rise and run south to Iraq.

They sound very distant and very remote from our world, but if Turkey ever does join the European Union, and most of those I've talked to here want that to happen, then Europe will share its south-eastern border with Syria, Iraq and Iran. Now that would concentrate the mind.

Moldova

Day Forty-six: *Chişinău*

I LOOK out of my hotel window in downtown Chişinău (pronounced Kish-i-now), expecting a panorama of Soviet drabness but all I can see is a sylvan carpet stretching across the city. Below me is a park, full of fine, tall trees, into which people are disappearing with various bits of equipment. I mean to ask the staff what's going on but they don't encourage contact.

The breakfast room, with high ceilings, huge paintings and long brocaded curtains, is a temple of scarcity. Everything has to be specially asked for, and even quite basic items, like milk or butter, receive the same response.

'Ten minutes.'

A request for toast is met with a look of exasperated disgust, as if I'd asked them to get a child off the street and roast it for me.

At least you know where you are. As more and more of the big East European city hotels are adopting the smile-at-everybody, 'Have a nice day!' school of insincerity, it's quite refreshing to find that saying what you mean and behaving like you really feel still survives here in Moldova.

I'm further cheered by a pleasant stroll in the Stefan cel Mare Park, where display boards, book racks and a small stage have been erected for what a lady organiser helpfully tells me is National Tongue Day. This raises all sorts of expectations and I'm quite disappointed when I learn later that the correct translation of the event is actually National Language Day. This is a celebration of the Moldovan language, and is a bit of a political hot potato as the language is basically Romanian, and yet a quarter of Moldova's four and half million inhabitants are Russian and its current government is communist. The tug of war between Romania and Russia for the soul of this tiny country seems to be Moldova's biggest problem.

'I hope that, if Romania will enter the European Union... Moldova will go to the European Union. Not to the Russians, to the West. That's my opinion.'

Olga is in her late twenties. Born in Moldova, she went to Romania at the age of sixteen to become an actress. She lives in Bucharest but comes home regularly to see family and friends.

She embodies the predicament of this young republic, the most fragile of all the post-Soviet newcomers. Stretching some 200 miles north to south, and little more than 50 miles from east to west, Moldova is an awkward compromise between an historically Romanian-leaning west, which used to be called Bessarabia, and an historically Russian-leaning east, separated by the Dniester River. The result of this split personality is that, tiny though the country may be (and I could find no English-language guidebook solely dedicated to Moldova), she has already nurtured two breakaway republics. One of these, called Gagauzia, has settled for autonomy within Moldova, but the other, which calls itself Transdniester, not only declared independence, but went to war to establish it. In 1992 thousands were killed and wounded, and though it has no international recognition, Transdniester is as good as lost to Moldova.

Once away from the hotel, the capital of this much compromised republic is a comfortable, almost cosy place to be on this warm and sunny morning. The Cactus Saloon in which I sit with Olga serves a fine espresso and its terrace looks out on colourful, tree-shaded streets. It feels more like California than the capital of a country ranked the poorest in Europe.

Big cities are an often inaccurate gauge of the feel of a country, so I'm pleased when Olga suggests I come out to meet her mother in the countryside an hour or so south of Chişinău.

The landscape is wide and open, with long rolling fertile slopes. The Russians used to call this the Sunny Country. Once off the main road the tarmac breaks up and sometimes disappears altogether, leaving us to negotiate villages on unmade muddy tracks, with horses and carts trotting impatiently behind us. The women wear headscarves, jackets and floral skirts and there seem to be few young adults around. There's strong evidence of religion, both Romanian and Russian Orthodox, in the shape of decorated crosses above well-heads and freshly painted churches and graveyards in better shape than most of the houses.

The road into Gradişte, Olga's mother's village, runs down a long avenue of walnut trees before turning to follow the course of a sluggish, willow-bordered stream. A man comes towards us driving a flock of geese. Neither agricultural nor industrial revolutions seem to have made much mark here.

Olga's mother Helena has lived on her own since her husband died seven years ago. The family house, built by her grandparents, stands, as is the way here, end onto, rather than facing, the road.

It's long and low with a tin roof and a blue-painted conservatory with stained-glass panels opening out onto a backyard full of cats and kittens, dogs and puppies, chickens and the occasional rabbit. The gardens at the back and front of the house are productive rather than decorative and, despite being the other side of seventy, Helena grows and gathers her own potatoes, tomatoes, cherries, apples, walnuts, plums, aubergines, sweet peppers, cranberries, raspberries, strawberries and watermelons as well as making wine from her own grapes. The house used to be heated with wood fires until gas came to the village, though because of a connection cost of 500 euros, she's one of only a handful who've taken advantage. The toilet is out in the garden.

Helena is a doughty lady of restless energy who gets up at four most summer mornings and pretty soon she's got me out picking raspberries, which have a fresh juiciness I'd almost forgotten was possible.

We talk a little about the old days when her husband was a local Party official and everyone worked on the collective farm. There was enough food and job security, even if nothing much ever happened, and it was tough for everyone after the glad hand of socialism was withdrawn in 1991.

When she isn't managing her sizeable estate she keeps abreast of things from the newspapers, reads her Bible and attends the local church, where congregations are routinely 100 or more, half the total population of the village.

Olga's older sister, the only one of the family's seven children still living in the village, comes by. She's been a teacher here for thirty years and seems downtrodden by it. She would desperately like to leave, but something in her eyes says that she knows she's left it too late.

Helena won't let us leave without cooking us a typical Moldovan supper. After she's said grace we tuck into chicken soup with home-made bread, a crusty cheese pie and pancakes stuffed with sesame, sunflower seeds and walnuts, washed down with a jug of her own white wine.

As we head back to Chişinău I muse on the contrasting lifestyles of self-sufficient Helena in her isolated village, and her daughter Olga, living in cosmopolitan Bucharest, chosen recently to be the face of Paco Rabanne in an ad campaign. The old and new worlds, one closed and secure, the other open, but insatiable. I know nothing much of Moldova but already I feel myself getting sentimental about it.

Day Forty-seven: *Chişinău*

Before I get too soft, I'm going to look at some of the less savoury realities of life in Moldova, in the company of Tatiana, still in her twenties. A tough and experienced journalist, she also works for UNICEF.

The village of Bieşti, two hours' drive north-east of the capital, is in one of the poorest parts of the country and the children here have many problems, including drink, drugs and the predations of sex-traffickers.

It's a little down at heel, but far from grim, with blue-painted metal fences and filigree ironwork decorations on guttering, roof-ends and fenceposts. A stern Second World War memorial commemorates the Russians (and Moldovans) who died fighting the Germans (and their Romanian allies). Opposite it, UNICEF has turned a run-down building into a community house, where the local children can work on computers, read, draw, learn acting and generally meet and talk. Many of them are just plain lonely, with fathers and mothers often forced abroad to earn money, leaving the older children to bring up younger families.

Today, on a patch of grass behind the war memorial, a group of children, with the help of a charismatic local UNICEF representative, are to put on a play they've written about the dangers of sex-trafficking. With the music of Peruvian pipes, Ennio Morricone, Celine Dion and others booming out over a P/A system, they present a powerful tale whose action follows three traffickers who come to the village (always depicted with a white backcloth) where the children do most of the work and the men sit around and drink. By various means they persuade local women to come with them to earn big money abroad (depicted by a black backcloth), where, of course, it all turns sour and they end up first having to beg and later to sell themselves into prostitution, which generally involves being raped first and turned onto drugs.

These adolescent children play rejection, anger and violence frighteningly well, but they also play compassion and grief with quiet force.

In less than fifteen minutes I learn a lot from them. That much of the work here, sorting and processing tobacco leaves, is poorly paid and dangerous. It demands long hours and can lead to cancer and leukaemia in the children. That most of the sex-traffickers are people from within their own community who have already made some money abroad. That the children are particularly at risk because so many parents, a quarter of the village population, are abroad at any one time, some of them going five or six years without seeing their children. That the women are taken predominantly to Spain and Italy to beg and Russia, Israel, Egypt and Greece for sex. That in this village children become adults from the age of twelve.

As Tatiana wryly points out, the only thing about the play which doesn't ring true is the happy ending.

Despite all we've seen, she says, 'If you ask at the end of the play who wants to go abroad, the majority would say, "I do".'

Later, back in Chişinău, Tatiana and I end the afternoon in the Giardina Publica sitting at a café and watching a curiously wonderful throwback to the old days, a communal tea-dance to which anyone can come along with or without partners and join in. The average age of the participants is probably not far short of seventy. They're all dressed with care and some elegance in the fashions of fifty years ago, and look, by and large, to be intelligent people of means.

A live orchestra plays ballroom favourites and there must be a hundred couples swirling around, all looking quietly happy.

Tatiana admires these people and the fact that they continue to take seriously what was very much a communal, Soviet thing. I ask if there is much regret at the passing of the old Soviet Union and she nods.

'Actually, a lot. I think people miss not the regime, but they miss the jobs and pensions and, you know, cheap food and good vacations.'

'And what about you?'

She replies without a pause. 'I also miss the Soviet period. Because I was young and I had my parents and my grandparents and everything seemed to be so beautiful.' She pauses and then goes on more thoughtfully. 'Logically, of course, I'm happy that it's not here and I can speak with you today. Twenty years ago this would be a crime.'

Tatiana sips a coffee. Behind her the band strikes up again, something Latin-American. 'It's important to be realistic. You miss the sensation of something, you miss the smell or the taste, but you cannot miss something which killed and made unhappy so many generations.'

The young Moldovans who never knew the Sovietic system, as Tatiana calls it, prefer a different kind of dancing, which she promises to show me when we go out to sample the vigorous and inventive night life of Chişinău. She's promised we'll go to a club where they make drinks with hot coals and mix cocktails by pouring the ingredients straight into the customer's mouth and shaking their head around. By the time I leave, which is obviously far too early, there's been no such head-shaking action, but a woman dressed as a schoolgirl is walking along the bar slowly shedding her clothes and heading for a pole.

Day Forty-eight: *Chişinău to Tiraspol, Transdniester*

This morning I rather tentatively enquire at reception about the possibility of getting laundry done.

'Where is your laundry?' asks the lady fiercely, as if I might have left it in Saudi Arabia or Macau.

The idea that the customer is always wrong might cling on here seventeen years after the collapse of the one-party system but tonight we shall be staying in a self-declared republic that finds places like this positively liberal.

It hasn't been easy to get permission to take a film crew into Transdniester, but there are two events which might have made things easier for us. One is a UEFA Under-21 international between Moldova and Switzerland being played in the capital Tiraspol tonight; and the other is Transdniester's National Day, when this schismatic republic that claims 2,000 square miles of Moldova will be celebrating its fifteenth anniversary. And breakaway republics love a bit of publicity.

The border is only 40 miles east of Chişinău. We have to negotiate three separate roadblocks at each of which Transdniestrian police and army check our papers beneath gantries proudly adorned with the emblem of the hammer and sickle, which, in the rest of Eastern Europe, you now see only in museums or flea-markets.

Once across the border all seems to conform to the *Lonely Planet*'s description of Transdniester as 'one of the last surviving communist bastions'. The sad town of Bender is a gauntlet of cheap and identical housing blocks. Camouflaged military checkpoints guard the bridge across the wide and muddy Dniester, and a Russian tank sits heroically on a plinth in the centre of a roundabout.

From here on, though, the picture is confusing. On the outskirts of Tiraspol is a gleaming modern sports complex, home of the local football club FC Sheriff, the personal property of one Viktor Gusan. It is in the newly built hotel here that we are to stay, and indeed hopefully talk to Mr G himself.

We pull up outside the main office, beside a stretch limo and next to a Mercedes-Benz dealership.

A number of black-clad, shaven-headed security men stand at the front of the building, eyeing us coldly. One of them checks our papers and talks into his mobile in that low Russian guttural which the worst baddies always use on TV.

It turns out that the hotel we were to stay in is not yet completed, so we will be given rooms in the Players' Academy. We drive around the huge site, which has two full-size floodlit outdoor pitches, one covered training ground, ornamental gardens and an Olympic-size pool (not finished). We're deposited finally at a freshly painted student dorm and canteen building.

The hard men in black eye us everywhere we go, phones up to their faces. The first person we see who's not in black seems amiable enough.

He comes towards us, beaming.

'Hello mans. You here for the match?'

We nod.

His face clouds as he sees equipment. 'But no filming. You know? No filming!'

One of the anomalies of the political split in Moldova is that the bulk of the country's industry is located in breakaway Transdniester, including armaments, steel, a textile business employing 15,000, and a shoe factory employing 6,000. Also on the wrong side of the Dniester is Moldova's oldest and most productive wine and spirit producer, Kvint (Cognacs, Vines and Beverages of Tiraspol). This 110-year-old enterprise in Lenin Street has recently been privatised and is now owned, surprise, surprise, by Viktor Gusan. It occupies a handsome set of red-brick buildings with a modern extension and I'm shown around by the well-built, strikingly vivacious Galina, who is clearly dying to tell us things but has not a word of English, and the rather more dour, Russian-born Dimitri whose default mode is definitely gloom.

'Is there any restaurant where we can eat in Tiraspol, Dimitri?'

'No.'

Their main product is brandy, and some of the classic bottles are on sale in Chişinău for 200 dollars (half a yearly wage for some). I notice that all their bottles have 'Made in Moldova' on the label. Dimitri explains that they have to print the country of origin and Transdniester is not recognised as a country. Apparently Moldova will only let them use the name if they register and this means paying tax to Chișinău.

There have been serious problems recently when the Russians, who take the majority of Kvint's output, used relabelling regulations as an excuse to embargo all Moldovan wines and spirits. This blockade has lasted six months and cost them eight million dollars' worth of orders already.

There seems to be no great sense of crisis emanating from the boardroom, where we're taken to sample their top brandies in the company of the dashing managing director, Oleg Byev.

As we sit round a long mahogany table, on whose immaculate white linen tablecloth stand nine brandy bottles, a set of cut-glass goblets, a bowl of fruit and assorted dishes of cold meats, cheese and olives, Byev is relaxed about just about everything. He's seen the company's output decline from thirty million litres a year in the Soviet period to ten million a year now, but, as a brandy-maker of forty years' experience, he welcomes the way the emphasis has changed from quantity to quality. His market is less protected, which means he now has to compete in an increasingly international arena on excellence alone.

I asked him how he felt when Moldova descended into civil war in 1992. His answer is philosophical, and perhaps conditioned by the fact that we were both holding glasses of very fine brandy, specially bottled for the 22nd Communist Party Congress in 1961 and known as 'The Party Spirit'.

'If war and peace were decided by wine-makers, there would never be any war.'

Dimitri was right. There is nothing to do in Transdniester tonight but have supper in the canteen and watch Moldova's Under-21s take on Switzerland. In the stadium, which would have many Premiership clubs boggling with envy, there are maybe 3,000 people, of whom half are UEFA officials and the other half security. Orange-jacketed stewards are in their element, looking nasty and being paid for it.

Switzerland win 3–1, which is perhaps why Mr Gusan is reluctant to give us the promised interview. Word has it he left the country in a private jet straight after the game.

Day Forty-nine: *Tiraspol*

It's Transdniester's National Day, and it's raining.

Tiraspol is not Venice at the best of times but in low skies and drizzle, it looks particularly dispiriting, as if the gods might be punishing them for not having their national day at the same time as the rest of Moldova.

The signs in the centre of town point two ways: west to Chişinău, east to Odessa, engendering a strong feeling of being on the outer edge of Europe as we know it. We park and follow a hardy group of celebrants to the long, wide main street where some thousand troops are lined up and students with red flags stand at intervals marking the course of the parade. A low and modest dais has been provided for a presidium of VIPs.

The most eye-catching element of the mix is the policewomen, dressed like 1940s Hollywood pin-ups in very short grey skirts, black high heels, epaulettes and jaunty caps, whose beauty shines even through the rain.

On the dot of ten o'clock two military jeeps, both with the hammer and sickle and garland of corn emblem of Transdniester on their sides, are driven down the ranks of soldiers. In the back of each, and quite delicately balanced, is an elderly general with a peaked hat the size of a steering wheel and a chest stacked with medals and decorations. As the generals draw level with each detachment, its troops let out fierce cries of loyalty, which roll down the line one after the other in a rather stirring Mexican wave of sound.

Then there are speeches, the main one from President Smirnov, recently re-elected for a third five-year term, after which the march-past begins. Up close the army looks young, scrawny and scared. They're followed by police detachments and a lone helicopter which emerges from the low cloud and flies slowly along the parade route with the rebel flag, red with two green stripes, hanging from its belly. It's followed at a suitable interval by two droning turboprops which perform a long and doubtless ambitious aerobatic display almost totally obscured by the clouds.

Apart from a ferocious exhibition of Ninja-like unarmed combat, most of the set pieces that follow the parade are cultural rather than militaristic. Noticeably missing are any of the heavy weapons which normally mark these big communist march-pasts. No rockets or missiles on low-loaders. And the only tank on show is the one on the war memorial.

A choir of children, all dressed in white, sing patriotic songs to their President, and there then follows a bouncy display of Russian dancing, all high-stepping, heel-slapping, leaping twirls, squat-kicks and rictus grins. This, more than anything, embodies what Transdniester is all about. Ever since they expelled the Turks from the land east of the Dniester in 1792, the Russians have been regarded here as natural protectors, and nothing that happened after the fall of the USSR has changed that. After the war with the rest of Moldova (and there are displays here showing atrocities committed by the Moldovan army), ninety-seven per cent of Transdniester's 550,000 people voted for independence.

Russophilia is what keeps the Transdniestrians separate. They may have a communist administration, but then so does the rest of Moldova, and from the activities of Viktor Gusan it's clear that it is as pragmatic a communism here in Tiraspol as it is in Chişinău. What cannot be reconciled are Russian (Slav) and Romanian (Latin) differences, and things will not have been helped by a bomb attack on a bus in Tiraspol only two months earlier. This will only give heart to those who prefer a Russian union to a European Union. And that, of course, includes Vladimir Putin.

Away from the parade ground there is much letting down of hair. Stalls have appeared under the trees in the centre of town, a Ukrainian musical group is playing heart-rending melodies and, as in Chişinău yesterday, it's the seventy-year-olds who lead the on-street dancing. I watch mesmerised as an old woman reveals a mouthful of monumental gold crowns as she's twirled round and round by an old man in a suit, who a moment ago had been a lonely figure sitting on a bench.

In the West, all this would be recorded, filmed, photographed. Looking around the crowd here in Tiraspol I can't, apart from our own, see a single camcorder, mobile phone or digital camera.

They're just watching.

Day Fifty: *Chişinău to the Danube*

Glebus Sainciuc (pronounced 'Sign-chook') is eighty-seven. He wears scarlet lipstick, a mass of blond hair, a long dress and high heels. He's caressing a microphone and miming to a torchy Russian song. When the song reaches its climax he bows low and whips off a mask to reveal angular, almost cadaverous cheekbones, a long, straight nose, big ears and a well-trimmed silver-grey moustache.

We all applaud.

We're in a high-ceilinged, single-roomed studio in a concrete block of identical studios built in the Soviet years especially for artists. Glebus, its owner, is a Moldovan mask-maker and perhaps the most famous artist in the country. Hung all over the walls and piled up on the floor, his masks are bold and irreverent caricatures of the rich and famous. Politicians, musicians, entertainers: all are given a larger-than-life glow.

When we picked Glebus up from his house in a leafy street of modest but attractive stone cottages earlier this morning, I was aware only of his physical fragility and delicate state of health. Now, in the studio, surrounded by his work and an audience, he is transformed. His eyes sparkle, he's reaching for his scrapbooks, making sketches of the crew, cajoling, questioning, demanding.

He is anxious that we shouldn't leave without drawing a cow.

'I ask everyone who comes here to leave a cow.'

He has an album in which he's kept them all. It's headed 'Cows of the World Unite'.

As Glebus entertains I talk with Lika, his son, a tall, thin middle-aged man with well-grooved features and a ponytail protruding from a New York Yankees baseball cap.

I comment on the remarkable energy of his father's antics with the masks.

Lika nods. 'He doesn't like too many people, doesn't like being crowded. He calls it the theatre of one spectator.'

I ask Lika how much freedom artists had in the Soviet times.

'You were free to paint anything, but you were not free to exhibit it, until it was not dangerous. Everything was politicised. Even now it's politicised, you see. We were so used to the system we cannot quickly get out of it.'

His father, who's trying to draw me, shouts at him from across the room to move me round a bit.

'In Soviet times, everything was allowed, except you couldn't find it. Anything could be read, but nothing was available. Communism was all predicated on hopes. This will happen, if not tomorrow, then in a hundred years' time.'

He pauses.

'Now we have become real.'

I wonder what he thinks about Moldova's place in the world.

'We are European. I don't say which is better, but we don't belong to East culture. The Dniester is the border between East and West. For centuries.'

He heaves a sigh.

'Maybe it shouldn't be, but it is.'

Later, driving south from Chişinău for the last time, we see, rising from the immense vineyards and long lines of walnut trees, a solidly impressive red and white painted concrete sign which informs us that we are entering the Republic of Gagauzia. Its 170,000 inhabitants are an unusual combination of Christian and Turkish. Half the size of troublesome Transdniester, Gagauzia stopped short of demanding full independence and became instead an autonomous region within Moldova.

The broad slopes are home to some of the best vineyards in the country, and as wine comprises thirty per cent of Moldova's GDP it's important for both sides to maintain harmonious relations.

In the capital, a nondescript town called Comrat ('Comrade'), the doorway of a church in the centre sports a large, ghoulish painting of John the Baptist's head on a charger and opposite, outside the town hall, the only extant statue of Lenin I've yet seen in Europe.

As if to emphasise the unusual arrangements between the host nation and its satellite, the Gagauzian flag of blue, white and red horizontal stripes flies above the administration offices alongside the blue, gold and red verticals of the Moldovan.

There is to be one last celebration before we leave Moldova. In the village of Văleni live a couple, well into their sixties, who have attained considerable notoriety in Moldova. A pair of staunch metal gates open onto a small courtyard, with single-storey outbuildings on three sides, in the centre of which is a long table set for a meal. Beyond that is a yard in which I can see sheds, bales of hay, milk churns, horses, goats, chickens, a flock of geese, a drum kit, four black Marshall amplifiers, a line of mike stands and a cluster of cables coiling through the dust.

A short, round, bright-eyed lady with a ruddy, weathered face welcomes us in. This is Lidia, known universally as Bunica, Grandma, who stole the show when she banged the drum on the Moldovan entry which took sixth place in Eurovision 2005.

None of which would have happened had not a young singer-songwriter called Roma, in search of inspiration, found himself down here amongst the sandy fields of the Prut valley, to see a man reputed to be a legendary drum-maker.

When he showed Roma his work, he asked Lidia to help him play some of the drums he'd made. The energy and power of this traditional music was to be enormously influential on Roma, who blended the music he'd heard into an ethno-folk-rock mix for his group Zdob si Zdub, for whom Bunica became the mascot.

Today he's come back to repay the debt by playing in her backyard.

In contrast to Bunica's bustling friendliness, Roma, a slim, pale boy, stripped to the waist and wearing a black peaked cap, is polite but preoccupied. As his name implies, he's Gypsy. Some others in his band are Russians. Lidia's husband Tudor helps here and there, trailing a little in his wife's wake. He, like her, is short, stocky and weathered. He wears a black trilby and beams cheerfully at everyone.

A meal is served up at the long table. A wonderfully filling fish soup is followed by duck with noodles, various salads, feta cheese and strong local wine, put away with convivial cries of '*Noroc!*'

After the meal Roma, used to playing big halls all over East Europe, gets his band together amongst the goats and the geese. Their trombone, trumpet, flute, pipes, guitars and drums are joined by Bunica and Tudor, their son, two daughters-in-law and assorted nephews and nieces; a Moldovan von Trapp family with embroidered jackets for the men and floral skirts and white headscarves for the women. Roma seems to draw such inspiration from their presence that he pushes himself into an extraordinary hornpipe dance, accelerating all the time, with lightning footwork that has those neighbours who've come along to watch up and on their feet, and a dog breaking loose from its kennel and racing around the yard dragging a length of unattached chain behind him.

It's a happy last image of a muddled country. As a local put it to me the other night, Moldova is a small, weak nation, twenty-five per cent of whose population has fled abroad. The police are on the make and the legal system is not yet strong enough to fight the rampant corruption. But they're not sly, superficial and duplicitous like the Romanians, they didn't kill people's grandparents like the Russians, and they're not like the Ukrainians 'who talk as if they're drunk all the time'. Maybe not a ringing endorsement of national pride, but a pretty good definition of what it means to be Moldovan today.

Romania

Day Fifty-two: *Sulina*

IF ANYWHERE deserves to be called new Europe it is the Danube Delta, where 46 kilos of sediment are added to the continent every second. That's forty million tonnes every year. Europe's second-longest river (after the Volga) rises from three springs in the Black Forest of south-west Germany and ends in three channels pushed through 3,500 square miles of delta. The Danube winds between the Black Forest and the Black Sea through ten countries and covers 1,770 miles.

The middle channel of the Delta, the Brațul Sulina, is the one through which we entered Romania from the Black Sea yesterday night. It was a fierce introduction, with a wild sea whipped up by a fierce northerly wind doing everything to push us away. There was relief all round when we finally found the protection of the causeways.

We found accommodation close to the river, at the Casa Coral, a restaurant with a cramped little nest of rooms to one side, with two attentive dogs and a dining-room door that is no match for the north wind. No sooner does anyone shut it than the wind flings it open again with a crash. The waitress has taken to locking it each time, which means the next customer to arrive has to hang onto their hat and bang loudly on the glass for attention.

There is a medal on the wall of the restaurant, set in an impressive black velvet box and struck in 2006 to celebrate 150 years of what must be one of the first, if not the first example of pan-European co-operation, a hundred years ahead of the EEC/EU. The European Commission of the Danube was set up by the

British, French, Prussians and the other victors in the Crimean War to develop the Danube as an international waterway, and to protect it against any takeover by the Russians.

As a result of the Commission's work the population of Sulina grew to 5,000 inhabitants, representing twenty-seven nationalities, and by the end of the nineteenth century it earned the unofficial name of Europolis.

The Delta is a desolate waterscape which even the most zealous pursuers would think twice about entering. Perhaps it's not surprising then that the area around it became the home of a people called the Lipovani, who originally fled here at the end of the eighteenth century to avoid religious persecution in Russia. Many of them are fishermen working the network of narrow channels around the town.

They're not easy to find. They go about their business discreetly in wooden canoe-like boats. This morning they're pulling in the nets they laid the night before. One end is attached to a sharp stick, which is plunged into the mud only a few feet below the surface, whilst the other end is reeled out some 10 yards and marked by plastic bottles. Once they've pulled in the nets they paddle down a side channel to a small island on which stands a long, high rectangular wooden building with a reed-thatched roof. This serves as cold store, workshop, supply depot, kitchen and dormitory. The fishermen leave their wives and families in Sulina on Monday morning and work through the week, keeping their catches of pike, bream and perch on ice, to be collected and shipped back to the town at the weekend.

They're taciturn, hard-looking men who come in off the water and sit at a table with plates of sausage and a bottle of vodka to warm them up. Around them, a crowd of dogs and cats, bred to keep the rats down, root around in the untidy mess of salvaged nets, discarded rubber boots and the detritus of grass and weeds hauled from the river.

Back in Sulina, at a pretty light blue and white painted house off a dusty backstreet, we meet some of the womenfolk they've left behind. They're an altogether more jolly bunch: buxom middle-aged ladies who have donned the traditional dress of deep blue skirts with silver bands around the hem, pale blue sequinned caps on the back of their heads, and floral scarves. We could be in the fields near Moscow. With their fair hair and blue eyes, they're textbook Slavs. They talk Russian and sing in Russian, sad songs about love and the Danube, and, like any self-respecting Russians, they have to stop the singing for frequent toasts in Stalinskaya vodka.

This is the Women's Institute with a twist. Just as their menfolk make a living from the long, anonymous channels of the marshes, the Lipovani ladies hint at hidden liveliness in the windswept, arid backstreets of this neglected little town at the very end of the Danube.

Day Fifty-three: *Tulcea*

A few miles from Tulcea, the biggest town on the Delta, a hotel has recently been built to provide seriously comfortable accommodation and an equally serious amount of information about this unique environment. Thirty slate-grey wood cabins look out over a labyrinth of water, reed-beds and low spits that provides shelter for millions of birds and very few humans.

Perhaps because he grew up with President Ceausescu's disastrous policies for the Delta, including toxic waste spills from a gold mine and plans to drain it and grow crops, Virgil Muneanu, a former governor of the Delta region, is almost fanatically dedicated to the preservation of the environment and the protection of rare birds. Ninety-five per cent of the world population of red-breasted geese are here. Three thousand pairs of pelicans breed every year, Arctic grebe and mandarin ducks migrating from Siberia stop on their way to and from Africa.

Pollution remains a constant threat, and he doesn't minimise Romania's responsibility.

'Romania has 1,000 kilometres of the Danube River and is one of the most important polluters, you know.'

The good news is that the reed-beds, which cover 300,000 hectares of the Delta, act as a natural filter, with the plants trapping much of the heavy metal and chemical waste that comes through.

Despite the fact that the wind is now blowing a steady rain across the marshes, Virgil is determined I should sample Delta life from an open boat. We negotiate the threads of clear water between thick stands of rushes and spits on which poplar, willow and small oak trees grow. In some places the water level has risen so high that some of the trees are left with only their upper branches above the water, as if making one last cry for help.

The Delta, or to give it its official UNESCO title, the Danube Delta Biosphere Reserve, is not an hospitable environment for humans, which is why there are only some 25,000 of them living in the whole area, and I have the feeling that Virgil, hunched beneath his cape, rain dripping off the end of his nose, thinks that's quite enough. His problems are all man-made, from the control of illegal sturgeon-fishing (feeding the world's insatiable appetite for caviar) to Ukrainian plans to develop their part of this fragile ecosystem for hunting and shooting.

The wind strengthens, the rain intensifies and we head for the jetty and the welcome shock of open fires and a taste of very fine Romanian wines.

Day Fifty-five: *North to Maramureş*

If Bulgaria is a big country grown smaller (they lost their Macedonian territories at the time of the First World War), Romania is a small country grown bigger. Wisely taking the winning side in that same war, they were rewarded with a slice of the dismembered Austro-Hungarian empire, which doubled their size overnight, making this, apart from Turkey, by far the biggest European country we've been through so far.

Unfortunately it has one of Europe's worst road systems, and with barely a hundred miles of motorway in the entire country, our ride up to the mountainous north is a long haul.

The region of Romania we're travelling through is the old kingdom of Moldavia, which, as it borders Moldova, makes the geography a bit confusing. But the further north we go the less it resembles Moldova's undulating lowlands. Beyond the heavily industrialised town of Suceava we're into the foothills of the

Carpathians, the greatest mountain range of Central and Eastern Europe, extending in a 900-mile arc from here to the Czech Republic. We climb steeply, following a series of hairpin bends through beech and spruce forest. There's a scattering of snow on the green verges and at the pass we're 3,600 feet above sea level. The air is biting but the view is grand, a receding perspective of forested ridges and alpine meadows studded with conical hayricks and intricately carved and decorated wooden houses.

Outside the village of Moldoviţa is a serenely located Orthodox monastery, built in the early sixteenth century by a man called Petru Rares, the bastard son of the great church builder, Stefan cel Mare (Stephen the Great) of Moldavia. When the Turks invaded Moldavia they allowed the monastery to stay open and ironically it was fellow Christians, the Catholics of the Austro-Hapsburg empire, who let it close, and from 1785 to 1935 the place was deserted. It's open again now and run by an order of Orthodox nuns.

At the head of the arch on the conical gatehouse of the monastery is carved a reminder of the days before Ottomans or Hapsburgs came this way. It's an aurochs, a European bison, not seen in the wild since the 1850s, with three stars above it, the emblem of the medieval principality of Moldavia. Inside the high stone walls of the monastery, like a pearl at the heart of an oyster, is a sensational surprise: a gloriously painted church, one of seven in the country, all unique to Romania, and all of them acknowledged gems.

What is so immediately striking is that the whole of the church is painted, inside and out, with every inch of its long, thin exterior walls frescoed in graphic detail, like a comic in stone and plaster.

Jesus rises in glory, flanked by prophets, apostles and evangelists. Man falls into hell, in a tumble of naked bodies prodded by black-tailed devils in an underworld populated by eels and octopuses. Miracles are reproduced with dramatic panache, saints are scourged and put to death. In one powerfully fantastic scene, an executioner with drawn sword stands beside a row of freshly decapitated martyrs, blood spurting from their necks whilst their severed heads, haloes still glowing, roll around on the floor.

Istanbul, Turkey On the Galata Bridge, which crosses the Golden Horn. The poster, sponsored by Istanbul City Council, bears the words of Kemal Atatürk, founder of modern Turkey: 'Our most sacred duty is to keep the Republic alive'.

Göreme, Cappadocia Among the extraordinarily eroded pillars of volcanic rock in what they call the valley of love. I can't think why.

Edirne, Turkey Dazzled in Edirne. With Selen in the Selimiye Cami mosque, masterpiece of the great Ottoman architect Sinan, who's buried in the grounds.

ABOVE: *Edirne, Turkey* Olive oil wrestling. Wrestlers in action. Buttocks can be used for leverage.

RIGHT: *Selçuk, Turkey* A simit-seller tempts the crowd with his bread rings coated in sesame seed.

Göreme, Cappadocia   A cold clear morning in Cappadocia. Perfect conditions for ballooning and a perfect way to see this uniquely weird landscape, highlighted by a blanket of freshly fallen snow.

Chişinău, Moldova Tucking into supper, Moldovan country style. Helena grows all her own vegetables, bakes her own bread and makes her own wine.

Chişinău, Moldova One of Moldova's favourite sons, Glebus Sainciuc (in the middle), with his son Lika in the studio where he makes faces.

LEFT: *Vişeu de Sus, Maramureş, Romania* The lumberjacks' train climbs up one of the most isolated valleys of the north Romanian province of Maramureş.

LEFT: *Sighişoara to Bucharest, Romania* Draculand. The soaring walls of Bran Castle, around which Bram Stoker built the Dracula myth; (BELOW LEFT) Dracula Schlock, on sale in the car park.

RIGHT: *Săpânţa, Maramureş, Romania* Some of Stan Ion Patras' work in the 'Merry Cemetery' at Săpânţa. Apart from anything else, a vibrant tapestry of local life. Stan himself, a lover of good drink and bad women, is bottom right.

ABOVE: *Belgrade, Serbia* Motoring down the Danube. Braca Petrovic shows me that his amphibious Porsche can still cut the mustard.

ABOVE: *Budapest, Hungary* Epic entrance to the famous Gellért spa. The therapeutic waters that emerge here have been an attraction since Roman times.

RIGHT: *Budapest, Hungary* The House of Terror is full of striking theatrical effects, like this Soviet tank trapped beside a wall of victims' photos.

There is a graphically depicted siege of Constantinople, which must at the time have been the equivalent of television news footage.

All were painted around the same time, anonymously, onto half a centimetre of rapidly drying plaster, with such skill that many of the frescoes have survived without restoration for nearly five hundred years.

The nuns who care for the church and the monastery cook us a wonderful vegan lunch. After an aubergine and tomato roulade, we have soup, then beans and gherkins rounded off with chocolate and walnut cake. They ply us with a distilled plum brandy called *palincă* which sends me quickly into a state of euphoria.

My last image of Moldoviţa is of a nun, all in black, bent over a vegetable patch with a low sun picking out the fine stone walls and turrets of the monastery behind her.

Nearly three hours later we're winding our way slowly behind logging-trucks up towards the 4,600-foot Prislop Pass. Once over it we're out of Moldavia and into the region of Maramureş, a small strip of beautiful but backward country hugging up against the Ukrainian border.

By way of introduction a thick cloak of dark coniferous forest almost smothers us as we run down the valley, gradually giving way to meadows and small villages with wooden houses whose high steep roofs mirror the ridges of high steep trees until night falls around us and the houses and the churches and the fields and the forest merge into one long darkness.

Day Fifty-six: *Vişeu de Sus, Maramureş*

After yesterday's surfeit of fine Carpathian scenery, my view from the window of the Hotel Gabriela at Vişeu de Sus is a bit of an anti-climax: a main road, a railway line and some semi-derelict industrial sheds, on one of whose doors the words 'Night Club' have been somewhat unconvincingly splashed in white paint.

It was yesterday's surfeit of Carpathian food and drink that did for me in the night. At a bar/restaurant next door to the hotel I had a pork stew with mushrooms: thick, rich and garlicky, and I certainly should have resisted mixing it with *palincă* brewed by our driver Andrei's father-in-law and dispensed from a recycled plastic bottle.

The result was a night of racing heartbeat and an awful inability to get selections from *The Sound of Music* out of my brain.

This is All Souls' Day in Romania, and in this conservative, rural, intensely religious corner of the country it's taken very seriously. We drive a short way over the hills and into the small side valley of the Iza River. The undulating countryside is fringed with low trees and wreathed in a chilly morning mist.

The small town of Ieud (pronounced 'Ay-ude') is situated in a fold of the hills, at the end of the road. It's been described to me as fervently Orthodox. Apparently there were no divorces in the town between 1787 and 1980.

It doesn't feel forbidding or strict, indeed as I walk through the lych-gate of the churchyard where today's celebrations will be going on, I'm greeted by two very jolly ladies in black headscarves, fur-trimmed jerkins and wide black skirts, who offer me doughnuts, special All Souls' Day bread baked in the shape of a bow, and a warming concoction called *afinata*, which tastes like fortified cranberry juice.

Colleagues of similar size, age and shape are tidying up the graves that surround the church, weeding, raking, laying out flowers, or in some cases simply arranging a decoration of petals over the black soil. From somewhere down in the town comes the insistent buzz of a chainsaw.

The priest, a tall, imposing figure with a black robe, long beard and a shock of thick grey hair just about held in check by a black pillbox cap, is already at work blessing the graves. He and an assistant chant prayers, sing responses and he then twice sprinkles holy water on each gravestone before moving on.

Had I not been at Moldovița yesterday, the wooden church at Ieud would have been one of the most delicately beautiful buildings I've seen in a very long time.

Built in 1364, it has two precipitously pitched, shingled roofs, one above the other, which sweep down and around the church, embracing and protecting it like sou'westers in a gale. At one end a tower rises some 30 metres, capped with a tapering witch's hat turret. The whole effect is of inspired simplicity.

The inside of the church, rather overwhelmed by its roofs, is intimate, dark and cave-like. Its walls and beams are painted with the same collection of haloed angels, saints, Incarnations, Last Judgements and Ascensions to heaven as at Moldoviţa, but as these are earlier the technique is simpler and less flamboyant.

I meet a ruddy-complexioned local man, Filimon Gheorge, who's there with his pale, intense son Ionut. They're both musicians.

Candles are now being lit all around the graveyard as families of those buried gather around their graves for the service. As Ionut puts it, it's a celebration of death, as important to these communities as celebrating birth and marriage. After a death, he tells me, everyone else in the family must wear black for six weeks. During that same six-week period male members of the family cannot take part in any festivity, drink alcohol or have sex and must go to the church every Sunday to pray for the souls of the departed.

As the priest, now with gold-embroidered robes over his black cassock, emerges from the church to begin the mass, there is something very affecting about all these families standing quietly, respectfully, alongside their dead.

We're invited back to Filimon's house for a meal and, as it turns out, a party. It has one of the increasingly few all-wood exteriors. Ionut tells me that in Ceausescu's time wooden buildings were discouraged and people persuaded to replace them with brick walls and aluminium roofs. The people up here are always the last to change, he says. They think of themselves as the original Romanians, because when the Romans came and colonised this part of Europe, the indigenous Dacians fled up here to Maramureş, where they remained unconquered.

As we sit around the table in a kitchen filled with cigarette smoke and musicians, a hard local cheese is produced, to be eaten with lard, onion, bread, salt and washed down with *palincă*, the all-powerful spirit which is rapidly becoming Mother's Ruin for me. This is followed by sausage and mash with *samale*, stuffed cabbage leaves, and a sort of polenta-like corn mush.

Filimon's wife, marvellously placid throughout, benevolently produces dish after dish, whilst her mother, who must be in her eighties, fetches fuel for the wood-burning stove. Ionut fetches beer and wine. Then cigarettes are stubbed out and the music begins. Good lively folk stuff almost completely ruined for me by the red-shirted, well-oiled drummer sitting next to me who hits the drum more violently and less rhythmically the more he has to drink, accompanying each strike with a manic high-pitched laugh.

I try a humorous response, with over-the-top wincing every time he hits it. This only encourages him to thump it harder and harder, until my wincing becomes real. Then he really laughs.

He rolls his eyes, and with a nudge and accompanying wink, he comes out with a line that has everybody falling about, and which poor Ionut has to translate.

'He says he can play the drum, and at the same time love a woman.'

Now it's my turn to laugh.

Day Fifty-seven: *Vişeu de Sus, Maramureş*

Every Monday morning a train filled with lumberjacks leaves Vişeu de Sus for the high forest of the Maramureş Mountains. At eight o'clock, with clear skies making for a bitterly cold morning, but holding out the promise of a beautiful day, we gather at the timber yard owned by a Swiss company, who have allowed us to ride up with them. Part of the attraction, aside from steam engines and lumberjacks, is that the 26-mile line is the only means of access to one of the most remote valleys of this border region.

Early morning at the lumber yard is anything but romantic. We stamp our feet against the cold as the sixty or seventy lumberjacks begin to gather, the majority of them arriving by foot or on horse-drawn carts. They're far from the rugged backwoodsmen of cliché. Ranging in age from teens to mid-fifties, these are tired men with craggy faces and chesty coughs. No colourful check shirts, rucksacks or all-weather mountain gear here. Instead they wear bobble hats, thin, often threadbare woollen jackets over shirts and sweaters and carry their belongings in plastic bags. There's a small shop and café nearby where the lumberjacks can buy supplies:

sausages, slabs of lard, bread and tins of food. At the moment it is full of railway workers in oil-stained overalls, smoking as if their lives depended on it and despatching brandies at the same time. Someone makes a joke and they laugh, more out of habit than conviction.

A lady in a headscarf makes us tea, which comes in small glasses, ready-sugared like in India. Through a dusty window I can see the sunlight beginning to creep down the mountain on the far side of the valley, turning its forested flank into a pyramid of gold.

Just before 9.30 a plume of smoke erupts from inside the yard and a tank engine, Romanian-built in 1954, chugs out pulling a flat-bed wagon stacked with wood for the boiler, another wagon with seats but open at the sides, a covered coach and two or three low-loaders for timber.

Maximum speed on the line is 30 miles an hour, but we seldom reach 20 as we move out of Vişeu de Sus, stopping at intervals to pick up more lumberjacks. It seems fast enough. One of the pleasures unique to the railway is the chance to have a snoop into people's back gardens and this is no exception. The houses we pass are old-fashioned, single-storey, with wooden slatted sides, outside toilets and wood-smoke curling from the chimneys. The grass cut from around them is stacked up in the pointed hayricks that are everywhere in the mountains and corn cobs dry in sheds beside piles of fresh-harvested pumpkins. Women look up from their rakes, scythes or axes as we pass. The men, I guess, are all on the train.

A card game is already under way on the open wagon in which we're travelling, and beer and *tuică* (the slightly less lethal, only once-distilled version of *palincă*) is already being passed around. I make a mental note to be well out of the way when this lot are chopping down trees.

Once out of the town we run alongside the River Vaser, the engine swaying, hissing and gurgling its way round the curves, following the sparkle of sunlight on the water. A pungent mossy smell rises from the gorge as the woodland closes in around us. The only stops now are for the driver and fireman to take buckets down to the river to refresh the engine. Only the increasingly acrimonious progress of the card game prevents it all from becoming stupendously idyllic.

We reach the first camps just after midday. The station buildings are dilapidated, some literally falling apart. Bellowed greetings. A few get off, one man recognising another with a fierce grab at his crutch. From somewhere two mattresses and a bedstead appear and are tossed so carelessly onto the wagon behind the engine that I assume they must be intended as fuel.

We move off again, out of the beech woods now and into thick conifer plantations. A man who's just got on offers me a cigarette. He shows me the box.

'Ukraine,' he says.

I nod and smile.

'Ukraine,' he says again, as if I haven't quite got it. 'Ukraine. Chernobyl!'

And he gurgles with laughter.

At the second camp, most of the lumberjacks, including the card-school, grab their carrier bags and jump down off the train, making straight for the toilets, and by the time we reach the third camp, within three miles of the Ukrainian border, we are almost the only ones left aboard.

Compared to the two we've just seen, the third camp is like Mount Parnassus. Modern wood cabins stand with the dark wood behind them, and the river and a flat strip of grassy floodplain in front. Here, a meal is cooked over an open fire. Another cholesterol fest, I'm afraid, with grilled lard and pork crackling proving quite irresistible, especially washed down with the deliciously cold, clear water of the Vaser.

I learn from our host that there used to be 500 lumberjacks working up here, but environmental pressure has reduced the amount they can cut, and now there's work for no more than 100.

The timber used to be floated down the river, a slow and costly process, but now everything depends on the railway and this eccentric Thomas the Tank Engine operation is the only reason logging can continue in these tightly enclosed mountains. Later, when we watch the lumberjacks at work, it all seems curiously casual. The weapon of choice is no longer an axe but a chainsaw, slung across the shoulder like a rifle. Once a tree is chosen and a directional cut made, the chainsaw goes through it in thirty seconds. Two men strip the trunk whilst the third brings up a spectacularly powerful all-purpose logging vehicle known as a TAF, one of which recently pulled a 27-tonne locomotive out of the river unaided. He hitches up not just the 70-footer that's been felled but two other trees as well, a combined load of over 3 tonnes, which is hauled effortlessly up a 50-degree slope and dragged away for loading.

It doesn't feel quite like the real world up here in the forest. When the trucks aren't working there is almost total silence. Maramureş is remote enough, but this must rank as one of the least accessible corners of Europe we've yet reached.

Day Fifty-eight: *Săpânţa, Maramureş*

President Ceausescu's bankrupt attempts to impose rural industrialisation lie scattered along the valleys of northern Romania. Factories and steelworks put down in the 1970s and 1980s are now reduced to hollow shells that border the main road, windows smashed, doors twisted on their hinges, creaking in the wind. The traditional rural life which Ceausescu sought to destroy still survives.

Take Săpânţa for instance. There are cars here, there are tourists, there are girls with nose studs and long painted fingernails, and at one point a Hummer, windows blacked out, cruises past us, avoiding cows being led up the street. But the couple who are showing me round have never owned a car. They get around quite happily by horse and cart. He's a farmer, born in Bucharest, where their daughter now lives. He wears a patterned sweater and a straw hat. His wife sits behind me on the cart, which, apart from the rubber tyres, could have been made any time in the last thousand years. She's entirely clad in black, the same colour as her mobile phone. Their horse is nine years old and does all the work on the farm. They can't afford a tractor and don't seem to miss it.

In other words they're happy. Hopelessly out of date, the likes of Ceausescu would say, but undeniably happy.

They drop me off at Săpânța's most remarkable attraction, a churchyard that's become known as the Merry Cemetery.

Instead of gravestones, the tombs here are marked with carved wooden crosses on which are painted, in bright primary colours, scenes from the life of the deceased, together with distinctive epitaphs in verse.

Most of them are the work of a local man, Stan Ion Patras, who made his first carvings at the age of fourteen, and died, at the age of seventy-one, almost exactly thirty years ago. Everyone says he was a happy man, keen on wine, women and song. Not really interested in money, he was quite happy to be paid in brandy. The graveyard glows with his trade-mark colour, 'Săpânța Blue', which he regarded as a symbol of hope and liberty, as green meant life, yellow fertility and red passion.

These densely packed rows of crosses provide a unique portrait of local life. Here are housewives cooking, farmers ploughing, hunters shooting, doctors consulting, carpenters carving, musicians playing. Dispensing with the well-worn iconography of death – skulls, angels, Grim Reapers and the like – Patras celebrates the routine pleasures of life, meals being eaten together, hay being raked, parents holding their children's hands. This doesn't mean he shirks tragedy. There are graphic paintings of a boy of thirteen struck by lightning, an explosion at a factory that killed three women, a twenty-seven-year-old killed by a train.

His idiosyncratic epitaphs, always written in the first person, accompany the scenes.

'Two evil-minded bandits hit me on the head and took my life away at age 22.'

'An evil man shot me in the back.'

This simple, faux-naif style can be deceptively powerful.

'I was called Marie Monghi. I was only a little girl going to nursery school. I was hit by a tractor when leaving my home.'

Like the All Souls' Day mass at Ieud, this singular place is another example of how tightly death is woven into the fabric of life here. It is seen as integral and inevitable, something to be respected rather than feared, but never ignored.

My last image of the Merry Cemetery is the carving above the grave of Stan Ion Patras himself. A jolly man, with a broad, lived-in face, a pug nose and a straw hat set at a jaunty angle. The only man who has ever sent me smiling from a graveyard looks just as I hoped he would.

Day Sixty: *Sighişoara, Transylvania*

The night sounds of Sighişoara are surprisingly soothing. As I lie in my superior garret at the Casa Cu Cerb, 'the House with Stag', the clock on the massive medieval clock tower strikes, with great restraint, every quarter, and every now and then celebrates the top of the hour with a rolling peal of bells, none of which intrudes, but rather enhances the atmosphere of this handsome little town, a day's drive from the northern borders.

The hotel, which numbers Prince Charles among its previous guests, looks out over a pretty cobbled square of painted houses with peeling stucco and tiled roofs with curving eyebrow windows set into them. It looks like a background to a Grimms' fairy tale. This isn't as fanciful as it sounds because Sighişoara was once one of the Siebenbürgen, seven towns fortified by Saxons from southern Germany in the thirteenth century.

The Magyars, terrified of the Tartars streaming in from the heart of Asia (as they themselves had done), gave the Saxons this corner of Transylvania to defend, and here they remained until the end of the twentieth century. Rudi Fischer, whose 'omniscient range of knowledge' was recognised by the great European traveller Patrick Leigh Fermor, remembers his mother attending a teacher training college in Sighişoara when it was still called Schässburg, and nearby Braşov was Kronstadt. They certainly took their task of fortifying seriously. Having organised themselves into guilds, each guild was charged with providing money for a tower. In a period of 200 years, sixteen towers were raised, of solid stone with red turreted roofs. The remains of nine can still be seen, including those of the Ropemakers, Butchers, Furriers, Shoemakers, Tinsmiths and Tailors.

My guide to Sighişoara, or Schässburg as the Saxons called it, or Castrum Sex as the Romans called it, or Segesvár as the Hungarians called it, is Ioanna, and she has a cold. Swathed in sweaters, a green and red velvet coat and a voluminous knitted scarf, she does her best to show me the town in which she grew up.

I ask her how she remembered it.

'It was a place to play. Play with my friends. I was a princess here. I used to walk around in my grandmother's underwear and high-heel shoes.'

It must have been a wonderful stage set for a young girl with a vivid imagination. The Old Town, or Citadel, is a mouth-watering collection of medieval, seventeenth- and eighteenth-century buildings. One of the finest is not a house but a covered stairway, the Scholars' Stairs, built to protect students climbing up from the lower town to the school. The broad stone steps are laid out in flights of six, corresponding to the days of the week, and the seventh step, as befits Sunday, the day of rest, is a landing. Ingenious and effective and, as people have been climbing up here for 380 years, pretty sturdy too.

There's still a school at the top and, after she's got her breath back, Ioanna recalls how she lived happily here with Hungarians, Jews and Germans.

'When I was little it was very good between people, no problems at all. I was eating German, playing German, talking German all day, but I hated the food, so I never learnt the language.'

Now most of her German friends are gone. Things began to change for them when Transylvania was handed over to Romania in 1918, but it wasn't until the Ceausescu years of the 1980s that they were made to feel positively unwelcome, and after the fall of the Berlin Wall most of them accepted an offer of a safe return to Germany.

Sighişoara's celebrity rests on more than being a mere Gothic bastion. On a wall a few doors down from the hotel is a plaque which informs the passer-by that Vlad Tepes, a.k.a. Vlad the Impaler, on whom the fictional Count Dracula was modelled, was born here.

For Ioanna, Vlad Tepes was a great man, a national hero who had fought bravely against the Turks and whose name has been gravely traduced.

I remember reading somewhere that Dracul meant 'devil'.

'No, no,' Ioanna shakes her head briskly.

'In 1431 his father was made a knight of the order of Draco, which means "dragon". It was an honour to be in the order of the Dragon.'

She mistakes my disappointment for disbelief.

'Draco,' she repeats, 'is from the Slavonian. It means dragon.'

'But he did a bit of impaling?'

'Everybody did,' Ioanna returns sharply. 'That's what they did then.'

I can't just let this drop. Transylvania may mean green fields and heartbroken Hungarians, but to those of us infected by Bram Stoker it means fangs and black cloaks and blood. After all, right below the plaque is a woman selling Dracula T-shirts, teeth and even a Dracula bottle opener. There are no dragons to be seen. The truth clearly doesn't sell.

Ioanna concedes the point and agrees to take me into the heart of the Carpathians tomorrow, to the village of Bran and the half-palace, half-fortress that has become known, irretrievably, as Dracula's castle.

Day Sixty-one: *Sighişoara to Bucharest*

'Transylvania had its high Middle Ages…its Baroque, its Enlightenment, all the historical ages that made Europe…that did not exist in Russia or in Romania, …Bulgaria, Serbia, Macedonia, Albania, Thrace, Greece and the Ukraine.'

These are the words of historian John Lukacs, quoted in Robert D. Kaplan's book *Balkan Ghosts*, and they neatly answer a few questions, like why the loss of Transylvania to Romania hurt the Hungarians and Germans so much, and still hurts. It also must explain the frustration of those who see Transylvania becoming synonymous not so much with enlightenment but with one of the world's most exportable fantasies.

When Bram Stoker created Count Dracula he created not just a monster but a monster people wanted to believe in. Dracula emerged, not just from death into life, but from fiction to reality.

Bran Castle, 17 miles south-west of the city of Braşov, soars dramatically from an unassailable crag. Red-tiled hipped roofs, a towering crenellated keep pierced by stone chimney stacks, all framed in golden autumn colours.

Though there is no evidence that Bran Castle had anything to do with Vlad the Impaler, apart possibly from a bit of besieging in 1460, people want to believe that these were the real walls he clambered round, and these were the actual lamp-lit windows he entered. So, around us, beside the car park, the Dracula industry is in full swing. For the drinkers, Vampire Pinot Noir or Dracula's Blood, for the parents, T-shirts and mugs, for the kiddies, severed hands, and for the clubbers, a Prince of Darkness disco, complete with twitching skeletons. And it could have been much worse. A proposal to rip up hectares of oak forest to build a Dracula theme park was successfully derailed by an alliance of Romanian environmentalists and the Mihai Eminescu Trust, a group set up to preserve traditional farming methods, of whom Prince Charles is a patron.

I walk up to the castle with Petre Moraru, an actor who makes a bit of pin-money playing Dracula at a club in Bucharest.

'It's Halloween coming up,' he reminds me. 'I'm very busy.'

In his opinion, the idea of human vampires was around long before Bram Stoker. The Romanian peasants were, and still are, deeply religious and nothing frightens them more than the idea of the Un-dead, the suspicion that a body might enter a state in which it's technically had it, yet the spirit remains alive. He had heard only recently of a stake being driven through the heart of someone who'd been terrorising a family.

Which, as far as he's concerned, can only be good for business.

The appearance of Bran Castle further blurs the boundaries of fact and fiction. It looks exactly like the sort of castle you'd find on a book cover or a theatre backdrop, and the interior is a set in itself. A combination of National Romantic and Arts and Crafts style, with lots of spooky windows, flickering fireplaces and winding stairs, it was decorated and furnished in the 1920s by Queen Marie of Romania and her court architect.

When the Turkish empire was breaking up in the late nineteenth century, the European Powers provided a complete make-over service for newly liberated countries, with a constitution, borders and a monarch. Thus Prince Charles of Hohenzollern-Sigmaringen found himself King Carol of Romania, even though he'd never heard of the place. (The Greeks were given a George, and the Bulgarians a Ferdinand.)

The castle is full of framed photos of Nordic queens and princesses, in silk gowns and Art Nouveau belts, all of them wholesome and handsome in a Rhinemaiden-ish sort of way, their sturdy white throats perfect vampire bait.

And suddenly he's there. Petre, in full Dracula costume, complete with black cloak, candle wax-spattered coat and white silk scarf, is ready to frighten the kiddies.

As the first group of schoolchildren toils up the steps, Petre puts in his teeth and starts to roll his eyes.

'In Transylvania you can see very strange things. Sometimes you can see blue flames in the forest, sometimes...'

At that moment his mobile phone goes.

'Might be some work,' he says, stepping nimbly out of character, and roots around in his cloak. The children love it.

Drive into Braşov to catch the train on to Bucharest. Sinister Saxon legends lurk here as well. The gloriously spacious Piaţa Sfatului, Council Square, is reputedly where the Pied Piper of Hamelin emerged with his children in tow. It's surrounded by beautifully proportioned buildings, including the fifteenth-century Council House, the Renaissance Merchant's House and, most striking of all, the Black Church, a huge edifice, bristling with pinnacles, which my guidebook assures me is 'the largest Gothic church between Vienna and Istanbul'. Its name comes from the way it looked after a fire in 1689. I found its sheer sides quite forbidding. And all the doors were locked.

High on the great slab of wooded rock face that rises behind the old town are picked out the letters B-R-A-Ş-O-V, in almost identical size and shape to the Hollywood sign in Los Angeles. It seems appropriate. When it comes to purveying fantasies, Hollywood and Transylvania have much in common.

The evening train to Bucharest twists and turns through the Carpathians, Europe's last great natural barrier. Every now and then there's a gap in the mountains and the sun spills through, bathing the beech and oak woods in a rich auburn glow.

Fall into conversation with a man called Emile. He has Latin good looks, long dark hair and piercing eyes.

As you might expect from a man reading a book called *On the Heights of Despair*, he's not one for small talk. But the book sparks off all sorts of connections and, as the shadows lengthen, we end up having one of those rambling discussions about the meaning of existence and so on, which I always imagine train journeys in Europe as the shadows lengthen to be all about.

Emil Cioran, author of *On the Heights of Despair,* was a Romanian philosopher who came out with cracking lines like 'without Bach, God is just a second-rate figure'. He propounded a nihilist anti-philosophy in which he argued that the only valid thing to do with one's life is to end it. He failed to live up to his own principles and died at the ripe old age of eighty-four.

Emile asks if I know Cioran's friend Constantin Noica? He developed the theory of non-history.

'Sorry?'

'His theory is that Romania has elected to be in eternity. To have no connection with historical time. We are in the middle of the crossroads of all nations, invaders, empires, and to survive...'

He leans forward. I lean forward.

'The Romanian people choose to be suspended in eternity.'

With immaculate timing the train roars into a tunnel.

By the time we've broken through the Carpathians, passed the oilfields and industrial flatlands around Ploieşti and are into the outer suburbs of Bucharest, I've learnt that Emile is a fan of Steaua ('Star') Bucharest, 'we are Latin people, we love football'; that Romania was a backward rural society, 'synchronised with Europe' in one great leap at the end of the nineteenth century; and that, in Emile's opinion, Bram Stoker was a prophetic writer who put his finger on one of our deepest anxieties, the fear of getting old and the desire for immortality.

A long day's journey ends at the ageless Athenee Palace Hotel, now the Athenee Palace Hilton, in Bucharest. A huge wedding dinner is under way. On my way to the lift I pass a gorgeously attired bride and groom standing outside the banqueting room preparing to make their entrance. They check their outfits compulsively, clear throats, lick lips, exchange quick, anxious smiles. Then the doors open, the crowd rises and, to the unmistakable whine of fresh-filled bagpipes, the splendid couple make their way in.

After a week and a half in the wilds of the north, I experience a short, sharp dose of culture shock.

Day Sixty-two: *Bucharest*

The Athenee Palace, now over ninety years old, has had a racy past. Comfortable and respectable as she is now, I rather yearn for the inter-war years when, according to one guidebook, 'the hotel became notorious for being a den of iniquity', or the 1950s when, according to another, she was reborn as an intelligence factory, 'with bugged rooms and tapped phones to reinforce the reports of informers and prostitutes'.

I can't help feeling I'm missing something as I head from my well-behaved hotel for a well-behaved hour at the National Art Museum. It's a five-minute walk from the hotel on Piaţa Revoluţiei, Revolution Square, and was once the royal palace. It's elegant enough, and wouldn't look at all out of place off the Champs-Elysées, but this is Bucharest and it faces square onto what was once the headquarters of the Central Committee of the Communist Party, from whose rooftop Ceausescu was helicoptered out of the city and executed, along with his wife, on Christmas Day 1989.

The communists knew how to build palaces. The National Art Museum could fit into a back room of the vast edifice from which Nicolae Ceausescu ruled Romania. A team of 20,000 labourers and 700 architects and engineers worked all day and all night for five years to provide him with one of the largest administrative buildings in the world, second only to the Pentagon.

The Art Museum is almost deserted. A pity, as there's some fine work here. I stand for quite a while before Brueghel's powerful 'Slaughter of the Innocents'. It's a timeless depiction of bullying oppression, pre-dating all the dark brutality of Europe's last hundred years.

It set me wondering where Nicolae Ceausescu would feature in the rogues' gallery of the twentieth century?

I look for some answers on a guided tour of Ceausescu's

Bucharest with Bogdan Moncea, an endlessly obliging and patient man who runs the highly successful Castel Studios just outside the city, where, amongst others, the film *Cold Mountain* was shot.

He reminds me that in the early years Ceausescu was seen as one of the decent communists, someone the West could do business with. His opposition to the Soviet repression of the Czech uprising in 1968 was seen as proof that communism in Eastern Europe was not so monolithic after all. Romania, under Ceausescu, was seen to be pursuing a national communism, and not just dancing to Moscow's tune. Added to which, Romania was a country of great economic potential, with a world-class aeronautics industry, reserves of oil and gas and, above all, a thriving agricultural sector.

But Ceausescu, a man with little formal education (according to Bogdan, he had only four years' schooling and could barely read or write), was more impressed by the achievements of the East. Taking Stalin's USSR, North Korea and China as his models, he embarked on a hugely expensive, ill-directed industrialisation programme, sacrificing a rich and profitable farming sector.

'In the forties and fifties we were the second food producer of Europe, after the French. Forty years later people were starving on the streets.'

Far from taking the blame for any failure, Ceausescu increasingly saw himself as the only saviour of the country. The man who embodied the Romanian nation, its people and its tradition.

In short, he went mad.

The country suffered. He destroyed churches, bullied non-Romanian minorities like the Magyars and the Gypsies and tried to increase the workforce with desperate measures like forbidding abortion or contraception, setting up the Baby Police to carry out compulsory gynaecological examinations and, in the process, creating an enormous pool of unwanted children.

Vast resources went not only into the construction of the Palace of the People, but also the clearing of a huge area around it to create his dream of a Centru Civic, 'a socialist capital for socialist man'. To make room for his version of Kim-Il-Sung's North Korea, he razed three and a half square miles of old houses, including sixteen churches and three synagogues.

Bogdan explains the thinking.

'The focus was on a central system, so everybody could be put together, receive electricity and heating from a central point. Everything was about control.'

One of the unwitting results of the bulldozing of old Bucharest was that half a million stray dogs, once pets of the 40,000 people thrown out of their homes, were released onto the city streets. Dog wars ensued until only the fittest survived, running the streets in packs.

Bogdan turns down the long boulevard that runs the length of the Centru Civic. Having learnt from his architects that the Champs-Elysées was the longest boulevard in Europe, Ceausescu demanded one longer and wider.

They dutifully delivered the Bulevardul Unirii, 32 feet wider and about 300 feet longer than its Parisian counterpart.

We sit and take a coffee in a crescent of stone-clad, classical pastiche colonnades on the side of what has now been rechristened Victory Boulevard. Bogdan agrees that after Ceausescu's fall things didn't change overnight. The old communists remained in power and not long after his death seven people were killed and 300 injured when they brought in miners to break up pro-democracy rallies in the capital. But now, despite the fact that two million Romanians are currently working in Spain and Italy, the economy is reviving and Bucharest is in the middle of a construction boom. A new generation of young film directors, who have won prizes in Cannes and Berlin recently, give Bogdan great hope. The press is free again and he welcomes the prospect of joining the European Union.

Both Bogdan and Emile talked of the importance of sport to the national morale and we have managed to secure an audience with the man who owns the most successful football club in Romania, Steaua Bucharest, winners of the European Cup in 1986.

It's rare to get a face-to-face meeting with such a stellar figure as George 'Gigi' Becali, and Bogdan is cautious.

'He's highly uneducated. Just a shepherd. He sold sheep, now he sells real estate.'

We turn up at the hour appointed at a large French-style mansion, once the Argentine embassy. A Mercedes Maybach

limousine, with curtained back windows, is being polished outside
a pair of gold-leaved wrought-iron gates.

We're shown into a house where workmen rule. A smell of
plaster and the sound of hammers and drills. Fortunately there's
a garden at the back with a table and a few chairs where we can sit
below a tall fir tree and wait.

Wait we do. For an hour and a half. Then, like the rising of
the wind before an impending storm, there is a flourishing of
mobiles and a flurry of instructions. Sitting minions stand and
exchange nervous glances. And round the side of the house
comes the man himself, in the middle of a swarm of attendants.
Gigi Becali is a short, trim, compact figure. Someone, I think,
who wishes he were just that bit bigger. His jaw juts firmly
forward, as if to compensate for a lack of height, and as he greets
me with a firm grasp of the hand, the word Napoleonic comes
to mind. Speaking through an interpreter, he apologises for
being late, whilst implying at the same time that I am lucky to
be talking to him at all. He's doing this as an act of hospitality to
visitors in his country. Typical Romanian hospitality, he adds,
warming to his theme. This is a great country and everything he
does he does for his country and for God.

His father hated communists. He once attacked Stalin with a
knife. This really makes me sit up, but it turns out that it was in
a restaurant and Stalin was in a picture on the wall. Still, he was
thrown in jail for it.

In the 1980s he made a lot of money from the family herd of
600 sheep, invested it in dollars and when the revolution came in
1989 was well positioned to take advantage of the chaos.

'In Romania at that time people would sell just about anything.
All they had.'

And Gigi was on hand to buy it. His acquisition of Steaua
seems less from a love of football than from a love of what the
team stands for, and of course, love for himself.

'Like any rich man, I like my image to be shown off.'

Perhaps because they've just been beaten 4–1 by Real Madrid
in the Champions League, Gigi seems less keen to talk about
specifics.

'Steaua,' he declares, 'is a symbol and a symbol has no price.' I get the impression that for Gigi, owning Steaua is a step towards owning Romania.

He clearly feels the hand of destiny heavy on his shoulder. He wants to start a new Christian-Democrat Party but only, he says, as an obligation to his people.

'Because God gives me all this power, all this money and everything else, so I feel I need to do this for my country and my people.'

God, one feels, is lucky to know someone like Gigi Becali.

At the end of our talk, or rather his talk, Gigi being not really into listening, we pose for photographs, Gigi now relaxed and expansive. He grips my shoulder, says something to my translator and even laughs. I ask her later what he'd said.

'He said did you know that you are having your photo taken with the next President of Romania?'

We all laugh together and shake hands in a cordial, manly way, but it's a disturbing encounter. The likelihood of a fiery religious chauvinist winning the Romanian presidency seems laughable. But as we leave I sense that for Bogdan and others like him it isn't such a joke. At the table in the garden Gigi is holding court. He has his jacket off and a thin, young, frightened-looking man is massaging his shoulders through a blue and white striped shirt. Half a dozen heavies in dark suits sit around guffawing and joshing. Forget Napoleonic, this is a scene out of *Goodfellas*.

Day Sixty-three: *Bucharest*

It's a grey, overcast morning for my visit to Ceausescu's Palace of the People, now known as the Palace of Parliament, the concrete, stone-clad behemoth that crouches over the city it devoured, like a great bird halfway through a meal.

Like anything to do with dictators it's designed to make you feel small and insignificant. Hence the 1,000 rooms, some as big as football pitches, the 4,500 chandeliers made from 3,500 tonnes of crystal and the one million cubic metres of marble.

'And it's not finished yet,' my companion points out. He's another Bogdan, Bogdan Oltianu, a Liberal Party MP and

President of the Chamber of Deputies.

His office is rather elegant, with a beautiful parquet floor, walnut panelling and a classical ceiling, which, at only 20 feet high, is one of the more intimate corners of the palace.

Oltianu is a slim, shaven-headed lawyer whose wife is expecting a second child any day now. As an eighteen-year-old he stood in Revolution Square the day Ceausescu's bluff was called. Now thirty-five, he's one of the up-and-coming Romanian politicians, by his own admission less interested in a tub-thumping international role than dealing with the urgent work of providing better schools, housing and hospitals in Romania itself.

His first concern is whether or not to take his tie off for our interview. He decides it should come off.

We walk through one of the mighty ballrooms, where a squadron of cleaning ladies is at work. Faced with a Herculean task, their mops glide slowly and silently from side to side as they move across the polished wood floor. Bogdan apologises for the mess, but there had been Halloween celebrations here last night.

Talking to him, I find out some interesting things about this colossus. For a start, Ceausescu, though he insisted on defining how it would look, was unable to read architectural drawings (the head architect, a woman, was only twenty-seven when she took on the job), so all they could do was build something, have him try it out and if he wasn't happy, knock it down and start again.

'Everything was rebuilt a couple of times. That's the way he liked to work.'

All the materials are from within Romania, all the marble, all the miles of oak and cherry wood, everything, was built, carved and installed by Romanian craftsmen.

And after all that, Ceausescu never lived here.

What does surprise me, but probably shouldn't, is that the people of Bucharest have not only become reconciled to this monster in their midst, but are becoming quite proud of it. Its grotesque scale has made it a major tourist attraction and sensible people like Bogdan and his colleagues, far from wanting it removed, are looking at ways to rent out their Parliament building for conferences, balls, trade exhibitions, anything to help pay an overheads bill which includes 200,000 euros a month for lighting alone.

It's getting dark as we plough through dense, stodgy traffic on the way to the home of a Romanian and international legend. In the 1970s Ilie Nastase was one of the most consistently successful tennis players in the world. He took the French and US Open titles and though he never won Wimbledon he was runner-up to Stan Smith in 1972, and Björn Borg in 1976.

It's not so much the tennis that makes me want to meet him, but the fact that in an increasingly managed, performance-led sporting world it's good to remember people like Nastase who played in their own, often profligate, way, unpredictable, passionate, over-excited, rude and wonderful to watch.

Unlike Gigi Becali, Nastase lives in comfort, but certainly not splendour, in one of a row of cheek-by-jowl detached houses in a busy suburban avenue. His house is like a mini rural castle, with turrets and wide eaves and brickwork painted an inexplicable shade of orange. The interior is even more eclectic, with carved wood, marble, Spanish wrought iron and veneered Chinoiserie milling around between sprayed concrete walls. There are pictures everywhere, mostly of 'Nasty' himself, arm round Muhammad Ali, or his former doubles partner Ion Tiriac; kissing lots of beautiful women. In one of them there's young Ilie, hair neatly brushed and wearing a blazer, outside the White House with Richard Nixon.

The man himself is no let-down. He's just turned sixty, has a wife of thirty and a baby about the same age as my recently born grandson. His moon face has broadened out but his hair is still as dark, lank and long as it was when he shocked the All England Club, and his eyes still as mischievous. He lopes about restlessly, showing me this and that, talking about the various business deals he's involved with, what his children are doing. It occurs to me that this is what it must have been like facing him on court.

He pours liberal glasses of Veuve Clicquot.

'My wife is importing it.'

In true Nastase style the glasses have no bases and have to be hung in plant-like metal holders.

I ask him about the Ceausescu years. He shrugs. They were not bad for him. As a successful sportsman he was granted privileges, both in travel and bringing in foreign goods, that were denied to the rest of the country. He was good friends with Ceausescu's children, but remembers once answering the President back at some official ceremony.

'He said I saw you swearing in Romanian, why are you like this? And I was stupid enough to answer him. I said I'm Romanian and I have a Romanian temperament.'

And the Prime Minister was next to me and he said, 'Careful, you might not be alive tomorrow.'

He doesn't paint a rosy picture of the country since Ceausescu's departure.

'I think people have more freedom, but they have less money. I'm talking about the general people, not the few of them that are very rich. Before they have money to travel and no passports. Now the freedom is there but they haven't the money.'

So angry was he at the state of his fellow Romanians that in 1996 he was persuaded to run for Mayor of Bucharest. He knows now he shouldn't have done it.

'I ran on behalf of the Socialist Party and they told me the only way to win is to promise a lot, and I didn't want to do that.'

He travels. To New York, London and Paris. A new biography is coming out. In it he claims to have made love to 2,500 women.

'Is it true?'

He grins wildly, clearly delighted to be asked the question, before finally opting for modesty.

'The writer, he asked me how many girls I sleep with? I said I don't know, I never count them. Thirty years, maybe three a month, four a month, five a month. He says that's almost 2,000. I said no, no 800, 900. He said it cannot be like this. First of all it doesn't look good for your reputation, it doesn't look good for my book. And then I said OK, 2,500.'

I don't know if he catches me glancing at the framed photo of his wife and child, but he adds rather sweetly, 'But you know for me the one who counts is the last one.'

He's playful to the end. I ask a rather stock question about what he thinks characterises a Romanian.

He grins mischievously.

'Cheating, lying...' and he gets no further before dissolving in laughter.

As we leave the house a figure comes up the street towards us. It's Mrs Nastase, carrying two bags of shopping. She looks exhausted.

Day Sixty-four: *Bucharest to the Iron Gates*

Bucharest is particularly well blessed with theatres and one of the smaller, more attractive of them is the Odeon, its old-fashioned classical façade squeezed between taller neighbours. They perform European classics, and currently have Shakespeare's *Cymbeline*, Oscar Wilde's *The Picture of Dorian Gray* and a play about the Marquis de Sade in production. One of their leading actors is Dan Badarau, a soft-voiced man of striking good looks, in his late forties, with long hair tied in a ponytail. He's a provincial, born and raised in the south-western town of Drobeta-Turnu Severin. He won one of only four places at the Institute of Theatre Drama School in Bucharest, from 400 applicants. As he has a couple of days off he's going back to see his parents and has agreed to escort me to his home town, and to put me back on the Danube.

We drive through flat, forgettable country. Towns and villages of small, red-roofed houses augmented with grubby concrete blocks, like chunks of overcrowded city broken off and dumped in uncrowded countryside.

There is nothing remarkable to see until we come to the village of Buzescu, an hour and a half south-west of the capital. Buzescu is a Gypsy Beverly Hills, and on the few hundred yards of Main Street are clustered the fanciful houses of successful Roma families, each one trying to outdo the other with another pinnacle or an extra silvery flourish.

Spiky turrets sheathed in beaten metal rise above balconies trimmed with filigree carvings which in turn spring from clusters of plaster columns. Some of them bear the owner's name, picked out in large metal letters and slung between brick chimneys. Many of these tinny mansions have forbiddingly elaborate gates covered in swirling tendrils of wrought iron, outside which large men with dark leather jackets hang about, exuding menace.

No-one knows exactly how many Gypsies there are in Romania, numbers vary from half a million to two million, but it's the largest Gypsy population of any European country.

This short strip of grand mansions, many of which are just for show, are symbols of success, in music, or trading cars or whatever, but the lot of most of the Roma people is not much different here than it was in Bulgaria. They are generally poor, ill-educated and treated with suspicion if acknowledged at all.

Beyond Craiova we pass fields of oil-donkeys and small yellow-painted derricks. In the middle of the nineteenth century Romania was the first country in the world to start oil exploration and was for a time the largest producer. Their oil reserves, coveted by Hitler, were largely the reason why Romania was forced onto the Nazi side for the first few years of the Second World War, resulting in the shameful rounding-up of Jews and Gypsies, many of whom were herded off to concentration camps in Transdniester. Romania now imports more than half her oil supplies.

As we draw closer to the Danube, low, wooded hills replace the monotonous flatness and Dan becomes quite nostalgic. These verdant valleys close to the Serbian border were where his childhood holidays were spent. He remembers playing cowboys and Indians, inventing stories and adventures. Like me, he always enjoyed acting things out, playing all the parts, and like me, his parents had been dead set against his becoming an actor.

By late afternoon, we're standing beside the Danube at Turnu-Severin, one of the most significant points on the river. Almost exactly 2,000 years ago this was where Emperor Trajan ordered the formidable limestone cliffs they called the Porta Ferrea (the Iron Gates), to be bridged, so that he could consolidate his conquest of Thrace and move north to take on the Dacians. A Greek, Apollodorus of Damascus, was given the epic task and he duly completed what must have been in its time one of the technological wonders of the world. All that remains now are the crumbling portions of two chunky piers below us, and a third which can just be made out on the far-off Serbian shore.

But turn the eye a few degrees north and you will see, depending on your prejudices, a powerful example of today's technological ingenuity, or one of the great outrages against nature.

The Iron Gates was one of the most famous gorges of the Danube. 'For hundreds of years,' writes Patrick Leigh Fermor in *Between the Woods and the Water*, 'rocks like dragon's teeth had made the passage mortally dangerous.' The first attempt to tame this lethal stretch of river was taken in 1896 when a safe channel was blown from the rock of the river bed, but sixty years later, lured by the potential of these mighty, rushing waters, the governments of Romania and Yugoslavia combined to build the turbine plant and linking bridge that we see today. It is quite a sight. The dam wall is 1,500 feet thick at its base and almost a mile long across at the top. It rises 100 feet above the Danube, and produces billions of kilowatts of power every year. Watching walls of water spilling over sixteen sluice-gates it seems a tremendous, almost inspiring achievement, except that the depth of the Danube, behind the dam, has risen well over a hundred feet. In effect the Portiles de Fer hydro-electric project has destroyed the very Iron Gates after which it's named. The drama of thundering, whirling waters has gone, along with the old frontier town of Orşova and a Turkish settlement with mosques and fortresses where, by legend, the Argonauts found the olive tree.

Leigh Fermor, so excited by the old Iron Gates, added an elegiac postscript to his book. The plant, he writes, has 'turned a hundred miles of the Danube into a vast pond.... It has abolished canyons, turned beetling crags into mild hills...myths, lost voices, history and hearsay have all been put to rout, leaving nothing but this valley of the shadow.'

I feel a similar, if less focused sense of loss and regret when, later, Dan and I stand outside the classical, pedimented Turnu-Severin theatre, where he first played on stage in amateur productions. It's now a library and cinema as well as a theatre and though it seems fine, if not exactly flourishing, to me, Dan finds it dowdy and run-down and apologises for wasting my time. He's even more dejected when we cross the street to an area he remembers as lively, full of coffee shops and other meeting places, and which has been flattened and replaced by a concrete fountain, no longer working.

Dry, rusty and filled with trapped litter, it is an awful indictment of the whole paternal concept of 'civic improvement'. He shakes his head.

'It's putting things here for people, rather than people themselves making what they want.'

I tell Dan, in an attempt to cheer him up, that it all reminds me of Sheffield in the 1960s and 1970s. Another area where our childhood experiences seem to coincide.

He's a good companion, Dan, but cursed with an apologetic nature.

Day Sixty-five: *On the Danube, Romania to Serbia*

A fierce and bitter north-east wind scours the banks of the river and sends curtains of spray flying up from the top of the dam. Not an ideal day for a boat ride into Serbia, but Dan is reassuring.

'We are going to the Kazan Gorge. It is beautiful, you will see.'

Sure enough, by the time we are upstream of the dam the sting goes out of the wind as the Danube is transformed from a recognisable flow of water into Leigh Fermor's 'vast pond'.

As our boatman, Sorin, heads us up towards a narrower, steeper channel I've time to take in the contrasts on either side. The Romanian shore is rocky and steeper, and the Serbian, greener, lower and more inviting. I ask Dan how the nations on either side of the Danube get on.

'Fine,' he says. 'You see we are both slaves.'

This produces another volley of apologies.

'Oh, I'm so sorry. Slavs! We are both Slavs.'

He thinks the Serbians good people, emotional, like the Romanians, but refuses to be drawn on whether or not there was gun-running between the two countries during the wars of the 1990s. (In 1989 Romania was the fifth-largest arms exporter in the world, and I know from my time with Captain Sablic in Rijeka that they supplied arms for Croatia.) He knows Serb actors, though, and speaks of them with both awe and respect. They're powerful, expressive, not afraid of pushing the boundaries and he thinks Belgrade theatre more daring and experimental than anything in Bucharest.

As we move into the Kazan Gorge, where a small valley enters the Danube from the Romanian shore, an enormous head is carved into the rock together with the Latin inscription 'Decebalus Rex – Dragan Fecit'.

It turns out to be less ancient than I thought; in fact, it dates from the 1990s. The carved figure, Decebalus, was a Dacian king who took on the armies of Emperor Trajan and is regarded as a great Romanian folk hero. Dragan, more prosaically, is a rich businessman who paid for it to be carved.

On this slightly ominous note of resurgent nationalism, we pass into the gorge itself.

Kazan means a cauldron and this gorge must once have been as fearsome as the Iron Gates. Steep grey cliffs, dusted with a few tenacious conifers, rise 1,000 feet on either side of us.

Dan points out that we are cutting through the mountains at a critical point. To the east are the Carpathians, which we've been in and out of for the last two weeks, on the west are the Balkans, which we haven't seen for two months.

It makes the Kazan Gorge, physically as well as politically, another European gateway. Now he's led me through it Dan must get back to Bucharest. He'll be in *Cymbeline* tonight. I'll be in Belgrade.

Serbia

Day Sixty-six: *Belgrade*

I'M APPROACHING the waters of the Danube in a car that's virtually the same age as me. Alongside me, driving, is Braca Petrovic, born in Belgrade in 1948, an intense, undemonstrative man with short greying hair. I look a little anxiously towards him because, though we're now a matter of feet from the grey-green waters of the river, he's not stopping. Nor is he going to stop. There's no time to say anything as Braca purses his lips, tightens his grip on the steering wheel and drives into the Danube. Water swirls higher and higher around the car. Braca looks wonderfully relieved, takes a right turn and strikes out for the far bank.

Fortunately the car we're in was meant to do this. It was designed to do it by no less a figure than Ferdinand Porsche, for the German invasion of Russia in 1941. Using a rear propeller worked by the driveshaft and capable of doing some 8 miles per hour through the water and 50 miles per hour on land, the Schwimmwagen, as they were known, were to be used in the crossing of the Volga, the only European river longer than the one we're in at the moment. They were vulnerable. Fifteen thousand were made, but they suffered heavy casualties, including 200 sunk at Stalingrad alone. This particular model, a four-seater, open-topped, bottle-green jeeplet, was raised from the Volga, painted with a red star and driven back to the Danube by the Russian army in 1944.

Braca acquired it, restored it and is very proud that it's the only one that can still be driven on land and in the water.

What's more, when we drive out of the Danube there is not a bead of moisture anywhere inside the vehicle.

Braca seems very Serbian in his curiosity and enthusiasm for all things mechanical. It's only as the day goes on that I find out that he's also Serbian in his industriousness, running the family café and catering business, a puppet theatre and dabbling in stage production as well.

I met up with him first thing this morning at an old garage opposite a police station in a backstreet of central Belgrade. Almost shyly, Braca took me round his eclectic collection of automobilia, ranging from a 1949 Ford Prefect to an 1897 Marot Gordon with a De Dion Bouton single-cylinder engine, and from a Fiat 'Jolly', a 500 converted by Ghia into a beach buggy with plastic seats, open sides and a tent-like canopy, to a magnificent 1929 tourer, made by Skoda.

He likes cars with a story attached and is especially proud of a 1955 Mercedes-Benz 300 called 'The Adenauer', after Konrad Adenauer, the Chancellor synonymous with the reconstruction of Germany after the war.

'With this car,' says Braca, 'the Germans told the rest of the world, "we are back".'

In case I thought he might be taking himself too seriously, he points out the two dummies in the car. One is Tito, sitting in splendour in the back. The other, driving, is Slobodan Milosevic, Serbia's one-time President who died in his cell at The Hague in March 2006, after his conviction for war crimes.

Another piece of history is the magnificent Packard, registration number Yugoslavia 1, in which the Russian leader Khrushchev rode on his first visit to Belgrade in 1955. Interesting, points out Braca, that, despite the Cold War, the leader of the communist world always preferred American cars.

It's not often you get a city tour in an amphibious car, but, on our way to the river, Braca laid one on for me. No-one seemed to bat an eyelid as we chugged through Republic Square, past the National Theatre, the National Museum and a statue of Prince Michael Obrenovic III, who is seen as the great liberator of Serbia from the Turks in the nineteenth century. We rattled along, at a steady 25 miles an hour, by the impressive walls of the Kalemegdan

Castle, started by the Romans and added to over the years by Turks, French and Hungarians, which guards the junction of the Sava and the Danube. Until 1918 the tree-fringed banks of the land called Vojvodina, on the far side of the Danube, were part of the Austro-Hungarian empire. In the great dismemberment of that empire that followed the Treaty of Trianon in 1920, Transylvania was given to Romania, and Vojvodina to the newly emerging Yugoslavia.

Because of its exposed position, on the edge of Europe's north–south, east–west divide, Belgrade has been constantly fought over. This Lazarus among cities has been destroyed some twenty times and always sprung back to life. In virtually my own lifetime, the Nazis devastated the city, it was fought over by Germans and Russians in 1944, and bombed by the Americans and British in 1999.

Braca, whilst no apologist for Milosevic, reveals a rare animation when I ask him about the Balkan wars of the 1990s, in which the Serbs are generally portrayed as the villains.

It was a political and religious war, he says, with all sides culpable, and surprises me by saying that despite the much headlined animosity of the Serbs towards the Muslims, there is a Muslim community of many thousands in Belgrade. Thousands of Turkish words survive from the Ottoman occupation, some of them for basics like bread and soup.

Above the roar of passing traffic I ask him about life in the city during the Allied bombings in 1999. Was the city brought to a standstill?

'Oh yes,' he smiles, swerving to avoid a bus. 'We have no vehicles. Very pleasant.'

With less of a smile he tells me that our boys hit a television building only a hundred yards from his house.

Day Sixty-seven: *Belgrade*

Spend much of the middle of the day crewing for a sailing boat out in the middle of the Danube, whilst the coldest wind of the coldest day of the journey held my head in a vice-like grip. We are racing other boats from the Zemun Yacht Club, named after a nearby Danube-side town even older than Belgrade. They're a nice laid-back group of people, mostly from the media, whose clubhouse is the steamy, bustling upper deck of a moored barge.

My captain calls himself Rambo Amadeus. Big man, big name. He looms over me, shades obscuring his eyes so I can never quite tell what to believe and what not to believe. He claims to have invented the term Turbo-Folk, a noisy, kitschy dance music that my *Bradt* guide describes as 'Balkan gangster rap, without the rap'. He has the physical presence of a gangland heavy and some of the opinions too. 'Television is stupid. Internet is cool.' In short, not the sort of person you associate with yacht clubs.

But he's funny and bright and a good enough sailor to have won this race had I not been crewing and asking him damn-fool questions at the same time.

His view of the war of the 1990s, and of war generally, is that it is a remorseless and inevitable process given that such large parts of national economies are tied up in preparations for, or defence against, war.

He says it got very bad in Belgrade in the late 1990s.

'If you threw your television through the window, nobody noticed.'

No sooner has he said that than he reconsiders.

'Actually no-one threw their TV out of the window.'

'Too precious?'

'Right.'

It's midnight. There is ice forming on the puddles on the dockside as I step onto the gangplank of one of Belgrade's riverside nightclubs. Belgrade has a reputation as one of Europe's great clubbing cities, and nightlife here seems to mean all-night life.

I get talking to Tijana, dark-haired, petite, currently working as singer and DJ on tour in Milan, Paris and Berlin, and Jelena, a blonde TV presenter who is retraining to be a film editor.

'I think people in Serbia still feel isolated,' says Tijana. 'If they're talking about other nations and countries it's always "us" and "them".'

Jelena nods and adds that less than three per cent of Serbians under twenty-seven have a passport.

'So they don't have a chance to see anything else.'

Tijana thinks this isolation has led to Serbs being very proud of themselves, and she adds, interestingly, 'There was never a real war in Serbia, so you don't get the same feelings as if you go to Bosnia or parts of Croatia. Belgrade always had this metropolitan glitter, it was the capital city of Yugoslavia too.'

'What happened when the bombs came?'

Tijana can't suppress a smile.

'It was the greatest party ever. Nobody had to go to school, to university, to work. And nightclubs were open all day, and nobody worried about going to bed early, and you could play your music as loud as you wanted and it was…it was crazy.'

Jelena doesn't think things are going to change for the better for a generation, and Tijana thinks things are improving in Serbia, but only slowly.

'I think there is no big hatred towards other nations in the Balkans…but this damned Serbian mentality is always coming to the surface. Like things started changing very progressively, then it all stopped with the murder of Dindic [a reforming Prime Minister assassinated in 2003] and the same mentality that brought Milosevic to the top of the country is now taking things in that direction again.'

I get back to the hotel late, but the lobby is buzzing with black-clad figures. For a moment they looked like soldiers, then I realised that they're all partygoers.

Hungary

Day Sixty-nine: *Esztergom*

JUNE 4 1920 was a dark day in Hungary's history. In the ornate elegance of the Grand Palais de Trianon at Versailles, a treaty was signed which, at a stroke, reduced the country to a third of its size. Land was lost north, south, east and west. Access to the sea through the port of Fiume (now Rijeka) was denied. There is hardly a route into Hungary which is not a distant reminder of national pain.

The Maria Valeria bridge on which I'm standing this balmy morning, looking down into a far-from-blue Danube, was originally built by the Emperor Franz Josef in 1895 to connect two provinces of an Austro-Hungarian empire which stretched from Switzerland to Russia. Now the empire's long gone, and the other side of the bridge is a foreign country. The bridge itself has suffered too, destroyed by the Germans in the Second World War, and not reopened until 2001.

The Austro-Hungarian empire was a political and religious balancing act, a polyglot conglomeration at a time when Europe was re-forming into independent nation states. Franz Josef's subjects were Catholic, Protestant, Jewish, Muslim, Greek and Russian Orthodox and they spoke a dozen languages. The First World War brought the whole unsteady edifice tumbling down, and from being part of the structure itself, Hungary became one of the pieces.

Not that you'd know it from crossing the bridge from what is now Slovakia. Hungary presents its credentials in immediate and dramatic fashion. On the first low hill, overlooking the river and dominating the border town of Esztergom, is a massive domed Basilica, more than 300 feet high. It's the largest cathedral in the country. Standing on the spot where the founder of the nation, King Istvan (Stephen) I, was crowned in AD 1000, it contains the tomb of the revered Cardinal Jozsef Mindszenty, who suffered imprisonment and torture for his resistance to both fascism and communism. Potent symbols of Hungarian pride are gathered together on this hill, of their long history, their independence and their religion.

And, for what it's worth, Esztergom has one of the biggest Tesco's I've ever seen.

Mercifully, not all of the city is on an epic scale. Down the hill below the Basilica are some small, attractive cobbled streets with carefully trimmed fruit trees and fat hydrangea bushes on clipped grass verges. In one of these lives Bishop Kiss-Rigo, my guide to the town they call 'The Cradle of Hungary'.

With his greying hair, ruddy complexion, quick, impish smile and way with a story, he seems more Irish than Hungarian, but he grew up in Budapest and first became a priest here twenty-nine years ago. He's the goalkeeper of his local priests' soccer team, and rather proud of the fact that they came fifth in last year's championships in Zagreb.

He's interesting about the Maria Valeria bridge. For a long time after the war there was no will to rebuild it. The politicians on both sides preferred it that way. He considers its much delayed reopening six years ago to be very important, a victory for co-operation over confrontation. And it seems to work. As I look back at it I can see people walking, cycling, even rollerblading, from one country to another.

We walk up the hill and talk a little about the communist days. As a priest he was never physically harmed but everything was, as he put it, 'under control'. Letters were opened, phones tapped. But he doesn't sound too happy with present-day Hungary. Corruption is bad, and getting worse.

By now we've reached the wide expanse of forecourt that leads the eye up to the mighty columned portico of the Basilica. I find myself becoming grudgingly Protestant about the intimidating immensity of the whole thing, and even the bishop himself agrees it's probably bigger than it need be. Completed in 1869 after fifty years in the building and intended as a glorious reaffirmation of national spirit and the Catholic faith after years of Turkish repression and Hapsburg Germanisation, it was modelled on St Peter's in Rome.

'It was to be a Vatican for Central Europe,' he says. The work so captured the imagination of the times that Beethoven offered to write a Mass for the opening but was turned down for lack of money. In the end Franz Liszt provided a Missa Solemnis without even claiming expenses.

The cavernous interior is full of people staring about in awe. Most seem to be tourists. Bishop Kiss-Rigo surprises me by saying that there was no great rush back to the churches after the years of communist repression.

'Faith is sometimes stronger in adversity,' he explains, without any great conviction.

Sixty-five per cent of Hungarians consider themselves to be Catholic, but church attendance is only around twelve per cent.

The most memorable space inside has beauty as well as bombast and that's because it was built over 300 years before the rest. It's a chapel with walls of red marble, saved from destruction by the Turks and reassembled in the body of the new Basilica. Impressive in a different way is the tomb of Cardinal Mindszenty. For some reason the current fails as we enter and with the darkness of the crypt broken only by oblique shafts of daylight, the power and simplicity of his memorial are extraordinarily effective.

'Vita Humiliavit Mors Exaltavit' it reads.

Life humiliated him. Death exalted him.

The drive through the enchanting Pilis Hills from Esztergom is a joy. We climb up over the escarpment, through graceful beech woods, and stop off at the country cottage of our guide and translator György, his wife Ildikó, and their soppily affectionate Belgian Shepherd called Zeus. It's a hot afternoon and Ildikó offers us a pick-me-up of mint, lime, sugar and a touch of white rum. It's a rare and gratifying pleasure on these long journeys to be able to sit and do nothing more than take in the unsensational tranquillity of fields and woods and distant hills. Summer afternoons don't come much better than this.

Day Seventy: *Visegrád*

It's mid-morning and a procession is making its way slowly through the riverside town of Visegrád, five miles and two bends downstream from Esztergom. Drums and trumpets are sounding, flags and pennants are fluttering in the breeze, and knights in armour are perspiring in the dusty summer heat. On and on they come; noblemen and women on horseback, citizens walking alongside, mothers with babies, burghers in the colours of their guilds, helmeted Tartar mercenaries from the East, with fur cloaks, barking out orders, Italians in vibrant red and gold tunics carrying huge flags of scarlet and deep blue high into the sky. Heavily robed bishops, archers with leather hoods, heralds in tabards, knights in black chain mail, horses in full armour, lightly dressed cavalry and plodding foot soldiers, and in the middle of them all, on thick-legged horses cloaked in coloured velvet, an unmistakable King and Queen.

The reason for all this is what György calls 'Middle-Aged Day', a once-yearly pageant with more than a hint of yearning for those golden days when knights were bold, and the boldest of all were to be found in Hungary. The serious historical context to it all is the reign of Matthias Corvinus (Corvinus referring to the raven that was the royal emblem). Matthias, still a teenager when he came to the throne in 1458, was the son of one of Europe's most successful warriors, Janos Hunyadi, a Transylvanian who spent most of his adult life fighting the Turks, defeating them, against all the odds, at the siege of Belgrade.

Matthias reaped the benefit of a breathing space of tranquillity to build up a reputation as a strong but civilised ruler. He taxed his nobles to raise a standing force of 30,000 men, known as the Black Army, but he was equally successful at attracting scholars and artists to his palaces, one of which was at Visegrád.

Visegrád (a Slav word meaning 'high place') guards the last loop of the Danube before it turns south to Budapest and Belgrade, and the remains of a thirteenth-century castle overlook the city. Matthias' Palace, too, fell into disrepair, and was submerged in mud until Janos Schulek, an archaeologist, rediscovered it in 1934. Partly restored, it is now the reason for, and location of, this celebration of all things medieval.

Hungarian day-trippers wander among stalls selling beer, sausages, books, jewellery, Attila the Hun DVDs and maps of pre-Trianon Hungary.

Meanwhile, the long procession spills into the palace grounds where the King and Queen of the day take their place in a Royal Pavilion, and receive solemn pledges of loyalty from the participants, many of whom then go back to join their families in the audience. Where else would you find a Teutonic Knight with his arm round a woman in turquoise hotpants?

A crowd of several thousand is entertained by all sorts of marching, music, pitched battles and feats of skill. The Italian contingent is led by a phalanx of gamine flag-bearers who toss flags and poles high in the air and catch them with infectious precision. A falconry display could have been a little dull but is immeasurably enlivened when one of the birds, poised elegantly on a post, raises its tail and sends a perfectly aimed jobby onto the upraised lens of a tourist's camera. A display of belly-dancing is a rare nod to the Ottoman past, but the highlight of the entertainment is a solo display of extraordinary skill from Lajos Kassai, the master of the art of horseback archery. At full gallop, aiming, firing and reloading as he goes, he sends six arrows from quiver to target in twelve seconds. On the next pass he fires at targets thrown up into the air, and hits four in succession, dead centre. In seventeen seconds he can shoot twelve arrows into a target.

As befits a member of the World Association of Horse Archery, Kassai knows his history. Did I know that the technique of backwards archery was the great advantage that Attila the Hun's men had over the Romans? Did I know that the Avars, another tribe from Central Asia, invented the stirrup? That an arrow fired at a gallop of 30 miles per hour will have double the piercing power of an arrow fired from stationary? The key to the success of the invading Huns, Avars and Magyars was the equestrian skills that came naturally to people who had been nomadic herdsmen for generations.

For Lajos, a powerfully built man with a shaved head and steely blue eyes, re-creating these ancient skills has become a way of life. He owns 15 hectares of a remote valley in which he has a riding school, archery courses, and a yurt to remind him of the roots of the ancestors he admires so much.

'Every Hungarian feels in his heart he is Attila.'

Further down the river in the direction of Budapest, a pretty little town called Szentendre (St Andrew) adds another piece to the jigsaw of Hungarian history. Szentendre was founded by Serbs fleeing north after the catastrophic defeat of their armies by the Turks at the Field of Blackbirds in 1389, and many more came later when the Ottoman armies recaptured Belgrade in 1690.

It has a handsome Orthodox church, next to which is what used to be the priest's house and is now the home of the Eredics, one of the hundred or so Serb families still left in Szentendre.

Kálmán Eredic, the elder of the family, started his group of musicians thirty-two years ago. Various members of the family have now joined him and in the secluded garden of what is largely a 300-year-old house, they play, on violins of all kinds (with Kálmán on the double bass), vigorous folk music that has not just Serb but also Macedonian and Croatian influences. Marta Sebestyen, one of Hungary's most celebrated singers, who sang the haunting folk song in *The English Patient*, has worked with the group over many years. With her wide emotional range and apparently effortless technique she can cope with any kind of material, but it's the songs of loss and longing that seem to suit this tall walled garden as the sun goes down.

'Melancholic,' she says apologetically, after we've all been reduced to reflective silence.

'Just like our history.'

A very un-melancholic meal follows, featuring a complex and delicious goulash, prepared over an open fire by Kálmán's short, dark, feisty wife Zita, and augmented with Hungarian wine and shots of *pálinka*. We're sent back to the Budapest ferry in high spirits, after hospitality so generous that I'm unable to remember whether or not music is the food of love, or food is the music of love. Time for bed.

Day Seventy-one: *Budapest*

The Hotel Gellért is an institution, and can easily feel like one as you open your door in the morning to find the palatial corridor outside full of shuffling figures in slippers and white flannel robes. Ninety years old next year, it feels as venerable as some of the clients who flock here to take the waters which have made it so famous.

Designed to market the hot springs that well up at the foot of Gellért Hill, and have been noted and recommended since Roman times, the luxuriously appointed hotel was opened with much ceremony in 1918. In France the last battles of the Great War were coming to an end and soon the peacemakers who were to dismember Hungary would set about their work, but the scale and aplomb of the Gellért harked back to the years of imperial confidence that had transformed Budapest into one of the great European capitals.

I've been up for some time studying an intimidating document called the Guide to the Gellért Spa, which fills me in, in considerable detail, on plastic admission cards, wristbands, barcodes and 'decency covers'. As advised, I leave my room, like all the other health-seekers, wearing the gown and slippers provided and carrying a bath cap and valuables in a plastic bag.

The first and easiest mistake is to assume that the hotel lifts will take you to the spa. Wrong. The baths are run, not by the hotel, but by the city of Budapest and are located in a completely different direction from the rest.

The lift is worth finding, not just because it's the only way down, but because it is a fully functioning museum piece, a wood-panelled cabinet set in a decorative cast-iron shaft, and operated by an Edith Piaf lookalike with hair dyed pitch black. As we descend she moistens her finger on a sponge pad, prises an admission card from a thick wad and hands it to me.

I step out of the lift, go through a door and find myself in a cavernous space the size of a large railway station. A big, arched Art Nouveau entrance decorated with ceramic tiles opens onto a galleried hall with porphyry columns, a vaulted roof with stained-glass panels and marble statues of naked maidens. It's a place for men with top hats and tails and women with long, satin ballgowns, not confused guests in bathrobes. One of two big boards on the wall tells me that the waters contain calcium, magnesium, hydrogen carbonate, sulphur and chloride, whilst the other describes the services offered, which include everything from Underwater Traction Mud Treatment, Gingival Massage and 'Inhalation for Pensioner', to Impulse Current Therapy, Salt Chamber and the frankly alarming Carbon Acid Tub Bath.

Display my card, barcode uppermost, and proceed through the turnstile, past the Ladies Only and Mixed pools into the changing area of the Gentlemen's Thermal. Here I'm given a rubber wristband and the aforementioned 'decency cover', which is little more than a tiny apron with a loose flap at back and front, and pointed towards another passageway.

I'm getting a little concerned by now, having seen no water of any kind, and fearing I might tumble unwittingly into the Carbon Acid Tub Bath. But there is light at the end of the tunnel, and splashing through a foot rinse, I find myself in a lovely arched chamber with a choice of 36° or 38° pools. Choose the hotter and recline against its enamel sides whilst water trickles soothingly onto my head from the mouths of marble cherubs.

Nothing is purely functional here. Every detail, from the stylish curve of a brass handrail to the maidens frolicking in a stained-glass oval in the roof, is there to create the feeling of having fun with some minor deities halfway up Mount Olympus.

The decency covers seem far from obligatory and the older bathers seem to have dispensed with them completely. This, and the fact that the slightest draught blows them aside, makes me a tiny bit apprehensive about entering the steam room. Of course I needn't have worried. The place is full of naked men in animated discussion about the stock market.

From my balcony I look out over the rumbling tramlines to the green girders of Liberty Bridge and the Danube, or Duna as it's called in Hungary, swirling by on its way south. It's a big river, wider than the Thames in London. In the nineteenth century there were two cities here, Buda, where I am now, and Pest, on the far, and flatter, side of the river. The Romans didn't even bother to try crossing here and left the Danube to mark the limits of their empire. Buda was part of civilisation, Pest was on the Barbarian shore. It was the bridges of the nineteenth century, beginning with the English-designed Chain Bridge in 1849, that sewed the two cities together into one great capital, Budapest. The Liberty Bridge was built at the height of the Austro-Hungarian empire in 1896 and is capped by two wrought-iron likenesses of a mythical bird, the turul, which is believed to have sired the father of Arpad, the leader who brought the Magyar tribe over the Carpathians and into Hungary. The sword of Attila, clasped in the hands of the turul, is an attempt to cling on to a more tenuous myth of Hungarian history, that the Hun in Hungary means descent from the great warrior himself. It's now pretty well accepted that the name comes from a group of Magyar-like tribes called the Onogur.

The Buda shore may have the height and the dramatic skyline of Castle Hill, but the building that most characterises the power and gravity of the city is the monumental neo-Gothic Parliament building over in Pest. It comes with the obligatory raft of staggering statistics: seventeen years in the building, 691 rooms, forty million bricks and a workforce of 1,000 men. For Ceausescu this would have been a kitchen extension, but when it opened in 1902 it was the largest Parliament building in the world.

I'm shown around it by an engagingly wise and witty man called Péter Zwack, an independent MP, and head of the family that makes Hungary's most popular digestif, Unicum. We meet up beside a huge, rather disdainful, bronze lion which reclines below the twin flags of Hungary and the European Union, both hanging limp and lifeless on this torpid morning.

Once inside we find ourselves on a wide red-carpeted staircase with stained-glass windows and gilded columns rising high on either side.

'It's far too big,' Péter mutters. 'There are only 386 members of Parliament. Which is about 186 more than necessary.'

But he can't deny the presence of the place.

'Six years ago I first mounted these stairs as a member of Parliament. It was an incredible feeling. Every Hungarian MP is called "Father of the Nation".' He smiles with not entirely mock pride.

'So, I'm a father of the nation you see.'

The red carpet leads inexorably up into a high-domed central hall and another iconic national image. In this case the iconic national image. In an impregnable glass case on a marble plinth set directly beneath the highest point of the 300-foot dome, and guarded by three soldiers with drawn swords, is the 1,000-year-old crown of Istvan I, father of the nation, which was a gift to him from the Pope. The gold cross on it is bent to one side, which apparently makes it even more special for it happened, so they say, when it fell from the young king's horse as he was being chased by pagans. At the end of the Second World War, the symbol of Hungary found its way into American hands and was kept in Fort Knox until 1978, when President Carter authorised its return.

Parliament isn't in session today so Péter and I have the Chamber of Representatives almost to ourselves. It's as extravagantly grand as an opera house, with panelling, desks and seats all carved from light oak with such fine attention to detail that there is even a numbered cigar rack in which members can leave their smokes before entering the chamber.

Though it looks an immaculate period piece, the Parliament building has been largely rebuilt after being bombed in the Second World War. Péter remembers life here at the end of the war as the British, Americans and Russians tried to flush out the occupying Germans.

'If you could hear the whizz of the bomb you were OK,' he recalls. 'When it fell silent that was the time to worry.'

Whilst dodging friendly bombs he was facing the much worse threat of unfriendly Hungarians. The Zwack family, like ninety per cent of Hungary's merchant aristocracy, was Jewish, and as pressure on the city increased the Germans began to round up and deport Jews on a massive scale. They were helped by the Arrow Cross, Hungarian Nazis, who Péter remembers as 'the real butchers'. They would take their victims down to the Danube, tie three or four tightly together and shoot one of them, who would then drag the others under the water. He himself was only minutes from being picked up when he managed to escape the city in 1944, returning eventually in 1987 to a communist country in transition from the hardline pro-Soviet days, but still capable of 'beating up young students with sticks outside the Parliament'. But he was totally taken by surprise by the abrupt fall of the communists, and the equally abrupt departure of Soviet troops from Hungary.

'I never thought this would change. I thought until my death we were going to live under communism here.'

He concedes that many problems remain.

'Under communism there was no corruption, no famine... everybody got something, but everybody got very little, and today with capitalism, especially the old people feel they had a better time under communism.'

While clearly a successful capitalist himself, he is not in favour of hunting down the old communists and settling scores.

'We should have closed it, like the Germans did in 1990, when they strictly filtered out who should be punished, who not, but in Hungary today, it's still a process going on.'

As the only Independent member of Parliament, he is, not surprisingly, the only one dedicated to rooting out corruption.

'OK, ten million people in the country. Out of that about three million pensioners on about 200 euros a month, and you have a million super-rich, who were close to power in the old days... and there's a real hatred towards these new-rich, with their gold chains.'

This results in the policy of envy which he feels is the curse of the country.

'There is no middle class in Hungary, which we had before. You have only the very rich or the very poor.'

We walk out onto the gleaming, freshly cleaned limestone terrace overlooking the Danube. The ramparts of Castle Hill rise up across the river, a hazy skyline of walls and roofs tiled in red and gold. This is undoubtedly the grandest city we've encountered so far, and despite his misgivings Péter is upbeat about its prospects. Money is pouring in and more foreign investment is coming here than into Vienna, making it currently the financial and business hub of Central Europe.

'The Soviets called us East European,' he says with a touch of asperity, 'which we are not, we are Central Europe. Call us East European, people don't like it.'

Day Seventy-two: *Budapest*

An example of the new entrepreneurial spirit of Budapest is their willingness to take risks. How else can I interpret an invitation from Katti Zoob, the newest, coolest, hippest designer in town, for me to model an outfit in her new show?

I am to have a fitting this morning and dutifully on time I arrive at a passageway off a busy, dusty street along which traffic off the Margaret Bridge pours into town.

Katti's is a fashionably discreet empire, a conversion of six apartments in an ornate, slightly shabby, cream and white-painted block, whose walls squeeze oppressively close around a narrow courtyard.

Inside, all is wood-strip floor and racks of expensive, elegant outfits. The sort of salon you'd take for granted in London or Paris but is the first of its kind in Budapest. Katti Zoob made her name in theatre productions. This is her first serious foray into the world of haute couture and only opened three months ago. Though she designs almost entirely for women she's anxious to broaden out into male fashion and I'm her guinea pig.

I'm taken upstairs to meet her in her workshop, past rows of inventive, unusual dresses in her trademark materials of chiffon, silk and taffeta.

I feel pleasantly and comfortably out of place.

Katti is in her forties, small, with a dark red glint to her hair, and dressed in a black top and a skirt of white taffeta with odd sections of fishnet on her legs and red silk slingbacks on her feet.

Despite her halting English, there's a playfulness about her which makes us get on right from the start. The theme of her show is to be Ördögi Angyalok, Evil Angels and Angyuli Ördögok, Angelic Devils.

'Michael, I want you to be a little bit devil, a little bit angel.'

'So I'm kind of bi-moral. A little bit good, a little bit bad.'

She looks baffled.

'I'm bi-moral.'

Now she looks interested, possibly even a little shocked.

'Really?'

I decide that it's better not to pursue this one and we get on with the fitting.

She has in mind a close-fitting black leather jacket with a white appliqué design of men, women, snakes and general coiling and couplings.

'Would you like a skirt?'

'Erm...well...'

'Black lace skirt with white lining?'

'A sort of see-through kilt?'

Fortunately she laughs at this and the skirt is dropped, in a manner of speaking.

Measurements are taken and I'm required to come in tomorrow for a second fitting. The big night will be in two days' time.

I like Katti. She's bright and inventive but her years in theatre have stopped her from taking herself too seriously. And I like it that she's always coming up with new ideas. I'm heading for the door when I hear her little voice behind me.

'D'you want wings?'

Day Seventy-four: *Budapest*

Almost exactly fifty years ago, in October 1956, students and workers gathered in Budapest to protest against a Moscow-led regime that had run their country with increasingly ruthless brutality since the end of the war. A statue of Stalin was toppled, the police fired into a crowd and only the second ever anti-communist uprising in Europe had begun. (The first was in Poznań in Poland earlier that same year.) It teetered on the brink of success. Moscow withdrew its troops and the new Prime Minister, Imre Nagy (himself an old communist), was the hero of the hour. There was real hope that they would remain free. Only a few months earlier, in February 1956, Premier Khrushchev had denounced Stalin and the hardliners in a secret speech to the 20th Communist Congress. The Americans had been encouraging all the occupied countries to do just what the Hungarians had done so there was a good chance that the West would help them. In the end neither Russian revisionism nor American anti-communism delivered. Khrushchev ordered the tanks back in, and the West, distracted by a futile war over the Suez Canal, sat and watched.

Soviet control was reasserted and remained in place for the next thirty-three years, though it gradually merged into a less repressive, more pragmatic Hungarian form that came to be known as 'Goulash Communism'.

Many Hungarians, especially the young, don't want to be constantly reminded of their communist past. For them the most important thing that's happened to the country happened on 1 May 2004, when Hungary was admitted to the European Union. The future is where hope lies, not the past.

It's mostly curious foreigners who make the trip outside town to Statue Park, where, amongst delphiniums and rosemary bushes, an enterprising private collector has gathered together some of the great Soviet monuments, including a 15-foot-high Lenin, coat-tail flapping and red flag in hand, a running sailor ten times life-size, and mighty heads of Marx and Engels. It's all a bit sad, these images which had such power to alarm or inspire or change the world, stacked together out here in suburbia, like garden gnomes on steroids.

In the shop by the entrance they sell various memorabilia: medals, recordings of old Soviet songs, and cans labelled 'The Last Breath of Communism'.

A much slicker operation and a more profound experience is to be had at the House of Terror, a part-museum, part-multimedia experience which graphically records the worst horrors of the communist period. It's suitably, and chillingly, situated at 60 Andrassy Avenue, the most feared address in Budapest, the very building that was at one time headquarters of the Arrow Cross fascists and, after the war, the AVO secret police.

From the garish grid of lettering which surrounds the exterior roof of the building, to the massive tank crouched in the darkness of the stairwell inside, the effect is dramatic and theatrical. Opened in 2002, it uses the most up-to-date multimedia effects, combining archive video and state-of-the-art sound and light effects. There is a courtroom where every surface is covered in a wallpaper of documents or box files, in which you can sit and watch compulsive footage of the secret trial of the leaders of the 1956 uprising glassily confessing to their crimes. Imre Nagy is the only one who doesn't appear brainwashed. He answers back his accusers even as he is sentenced to death.

A wall of photos identifies members of the AVO political police. Someone points out that some are still around, one a writer, another a TV presenter.

Another display shows communist posters of the period, full of happy smiling faces rejoicing over industrial targets exceeded, and workers grasping hands in the fields, whilst one warns of the perils of the imperialist, bourgeois Colorado Potato Beetle, America's latest weapon against the people. Elsewhere there is archive footage of the Hungarian football team in 1953 inflicting England's worst-ever defeat at Wembley, six goals to three.

Most effective of all the presentations is a glass lift set in a black shaft which descends imperceptibly slowly to the death cells below whilst on a screen a man describes what it was like to have to clean up after the executions. His testimony is all the more chilling because of his completely matter-of-fact, unemotional delivery.

The House of Terror, on which no expense seems to have been spared, makes clever use of a series of ingenious and often abstract set pieces which leave you in no doubt that communism was a very bad thing indeed.

But the other atrocities perpetuated at 60 Andrassy Avenue, such as the torture of Jews by the Arrow Cross, have so little space, that I'm left feeling hugely impressed, but a little manipulated, by this extraordinary place.

For the moment my mind is taken off any other thoughts of doom and gloom by the imminent prospect of having to appear, for the first time in my life, on a cat-walk.

Katti is remarkably calm, finding time, even as the carefully chosen guests are taking their seats in the long, mirrored room, to sew a devil's tail on the bottom of my slinky leather jacket.

People rush around backstage making last-minute adjustments, the sound system plays up, and as eight stunning models and myself slip in and out of outfits in the communal area, I have to remind myself that for once this is not fantasy. I am the only man in the girls' changing room.

Adrenalin levels creep up as the time comes for Katti to step out and confront the movers and shakers of Budapest society. At a given signal, funky music with a heavy bass beat silences the audience. Katti takes a bow, introduces the show, then introduces me. I've seen enough models at work to be able to put together a parody of swinging hips, and the twirling black tail is a great success. I give a short speech, which is listened to with far more respect than a man with a long black tail deserves, and that done I sit back and watch eight of my fellow models strut their stuff, each one changing outfits, and often make-up as well, eight times. Tall, small-breasted, with very high heels on the end of very long legs, they walk like thoroughbred horses, flicking out their legs as if cracking a whip. Sixty-four passes in thirty-five minutes. Respect.

Have no luck afterwards with my attempts to join the Hungarian Models' Union. Not even associate membership. Oh well, perhaps it's for the best. I shall be leaving for the Ukraine tomorrow.

Day Seventy-five: *Budapest*

Budapest is a city of confident landmark buildings; some of them, like the Castle and the Royal Palace, have outlived their original purpose, or in the case of the Parliament building are too big for their present purpose, but all have a sense of style, scale and swagger. A quick visit to the revitalised riverside area of South Pest shows that the monumental tradition is not forgotten. The grand (my guidebook prefers 'overblown') Palace of Arts complex includes the largest concert hall in Europe, and the new National Theatre next to it is not just big but very wacky, with blue carpet on the outside walls, life-size bronze figures of famous actors and actresses sitting on seats and benches in the park around it, and the classical façade of the previous National Theatre beside it lying half-submerged in a tank of water. Practical and functional are not the first words that spring to mind when describing Budapest's architecture. These buildings have a purpose, of course, but far more importantly they must be celebrations of that purpose.

Bearing this in mind, I take my last bath, and Budapesters love to bathe, at the lushly ornate Széchenyi Gyógyfürdő, where healing spring waters bubble up from over 4,000 feet below the ground. There can be few places in the world where water is as lavishly celebrated. Even the word 'Gyógyfürdő', meaning a spa or medical baths, suggests something surreal and fantastical.

From the outside the baths look like a small Baroque palace. Inside is a domed central chamber with mosaic-tiled passageways leading to private bathing boxes and a hospital where patients are sent for special mineral treatments. White stucco erupts like fungus from the walls and semicircular panels depict, on one side of the room, Venus being bathed by four robed cohorts and on the other, Neptune assaulting a mermaid.

For a moment it's quite possible to forget that you've come here to get yourself wet. The very act of undressing seems to belittle the surroundings, but step through to the three steaming pools and you may, on a busy day, be in the company of a couple of thousand others. These are pools for hanging around in. There are no lanes and no Olympic wannabees cleaving the water. The most competitive activity is probably chess, which is played to a very high standard by men and women half-submerged, of course, in water.

A hundred miles or so east of Budapest the cultivated fields give way to an immense emptiness, a flat, unbroken, oddly hypnotic expanse of land known as the Puszta. Once a swampy flood plain, it was drained in the mid-nineteenth century and is now home to herds of magnificently horned Hungarian Grey cattle and the herds of tourists who come to see them.

It's quite late, and the sun is setting spectacularly in a cloudless sky as we reach the village of Hortobágy, (pronounced Horto-bodge). By the time we find the *gulyas*, the cowboys, and the horsemen they call *csikos*, they're preparing food at the end of the day, gathered around a collection of neatly thatched buildings with whitewashed walls, only accessible after a bumping ride across the hard-baked grassland.

A herd of Hungarian Grey cattle, big as stags and solid as armoured cars, kicks up the dust as they're moved towards the tall uprights and crossbeams of a well that reminds me of the shadoof-like irrigation systems in the Saharan oases.

I try to help out but am rather clumsy with it. A hefty tug on the rope sends the bucket down into the well and another pulls it back up. The knack is to catch the leather bucket at the right moment to use its own energy to tip it effortlessly into the gutters that flow through into the water troughs. I can't get the tipping point right and I lose the whole momentum and have to start again. Aware of increasingly disgruntled bovine faces looking up from the trough, I hand over to my instructor, a small, podgy, ruddy-faced man in a black semicircular hat, like a French parish priest, who executes the same movement with exquisite grace, over and over again.

I'm taken off watering and put onto cooking. First of all helping to split logs for the fire and later to cut up onions and peppers and put them into a big cooking-pot of goulash. The knife they give me could barely cut butter and I'm aware of the hard men of the Puszta looking at me with ill-concealed despair as I struggle to peel an onion.

With the goulash eventually bubbling away, they find something they can entrust me with, scattering paprika into the pot. So well do I do this that I'm put onto stirring.

Meanwhile, a herd of tall, sleek lissom horses, straight from central casting, gallops into view accompanied by the *csikos*, who are top of the hierarchy out here on the Puszta.

They wear a loose robe in the same indigo blue as the Tuareg of the Sahara, but they wear it with a black waistcoat, a broad black hat with a feather inside its upturned brim, and a pair of knee-length black leather boots.

Despite their slightly camp attire, these are men who are well in touch with their masculine side. Without a saddle in sight they gallop about cracking fearsomely long whips, and sending well-fed dogs yelping happily off to round up equally well-fed cattle. Others leap, not just on their horses, but on each other, forming perilous pyramids on galloping horses. One man, standing bareback, controls five cantering horses at the same time.

Once the frenetic performances are over, and the goulash is done and the beers are out and the dying sun is just a scab of red above the horizon, a great peace descends on the plain. The immensity of the land mirrors the immensity of the night sky and voices drop and for a moment the only sound is the gentle clink of cow bells. This is one bit of the Puszta experience that can't be faked. And it makes the journey here worthwhile.

Day Seventy-six: *Hortobágy to the Ukrainian border*

Back to Debrecen to pick up the night train to L'viv. The stock is quite elderly but they've done their best to brighten up the compartments and there are flowers absolutely everywhere. Unfortunately they're plastic flowers and when they're combined with plastic hanging baskets, as they are in the corridor, they can be quite uncomfortable to squeeze past. There are two attendants, a blonde Ukrainian lady, around forty, I estimate, and a deeply tanned Hungarian colleague who keeps appearing with his shirt half-off, revealing a well-toned bronzed chest. As there is no food or drink to be had on the train, there isn't a lot they can do, except prepare our beds for the night.

At a quarter to eleven we arrive at the last station in Hungary, a nondescript place called Záhony. A squad of Hungarian border guards, suntanned country boys, pass through, gawping in astonishment at our thirty pieces of baggage. They smile a lot and the last one shakes my hand as he leaves. I put my watch on an hour to Ukrainian time and wait, as you often do on international trains, in limbo-land. Eventually we edge creakily forward towards the border. Less than ninety years ago we wouldn't be leaving Hungary at all, just carrying on into that part of their empire called Galícia.

In the last century Hungary joined two world wars in order to preserve or regain territory and ended up on the losing side in both of them. Her population has halved, her land has been cut by two-thirds. The Hungarians know they should be bigger. They have talents in abundance: this is the country of Edward Teller the atom scientist, Rubik of the cube, Bíro of the biro, Bartok, Liszt, Kodaly and Tony Curtis. Budapest has some of the most sumptuous buildings in Europe. But, in contrast, say, to the Balkans, nationalism in Hungary is no longer a big issue. They're above all that. Despite everything, they still believe they are the heart of Europe.

My musings are brought to an abrupt end as we squeak to a halt at Chop, and it's the turn of young Ukrainian guards to examine the train and its contents. Wearing camouflage fatigues, they come through with large, amiable Alsatian dogs who sniff us all most politely.

Now history intervenes once more. When the Bolsheviks took power in Russia they decided, for reasons of national security, not to adjust their railway gauge to that of the rest of Europe. This means that at half past midnight we're shunted into special sidings where the wheels of each coach are loosened and the whole thing raised a couple of metres in the air on hydraulic jacks.

We're out filming this cumbersome procedure when a bleary-looking passenger in a pair of pyjamas appears at the open door, takes one look at the 6-foot drop beneath him and disappears rapidly back the way he'd come.

Working under floodlights wheeled along beside them, the train-gang slide out the old bogies, slide in a completely new set, lower the train and tighten the new ones up. The whole process of changing every set of wheels on the Budapest–L'viv express takes a little under an hour.

At two o'clock we're on our way again, travelling north and east, close to the Slovak-Ukraine border through the valleys of Ruthenia, the old Latin name for Russia, and into Galicia, an ancient land that once stretched from southern Poland to the Carpathians. Magical names. The stuff of dreams.

Ukraine

Day Seventy-seven: *L'viv*

FIVE-THIRTY. Move my vase of plastic yellow roses out of the way and push aside the scrap of lacy curtain. It's dawn, but there's precious little light coming in. Everything outside has changed. The flat Hungarian plain has been replaced by the steep, tree-fringed fields and hills of the northern Carpathians, the sunshine and clear skies of the last two weeks by streaming rain and low cloud. Our Ukrainian stewardess, back in her own country, and in sole and effortless control of the coach, is already up and about, bringing us glasses of tea in stainless-steel holders as we gather and gaze out at the gloom. She beams at us in motherly fashion and says how much nicer it is to squeeze past us than past the beer bellies of her fellow stewards.

Outside, the hills become small mountains, their summits hidden in the cloud. Villages and farms huddle more tightly into the valleys. They look bleak this morning, all grey walls and roofs. The stations are rough and ready. At one a pack of barking dogs patrols the platform and there are no passengers to be seen. The fields look strangely familiar, full of the same cone-shaped haystacks we saw in Romania; Carpathian landscape, sylvan and unspoilt, which, even on a moody morning like this, makes you want to be out there, in the middle of it.

Sip my tea and mug up on the country ahead in Anna Reid's book about the history of the Ukraine, *Borderland*. I learn from her that the first line of the Ukrainian national anthem translates as 'Ukraine is not dead yet'.

Whoever supplies the signs at L'viv station must have had a

good few years as the city has changed its name four times since the end of the First World War. Known as Lemberg when it was a part of the Austro-Hungarian empire, it became Lwów, part of Poland, in 1919; Lvov, part of the USSR, in 1945; and L'viv, part of the Ukraine, from 1991.

This is what it has wanted to be for a long time, for the city has been at the forefront of Ukrainian nationalism for 150 years. When independence finally came L'viv couldn't wait to replace its Lenin with a grand memorial to Taras Shevchenko, the nineteenth-century poet often called 'the father of the Ukrainian language'.

Any idea of L'viv being a casualty of a promiscuous past is dispelled as soon as we're into the heart of town, which is full of beautiful buildings and generous squares in an unexpectedly rich mix of Baroque and Renaissance styles. Its centre is intimate and perfect for walking and exploring, except that it's pouring with rain and the whole of the Old Town is being dug up and relaid.

This hasn't put off the organisers of a sizeable political rally which has attracted a few hundred umbrellas onto Svobody (Freedom) Square. Ukrainian politics is still volatile after the Orange Revolution of 2004 raised hopes of a new era of reform and Western-style democracy. Since then the liberalisers have split amongst themselves and the more conservative Russophile parties are recovering ground.

L'viv feels European. There's an Opera House as strikingly neo-classical as anything in Paris or Vienna, both Catholic and Orthodox churches, and on Rynok Square, a glorious collection of merchants' houses, with names like Venice House and the Italian Yard. The town hall has a neo-Florentine tower. This was a city on the lucrative route between Europe and Asia, a prosperous city which thrived on trade and tolerance. But there is evidence in the remains of the old Jewish quarter, still unrepaired, of what happens when both trade and tolerance break down. In the pogrom between 1941 and 1944 the Germans, aided by Poles and Ukrainians, emptied the city of its entire Jewish population, most of whom were killed in local concentration camps.

I walk around in the rain, lured by a seductive network of courtyards, stairwells and back alleys, struck by the detail on the walls and façades and cornices. Lions everywhere, of course, L'viv,

Lvov and Lwów being derivations of the Latin, Leo. I poke my nose down dark passageways, at the end of which are dimly lit bars, which, for some reason, I'm wary of entering.

L'viv is proving to be a mysterious and intriguing gateway to the second-biggest country on my journey. As far as new Europe goes, Ukraine, I feel, will offer more questions than answers. But just over sixty years ago there was a meeting on what is now Ukrainian soil that provided me with a reason for making this journey. Over a few days in February 1945, Churchill, Roosevelt and Stalin met at Yalta in the Crimea and shaped the Europe that my generation was brought up with. This is somewhere I have to see.

Day Seventy-eight: *L'viv to Yalta*

Driving out to the airport I realise how much we travellers judge cities by the bits that look best. Old L'viv is handsome, rightly judged to be a World Heritage Site, but the majority of its three-quarters of a million citizens live in run-down neighbourhoods and shabby, blackened concrete estates well beyond UNESCO's restorative reach.

They should, however, consider listing the airport, one of the most eccentric terminals I've ever checked into.

We lug our bags up the steps of a grand neo-classical façade and through doors that lead into a miniature classical temple. Not a check-in gate or a baggage trolley to be seen. Instead a circle of ornately stuccoed columns and murals depicting joyful agrarian toil. The departure board is exactly that, a wooden board with departures on it, screwed high onto one of the walls, with the names of flights and destinations painted in Cyrillic script some years earlier. The whole place seems to be run by three middle-aged women, the sort you might find in an old-fashioned dress shop, but less helpful.

The chamber echoes with the sound of heels clicking to and fro, of anxious enquiries and raised voices.

Eventually someone points out a travel-worn Antonov AN-24 belonging to Donbass Airlines which will be our transport to the Crimea.

As we walk out to the plane I take one last look back at the airport building, just to make sure I didn't dream it, and am glad I do, because otherwise I'd have missed the tour de force – a glorious colonnade of statues on the outer wall, welders with goggles and miners with lamps interspersed with diaphanous maidens holding baskets of fruit and sheaves of corn. A glorious fusion of Watteau and Soviet Realism.

The flight is basic. Our plane is a fifty-seater turboprop with very little sound insulation and a stewardess who distributes snacks as if passing out live grenades.

Our flight across the wide and watery Dnieper Basin is largely uneventful, until we are just coming in to land at Simferopol in the Crimea. The undercarriage is down and we must be less than a hundred feet from the tarmac when there is a piercing scream from behind us, and a steward looking hot and anxious runs up the aisle, stops for a moment to stare out of the port window, then races on into the cockpit, followed by the stewardess who shouts, reassuringly, 'Someone tell me what's going on!' before being calmed by the passengers.

It all happens too quickly to be anything other than confused, but after we land there's some muttering about the landing gear not being quite fully extended. But we're on time and anyway, no-one knows where to complain.

Simferopol, the Crimean capital, and Yalta, its chief holiday resort, are linked by a world record: the Number 52 trolley-bus route. Covering 51 miles in three hours, it is indisputably the longest trolley-bus route in the world. It was opened in 1959 as cheap travel for the masses and not only is it still running three services an hour, it's probably long overdue for a green transport award.

I pick up a Number 52 outside the main railway station. Whereas L'viv couldn't wait to get rid of their Lenin statue, the great man is still to be found by the roadside in Simferopol, comfortably reclining on a plinth surrounded by scrubby grass.

The Number 52 is packed, and stops so frequently to let people on and off at the scores of informal roadside small markets that I worry we shall never leave Simferopol, let alone reach the Black Sea. But once out of the city the crowds thin and the stops come every half-mile or so.

There's something surreal about a trolley-bus in the countryside. They seem such an essentially urban vehicle that to be in them as they trundle up through pine forest is a little disconcerting. For a while roadside billboards, advertising property, mobile phones, booze and Sobranie cigarettes, reassure us that nature isn't totally in control, but soon even these disappear, leaving the Number 52 alone with the crags and the clouds. Then, quite suddenly, our trolley-bus emerges at the head of a 2,500-foot pass, marked by a monumental concrete arch, and stops briefly before heading downhill past scree slopes and rock falls, through woodland and a few green fields, until there in the distance is the thin, blue line of the Black Sea.

The descent is the trickiest part of the Number 52's route, as the combined effects of our momentum and the twists and turns of the road can easily dislodge the antennae from the overhead cable. But our driver's up to the challenge and brings us safely down past newly planted vineyards and more property adverts whilst old Soviet-era trucks grind by reminding us of a less capitalistic past. Another reminder is that the cost of this most epic of all trolley-bus rides is ten *hryvna*, about one pound.

Yalta is heaving. It's a summer weekend in the Crimea and the holidaymakers are out in force, cars squeezed onto every inch of road, people squeezed onto promenades and sunbathers spread like seals across the rocky beach. Along the front a concrete Spanish galleon, full of snack bars and restaurants, rears up from a concrete frame, and a pirate ship is home to an up-market sushi bar. The obligatory disco beat thuds out. Yalta, where the fate of post-war Europe was decided, turns out to be Blackpool without the sand.

Anya, a local twenty-one-year-old, hoping to be a journalist and speaking excellent English, walks around with me. She tells me that though most of the visitors are Ukrainian and Russian, Crimea is not completely one or the other. It's a bit of a maverick, officially an autonomous republic, representing eighty ethnic groups, with its own flag and parliament. In a 1991 referendum held by President Gorbachev, eighty-eight per cent of Crimeans voted in favour of keeping the Soviet Union intact.

We stop in a sea-front piazza where there is a modern installation, all cable and stainless steel, celebrating the resort's twin cities, and from which I learn that Yalta is twinned with Margate.

Behind us is a McDonald's and opposite it an enormous statue of Lenin. I ask Anya why they would have left this standing. The Lenin, not the McDonald's.

'There are many people who have positive memories of the Soviet days,' she says as we gaze up at him.

'You cannot tear a page out of history, can you?'

I know what she means, but it was Lenin himself who said: 'Sometimes, history needs a push.'

Anya's a good diplomat. Just recently Russia had turned off gas supplies to the Ukraine, but when I ask her if it had soured relations she shakes her head firmly.

'This is only politics.'

Day Seventy-nine: *Yalta*

Yalta is on the same latitude as the south of France and in the nineteenth century the balmy climate and the beauty of the rocky coastline attracted wealthy and well-connected folk who wanted an escape from the hard Russian winters. They employed the best architects, craftsmen and gardeners to create summer palaces on the pine-clad slopes of the mountains.

In the last months of the Second World War, with Germany on the brink of defeat, Yalta's great nineteenth-century mansions offered a safe, comfortable and suitably stately get-away for the Big Three, the leaders of the Soviet Union, the USA and Great Britain, to sit down and wrestle with the implications of victory.

Churchill and his team were installed at the Vorontsov Palace, a combination of Scottish baronial and Oriental fantasy built by English architects in the early nineteenth century for Count Mikhail Vorontsov, Governor of the Crimea, who spent several fortunes on the place and never lived here. The German army had only moved out ten months previously and when Churchill arrived for the conference with Stalin and Roosevelt in February 1945, it was cold, dark and a little grim.

Today it's beautiful. The palace has been restored and though the Gothic walls and towers facing the mountains remain a little forbidding, the seaward side is light and graceful. A long glass conservatory with ceramic tiled floor is well stocked with plants and rather twee Italian marble busts and there are some splendid interiors, including the Blue Room, entirely decorated like a piece of Wedgwood pottery, all of which are tended by an all-female army of cleaners and curators.

The gardens are equally well tended and a wide flight of steps leads down from the flamboyant arabesque south entrance, flanked by three pairs of white marble lions. One of the lower pair is in a blissful state of semi-sleep, paws crossed, head on one side and looking deeply content. Churchill was very fond of this lion and described it as 'Like me, only without the cigar'. He asked Stalin if he could have it, but his request was turned down.

Today the Vorontsov Palace is the centrepiece of a park complex and tour groups pose beside Churchill's favourite lion and wander through the huge rooms that the British delegation of 1945 suspected were bugged by Stalin's people. One of the British delegation noted in his diary that in a private conversation someone mentioned having seen a large, very empty fish tank. Two days later it was full of goldfish. Another private exchange about not being able to find lemon peel for the cocktails resulted in the arrival of a large lemon tree in the conservatory.

Churchill, meanwhile, was more concerned about the amount of work there was to do and the short time set aside to do it.

'I do not see a way of achieving our hopes in five or six days,' he wrote. 'Even the Almighty took seven.'

Every day the delegation was driven the three and a half miles to another palace called the Livadia, where the conference meetings took place. Built in 1911 for Russia's last Tsar, Nicholas II, it's also set in luxurious gardens on the thickly wooded slopes overlooking the Black Sea. A long, elegant neo-classical façade in white Inkerman stone with a Carrara marble portico promises much but it's quite dull and gloomy inside.

In 1945 the delegations met around a long table in a white-marbled dining room and there was a smaller round table, which can still be seen, for intimate talks between the leaders and their closest advisers. Roosevelt, the American President, was partially disabled with polio and to make it as easy as possible for him to get to the conference table, an adjoining room, the Tsar's Grand Reception Study, was turned into his bedroom. The smallest of all the main rooms is the billiard room, panelled in English chestnut. It was here that the treaty was signed after six days' deliberation. The photo-call that followed and produced the famous images of the three leaders looking very cold took place in the Italian garden, a small formal garden onto which all the ground-floor rooms give access. With its Renaissance restraint and Italianate decoration, the Livadia Palace is incorrigibly Western European in style, yet by all accounts it was Stalin the Russian, twenty million of whose countrymen perished in the war, and whose armies already occupied most of Eastern Europe, who was in the driving seat at Yalta.

The treaty may have been signed in an English-style billiard room but the advantage went largely east.

Roosevelt died of a cerebral haemorrhage two months after the conference ended. Churchill was voted out of office in Britain three months after that. The Soviet Union was allowed to continue occupying countries like Estonia, Latvia and Lithuania, and the Polish government-in-exile in London was excluded from elections in Warsaw. Almost exactly a year after the back-slapping and the hugs in the Livadia Palace, Churchill, in a speech at a small college in Fulton, Missouri, declared that 'from Stettin in the Baltic to Trieste in the Adriatic, an iron curtain has descended across the continent. Behind that line lie all the capitals of the ancient states of Central and Eastern Europe.'

Forty-three years later the iron curtain was lifted and today it's girls in miniskirts who are being photographed in the garden where Churchill, Stalin and Roosevelt once sat.

By a neat coincidence the very last act of the drama was played out not ten miles from here. If you follow the winding coast road south and west you will come to the little headland village of Foros. Here Mikhail Gorbachev, the man who more than anyone else was responsible for lifting the iron curtain, had a summer cottage. His house arrest here in August 1991 precipitated the final collapse of the Soviet Union.

Day Eighty: *Kiev*

During the filming of *Pole to Pole* in 1991, I met a man called Vadim Castelli on a train travelling through the USSR from Novgorod to his home in Kiev. Vadim was a Ukrainian nationalist, frustrated and helpless at being a part of the Soviet Union. I remember feeling sad when we parted, because I was free and he wasn't, I had a country and he didn't. I could travel wherever I wanted and he couldn't.

This morning, fifteen years later, I'm waiting to meet him at a café beside the Gap and Mothercare stores in a shopping mall in Kiev, capital of the Ukraine.

He looks as I remember him. Fair hair, beard neatly trimmed, but in his white T-shirt and black jeans he looks almost younger than when we last met. Certainly less anxious, less preoccupied. He tells me he's just done his own European travel series for Ukrainian TV, and from his description of the route, I'd say Vadim has travelled a lot further than I have.

I ask him what it felt like to be so suddenly precipitated into independence.

'First of all there was a feeling of bliss. A feeling like "God this is impossible that I've seen it in my life." Then there was a feeling of anxiety. For many people...the Ukrainian national idea had been eradicated, so many people felt part of that anonymous global community called the Soviet Union. All of a sudden you have to become part of something smaller, a part of a nation where you have to make your own decisions. Many people can't get used to that even today.'

We walk out onto Maydan Nezalezhnosti, Independence Square, and an extraordinary sight greets us. On both sides of Khreshchatyk, the main street that bisects the square, is a tented encampment. A medieval army with banners and emblems instead of weapons. Ukraine may have achieved independence but they're still fighting over what to do with it. As at the heart of most politics, the struggle is between reformers and conservatives, intensified here by the differences between Russian Ukrainians and Ukrainian Ukrainians.

Vadim confirms the impression I've begun to form already.

'Ukraine is almost a divided nation. A lot of people living in the west and the centre want Ukraine to be part of the normal European Community. But there are many who believe our historic path should lead us into Russia, and it's very difficult to find a compromise between different mentalities. You have to show them that walking towards Europe is more practical than walking towards Siberia.'

It's a difference neatly characterised by Vadim and Igor, our good-looking but dour fixer. Vadim is the intellectual, Igor, the pragmatic ex-soldier (he served with the Soviet forces in Afghanistan) who instinctively looks east.

The tents in the square are primarily those of the supporters of the Democracy Party, headed by Julia Tymoshenko, the attractive, ambitious woman who embodied the mood of the Orange Revolution two years earlier, but who was dropped as Prime Minister by the other great hero of that revolution Viktor Yushchenko (the man whose face was disfigured by what is thought to have been dioxin poisoning). He was forced into an unsatisfactory working arrangement with his conservative rival Viktor Yanukovych. The Tymoshenko camp with their red heart logo make much of the wholesome good looks of their leader, and she in turn sells herself, Vadim thinks, as the essence of Ukrainian womanhood.

'Ukrainians like being run by The Mum.'

Igor mutters darkly as he leads us to a riverboat restaurant by the Dnieper. He defends the old Soviet regime, saying it was they who kept the Ukrainian economy going. I daren't mention Chernobyl.

In the afternoon we walk up the hill to the Parliament building around which the blue flags and banners of the conservative Party of the Regions are flying. They look to be an older, more traditional crowd than those in Independence Square, less sophisticated, less well-off, the harder faces of working people.

In amongst the blue banners are a few old-style communist placards with the hammer and sickle rampant. Igor tells me these are industrial workers from the Donetsk region showing support for their man Yanukovych, who campaigned under the slogan: 'Hope is good, confidence is better'. Since the heady days of the Orange Revolution they've seen their support rise by almost twenty per cent.

He says they may be rougher, more plain-speaking folk but they're here because of their beliefs, whereas the Tymoshenko supporters, he alleges, are paid 100 *hryvna* every day just to turn out.

Even as we watch there are noises off and a line of red Tymoshenko hearts can be seen advancing up the hill. Raw, nervous young policemen moisten their dry lips. Behind the scenes their plain-clothes colleagues move discreetly about giving orders on radios to the black-clad riot police. But, so far, it's all just noise.

Day Eighty-one: *Kiev*

One reason why the political argument being played out on the streets of Kiev has been relatively free of violence, is that it has been allowed to take place in an almost party-like atmosphere. Celebration has become more important than confrontation. In the new vocabulary of Ukrainian politics, separate camps means whether you prefer your tent to be of polyester or ex-army canvas and a political party means dancing to a group on an outdoor stage.

This new face of politics, so completely different from the old days of grey men on balconies, is characterised not just by Julia Tymoshenko herself but also by her activist daughter Eugenia and her remarkable husband, a strikingly tall man with a powerful physique and eyes that slant distinctively upwards at the sides. The couple are an image consultant's dream. If Eugenia represents the national stereotype of fresh-faced beauty, he looks the very personification of the Ukrainian folk hero, the warrior Cossack. In fact, his name is Sean Carr and he's a biker from Leeds.

Their story is full of wonderful twists and turns. Eugenia was sent by her parents to be educated at Rugby, the English public school on which *Tom Brown's Schooldays* was based. She and Sean first set eyes on each other at a hotel in Egypt, attracted by a mutual interest in biking and the music of Sean's group, The Death Valley Screamers.

Having already broken so many conventions, the biker and the public schoolgirl are hoping to try and break one more and have a woman elected as President of Ukraine.

This morning they've invited us to visit them at their house just outside Kiev. Not a problem, except that Sean insists on driving me part of the way there on his motorbike. I don't know a lot about high-performance bikes, but a passenger saddle would have been nice. I cling on to my fellow Yorkshireman for dear life as he throttles his silver and chrome beast, streaked with a red flame motif, through the plantations of ramrod straight pine trees.

Just as I'm wondering if the shape of my face might be permanently altered by the blasting on-rush of air, Sean throttles down the engine to a deep gurgling rumble, makes a sharp turn off the road and parks up on a sandy track outside a well-fenced, rather bland, modern-ish house.

I unhook myself from the SS 'Vengeance' and follow Sean inside. Given the febrile atmosphere of current Ukrainian politics I'm not surprised to see CCTV cameras around the walls and a Rottweiler padding after us. We talk in the garden. Eugenia and Sean make no secret of the fact that the street politics is a protest at what they see as the corruption and illegitimacy of government, against the culture of secret deals behind closed doors. Her mother, she says, is the only one who's remained true to her word.

Sean tries to keep his band separate from the politics but it's not easy. They're hugely popular here in Ukraine.

'I mean, we've had seventy-year-old grandmas coming down wearing Death Valley Screamer shirts. It's like, hang on a minute, what's going on here.'

His mother-in-law is a cautious supporter but, according to Eugenia, would prefer it if he didn't take his shirt off on stage.

Eugenia emphasises that Ukraine is a very young country, trying to deal with a democratic parliamentary system in a country where the rulers were used to getting their way. Openness of the press, consultation with the people are new concepts here.

The big difference, of course, is that things don't happen in a vacuum any more. The eyes of the world were on the country during the Orange Revolution.

Eugenia nods and smiles.

'After the revolution, everybody found out about the Ukraine, but now in a positive way, you know, rather than just knowing about Chernobyl.'

They're a dedicated pair, and seem seriously committed to their task, but Eugenia looks tired and it's clear that changing Ukrainian politics is not as easy as it seemed to be two years ago. I ask her how she would define what they're fighting against.

She sighs.

'Oh. We're fighting the old communist mentality. You know...'

On this last evening in Kiev, I walk with Igor, who clearly sees some value in the old communist mentality, up on the hill overlooking the Dnieper where the huge statue of Mother Russia dominates the west bank of the city. Donated to the people of Kiev by the Russian leader Brezhnev in 1977, it's finished in panels of silver-grey titanium and stands 320 feet high. Visitors can climb up her left arm and, from on top of the shield, look across to the other side of the river where row upon row, wall after wall, of housing blocks are caught in the red glow of the setting sun. Two million of the city's three million-plus population live over there. 'Sleeping Kiev', Igor calls it.

There is a huge military museum up here comprising weapons, tanks, rockets, relief murals, all commemorating the Soviet achievement in the Second World War. Except they don't call it that. They call it the Great Patriotic War.

Perhaps this was the key to Stalin's success at Yalta. The Soviets were never culturally or ideologically compatible with the rest of the Allies. The Second World War was not presented to the Russian people as a world war, a collaborative effort, worthy of equal rewards. It was about the preservation of the system that had made the USSR only the latest embodiment of Mother Russia's timeless aspirations. Their boys fought and died for the liberation of their homeland. In the process, other homelands were drastically affected, and many didn't like it. Estonia, Latvia and Lithuania, for instance, for whom a brief taste of independence came to an end in 1945.

Day Eighty-three: *Tallinn*

MY FIRST sight of the Estonian coastline. Well, second really. I'd seen it before, in 1991, but technically it wasn't the Estonian coastline then, it was the coastline of the Soviet Union.

It lies low and modest, but even at a distance I can see early signs of the great change that has overtaken Estonia in the fifteen years since I last crossed the Gulf of Finland.

The old spires and towers to the west now have competition to the east, where a clutch of modern skyscrapers, the first shoots of a business district, have sprung up. Tallinn now has a New Town and an Old Town. The dockside, gloomy and unwelcoming before, is now extended and expanded and a network of tube-like jetties spreads its tentacles between ship and shore. Tallinn is open for business. Which is as it should be. Estonia's strategic position midway between Scandinavia and Russia makes it an ideal entrepot port, but it was always a small country and needed support from powerful outsiders. The Danish, Swedish and even German overlords allowed the Estonians to keep some elements of their culture alive, but the Russians were less tolerant neighbours and for forty-six years after the Second World War it became another republic of the USSR. When we landed here in 1991, the presence of a Soviet army, 180,000-strong, confirmed the occupation of a country that had known only twenty-two years of independence in the last 500 years of its history.

Now the army's gone and the tables have been well and truly turned. The Estonian economy is booming. Annual growth is in double figures, the budget is in surplus, and *Time* magazine recently described the country as 'one of the most technologically advanced places on the planet'. Just to rub it in, those Russians who have stayed on are not allowed full citizenship until they have learnt Estonian.

It's a complicated language, comprising 33,000 characters, so most Russians don't bother. They remain here as second-class citizens, which is about the only thing the European Union, which admitted Estonia in 2004, is not happy about.

Day Eighty-four: *Tallinn*

It's early evening when we turn off the road about 20 miles west of the city and follow a track that leads to a modern house built like a pyramid. We park on a grassy strip alongside a line of Volvos and Saabs, whose occupants are busy moving logs and laying them on a stack in front of the house. The smiles of greeting are polite but cool, except for a slim young man with a shaved head and intense gaze who smiles broadly and clasps me to him. This is Margus Aru, whose house this is and who is supervising the building of the fire. It all looks very much like any suburban summer barbecue. The difference is that what's going on this barbecue are the guests.

Margus tries to be reassuring, as if this were no more stressful than a visit to Ikea.

'We start. We come together. We feel good things together and do fire-walking.'

I ask him if this is a particularly Estonian thing.

'Not so much, but Indian people I have heard, and South American and...' he shrugs as if this line of questioning is missing the point, 'Vikings.'

The point of the exercise is, he says, to conquer fear. I suggest that fear can be a very useful way of preventing you doing something very silly.

Margus smiles, pleasantly, but dismissively. His little son walked on hot coals at the age of four. When he asked him if he'd found it very hot he merely answered 'Was it supposed to be?'

The build-up to the walking is long and slow. Occasionally two or three young musicians, who look more than naturally relaxed, will start some desultory drumming, whilst Margus whirls a piece of plastic piping around his head producing a high-pitched moaning sound.

No-one really knows quite what to do or how seriously to approach the whole thing. The only ones who seem to be really enjoying themselves are Margus' six-year-old son Christian and his friends, who charge around shrieking, screaming, chasing and generally scuppering any attempt at contemplation. Meanwhile the long pyre of wood blazes merrily away. Margus says that not much will happen until the sun goes down, which, as we're now at Scandinavian latitudes, will not be before eleven.

There is a very practical reason to wait for sunset, he says. It's important to be able to see that all the flames have gone, otherwise the fire walk could be very dangerous. As if strolling over a strip of burning embers half the length of a cricket pitch might not be dangerous.

As the walking hour approaches, the twenty or so people here, nice, well-behaved middle-class folk of all ages and sexes, begin to move closer to the fire. Some are silent and still, some make strained attempts at chanting; most are looking to Margus for a lead. The evening is turning quite sharply colder.

A pail of water is fetched and a cloth dipped in it and laid at the end of the strip of embers. The music becomes more insistent. Everyone seems mightily relieved when, at last, Margus moves to one end of the glowing embers, and begins softly issuing instructions.

Breathe deeply in and out. Swing the arms loosely from the waist, palms flat and open to release the spiritual energy.

'Think of yourself only in the present. Clear your mind of past and future.'

I can see faces struggling to come to terms with the reality of mind over matter. Like how does it work and will it be enough to get me across a five-metre-long bed of fire. In the background the children romp around with unquenchable energy, wearing bits and pieces of plastic armour, matter firmly uppermost in their minds.

With a last deep breath and holding his palms outwards, Margus walks. I count ten paces to get through the fire. That's ten times the feet are pressed against red-hot ashes. Then he turns and calmly and unhurriedly walks back again. That's twenty times. He's followed almost immediately, and with admirable sang-froid, by a very large man whose body-weight must press his soles onto the fire like steaks on a grill. He's followed by Margus' striking blonde wife Evelin, carrying their new baby across the fire, like a Nordic madonna.

A middle-aged woman in a yellow coat who has been psyching herself up all evening comes to the fireside and waits, looking down. Then she goes and at the far end I see for the first time a reaction. Joy and relief almost verging on ecstasy. A younger woman can't make the decision. She stands rooted to the spot looking down at the fire with intense concentration, then turns away.

We pack up our equipment. I haven't been at all stirred to participate. All I'm thinking of is my hotel bed, warm but not blazing.

Margus remains friendly but un-pushy. He hugs me again and I know he thinks I could have done it.

Just then, as we are walking to the van, I hear a shout from the fire behind me.

'Ow! That is hot!'

And as we head back to Tallinn I don't feel quite so bad.

Day Eighty-five: *Tallinn*

Sun shining strong and unhampered. With the ferries arriving from Sweden and Finland by the hour rather than by the day, as they did when the country was part of the USSR, the picturesque streets are filling up and all seats are taken at the cafés that surround the wide, traffic-free, and now totally wi-fi Raekoja Plats (Town Hall Square).

A good day to get out of town. We turn north, off the main road to Russia, and wind through gentle coastal scenery to a small village called Viinistu. The sea takes the edge off the heat of the day, and having passed a cluster of weatherboarded houses with flowers spilling over their wooden fences we come across a sight that brings us up with a jolt. In a wide concrete yard, running down to a small harbour, is a collection of suitcases, all apparently identical and all, like the yard itself, made of concrete.

They're part of an art collection gathered together by Jaan Manitski, a man of exactly my own age, trim, bespectacled and crisply turned out in chinos and an open-necked shirt. For him the concrete suitcases mean a great deal. In 1944 the occupying Germans retreated from Estonia and the Soviet army began to move in.

'Many, many Estonians left,' explains Manitski, and he gestures out to sea.

'From this coastline here many small fishing boats left to Finland or Sweden and most people could only bring with them a suitcase, and when the small boat was crowded they even had to leave that on the shore here.'

Jaan's family, who had lived in Viinistu for as long as any of them could remember, was among those who went into exile. His travels led him eventually to Sweden, where he prospered, becoming business manager for Sweden's best-known export, Abba. He was successful and respected but one thing was missing.

'Even if I lived abroad in different countries for forty, fifty years, I was still in my heart an Estonian.'

In 1989, just before Gorbachev's reforms sent the old Soviet system into meltdown, he came back to his homeland and to Viinistu. He tried his hand at various things that took his fancy, including growing mushrooms, before being persuaded to take a more serious role, spearheading his newly independent country's transition to a free-market economy. He was even prevailed upon to take the job of Foreign Minister, an office he vacated after a year, causing extreme bureaucratic consternation by not bothering to claim his last month's salary. Since then he has concentrated his energy and abilities on his birthplace, buying up a defunct local fish-processing plant and transforming Viinistu into one of the most vital and lively art centres in the Baltics. The fish factory has been sympathetically transformed into galleries, restaurants, a conference centre, an auditorium and a hotel. As we speak, diggers are at work constructing a wall for a new marina.

We walk down to the water, clambering over a rocky beach.

Jaan wants to show me what they call here the Baby Stone. It's a huge, black, seaweed-stained rock which, according to local tradition, is where babies come from, Viinistu's equivalent of the stork. During the years of Soviet occupation the coastline was off-limits to bathers and fishermen alike, a sealed-off military area with wire fences and searchlights.

Since the Soviets left and access to the rock has been restored, there has, Jaan says, been a baby boom.

He claims personal experience.

'I went there to check the Stone a number of years ago and we have a small boy of five, and then I went there once again and there's now one of two years old. So...' the sixty-two-year-old grins a little sheepishly, 'it works.'

He talks about the craziness of the old Soviet economy. 'A big shoe-making factory in Tallinn produced left-foot shoes...the right-foot shoes were made in Irkutsk.' He has his own ideas as to why Estonia has recovered so well and made such progress, citing a young government, with a Prime Minister in his early thirties, and the fact that it's much easier to make big changes in a small country.

'We started from scratch or even minus...but the keystone to start up a new society and a new life in this country was a successful privatisation. And this,' he gestures around him, 'is an illustration of that process.'

The noise from the building work at the harbour becomes so loud that he sends someone to ask the workers to stop. I can't help noticing that the only language they seem to understand is Russian. It's beginning to look as if hi-tech-loving Estonians don't do the manual labour any more.

I have an afternoon appointment with the doctor. I'm quite unusually anxious, not because of what they might find out, but because of their method of examination, for this particular clinic specialises in something called hirudotherapy. To the uninitiated, leech treatment.

Leeches have had a generally bad press and a quick look at the dictionary doesn't help.

'A blood-sucking annelid worm. To cling to like a leech. To drain.'

I've been warned about their unwelcome attentions for walkers in the tropics and how they have to be burnt off the skin with cigarette butts. So why am I offering my aged body to them in a remote corner of the Baltics?

Well I guess we all want to feel better, especially after months on the road, and I'm a sucker (excuse the pun) for any form of revitalisation.

'What do you want me to take off?'

'Small striptease,' orders Lyudmilla Agajeva, one of the clinic's most experienced hirudotherapists, in heavily accented Russian.

Ms Agajeva must be in her fifties, buxom in a generous, motherly way. As far as she is concerned, leeches are it. They are an ancient and proven way of treating impotence, high blood pressure, high cholesterol, hangovers and the problems of overdoing it generally. She smiles reassuringly as I lie on her consulting couch. Hers are the very best leeches. They've come all the way from St Petersburg.

She extracts three of them from a bottle and lays them on my right-hand side, just below my ribcage. One keeps slithering off but the other two waste no time digging themselves in with what I'm told are 300 teeth, arranged around a three-jawed mouth.

Ms Agajeva is not happy.

'One is lazy,' she says, disapprovingly.

'Maybe it's a teetotaller.'

The other two have now punctured the skin and are tucking into my blood. The sensation is not painful, but it is uncomfortable, like a low-level electric shock or a nettle sting.

It will not last long, I'm promised, though I can still feel sharp discomfort after fifteen minutes. This is the leeches putting in anti-coagulant so they can do their work, checking out your blood, removing what's bad and replacing it with what's good. Selfless little buggers.

Every time I look down the leeches are getting bigger. They've only been at it twenty minutes and already they've swollen to twice their size. They lie there, black and glistening, like satisfied slugs. Ms Agajeva nods approvingly. They like me.

Alarmingly, I sense a trickle of moisture spilling down my right flank from the direction of the wounds. I'm assured that this isn't my blood, it's the leeches sweating. So not only are these three little workers cleaning out my bloodstream, they're perspiring with the effort. I begin to feel absurdly grateful to them and when, after fifty minutes, the time comes to pull them off me I feel we've bonded, become friends, shared something very intimate. But no time for sentiment. Having done their work they are unceremoniously disposed of in a solution of caustic soda, never to suck again. Leeches used to be reused, but not in these days of HIV-Aids.

Lyudmilla (I feel I can call her that now) dresses my wounds with a thick long pad and lots of plaster. During the 'procedure' as she calls it, around 25 millilitres of blood will have been removed, but after the procedure as much as 200 or 300 millilitres could leak out. I'm to take it easy, avoid alcohol and not take the dressing off until tomorrow morning.

Back in Tallinn the rush of relief at having completed the leeching and a light-headedness from the effects demand some kind of recognition, and I end up celebrating with more than a glass of wine or two in the excellent restaurant of the Hotel St Petersburg.

Day Eighty-six: *Tallinn to the Latvian border*

Wake to a re-run of the scene from *The Godfather*. Bloodstained duvet and a thick, dark wodge of dried blood on my T-shirt. Look round for the horse's head but mercifully I'm alone. In the bathroom I gingerly begin to peel off the dressing, but gingerly clearly isn't going to shift Lyudmilla's industrial sticking plaster so eventually pluck up courage and rip it off with one sharp tug. An ear-splitting noise as if my entire stomach had opened up and I'm left holding the mobile equivalent of 300 millilitres of blood. In my side are three small purple circles with black puncture marks in them, blood still gently seeping from one of them. Tidy up as best I can and feel quite glad that I shall be checking out of this charming hotel this morning and should be well on the way to Latvia before the blood-soaked evidence is discovered.

From well-trodden Tallinn we turn our backs on the Baltic coast and head south and east to the less visited end of the country, near to the Russian border. The road, never busy, takes us through the town of Tartu, Estonia's second city, whose 370-year-old university became, in the nineteenth century, the focus of that upsurge in Estonianism known as the National Awakening, when many of the cultural foundations of present-day Estonia were laid.

We take a coffee break at the self-consciously literary Café Wilde, named not after Oscar but Peter Wilde, who published the first medical textbooks in Estonian. This doesn't stop them having a bronze sculpture of Oscar Wilde, seated on a bench outside. The current owner of the café believes that the Irishness of Oscar Wilde resonates with Estonians. Both countries are on the edge of the continent, both love singing and mythology and both have been transformed by the cyber-revolution.

An hour's drive through uncut meadows carpeted with wild lupins brings us to the secluded little town of Värska in an area settled by a few thousand members of the Setu people. In a sense the Setu are victims rather than beneficiaries of Estonia's independence, as a third of their land is in Russia and, Estonian-Russian relations being what they are, many families are separated. The culture has been kept alive, rather successfully, by a group of older women, uninventively dubbed the Singing Grannies, who preserve their traditions through folk songs and costumes hundreds of years old.

These Setu matrons, with more than a touch of the Women's Institute about them, are tougher than they look. Marshalled by the formidable Vera, whose powerful features radiate a mixture of stern discipline and timeless patience, these mature ladies, some of whom can only get into the room with the aid of a stick, don traditional headdresses, complex necklaces and heavy silver breastplates to sing sweet harmonies, quite beautifully, without any accompaniment.

Later in the afternoon the King of the Setu drives round to talk to us. King Ritzier, a handsome young man who in his national dress looks a bit like an estate agent appearing in a pantomime, seems tired. I sense from him that the good days are over. The Setu were farmers and their culture, he explains, drew its strength from the woods and the forests. This pagan tradition has been diluted over the years and Christianity mixed in through the influence of the Russian Orthodox Church. The re-drawing of the border has divided the *Stoma*, as they call their land, as never before and their Russian roots have made life in Estonia a little more difficult.

I leave the singing Setu with admiration and a little sadness. They're a small group with no big friends.

It was the Soviet occupation that began in 1944 that turned the Estonians so bitterly against their mighty eastern neighbour, and at Vaster Rosa, a village close by the Latvian border, is a network of tunnels and dug-outs that were built by the Forest Brothers, a resistance network that kept up a guerrilla campaign against the Soviet army for almost twenty years after the Second World War ended. Moving by night and under cover of the great Baltic forests, they blew up bridges, attacked convoys and generally stung the Russian bear wherever possible. The authorities reacted by deporting over 20,000 Estonians to Siberia, whilst bringing in thousands of workers from other parts of the Soviet empire to keep the country running.

Accompanied by a son of one of the Forest Brothers, now a portly and prosperous farmer, I climb a low hill (quite a phenomenon in a country whose highest point is less than 1,000 feet) onto a ridge covered with holes dug 10 feet into the earth. These claustrophobic timber-lined chambers often sheltered entire families. We squeeze down into one of them. It's a cool and refreshing retreat from the mosquitoes and the thick summer heat, but almost impossible to imagine living down there for months, let alone years. My friend showed me one of the reasons why they were able to bear this troglodytic existence – a large bottle of a clear grappa-like liquor, which was the Forest Brothers' secret weapon. They jealously guarded its quality, which could only be tested by the imbiber pouring a glass, sticking his forefinger into it, then passing his finger over a candle. If a flame burnt around the finger then it was the real thing. Still smarting from the leech holes in my side, a charred finger seems a small price to pay and after a couple of glasses I don't feel anything anyway.

Not far along the road we come upon what must surely be one of the world's most peaceful border-crossings. The silence only broken by the chatter of birds and insects and the very occasional, almost furtive, car. The name of the crossing, Ape, seemed strangely suitable in the middle of a forest.

On two long poles above a modest cabin fly the blue, black and white stripes of Estonia, with the flag of Latvia, white stripe on a dark red background, fluttering alongside. The combined population of both countries may amount to only half that of London, and yet they take their independence seriously. Beyond Ape lies a new language, a new currency and a whole new history.

Latvia

Day Eighty-seven: *Aluksne to Riga*

STILL CAN'T get used to the brevity of the nights up here in northern Europe. Scarcely has the sun gone down than it's up again. Morning sunshine blitzes through the fragile curtains from four o'clock onwards.

It seems hardly necessary to push the curtains back, but I do, only to be greeted by the sight of a decommissioned industrial plant below me. It looks to have been abandoned some time. There are piles of rubble, patches of thick oily slime and entwined around this whole mess are the discarded entrails of a heating system, cladding peeling off the pipes.

From a small station in Aluksne, a narrow-gauge railway runs for just over 20 miles south-west to the town of Gulbene. It's all that remains of a longer line, opened in 1903, built by the Tsarist authorities when Latvia was part of the Russian empire. A hundred years later it was saved by the new European empire, the EU, under an industrial heritage preservation programme.

Thank God for empires, I feel, as I climb aboard, for I've seen few services as modestly appealing and manifestly uncommercial as this one. A single diesel railcar, complete with guard and ticket collector, rocks and sways through woodland and meadows of wild flowers, stopping at eight small halts to pick up and put down the locals. A lady with a bucket of cut flowers in her huge, wide arms settles opposite me, two seats down from a man with one leg, who, with a cheery farewell to the guard, hops off at one of the stops and disappears into the birch woods.

The terminus at Gulbene breaks the mood. No picturesque

woods here. A big, rather gloomy old station built for busier and grander times and a plaque on the wall whose chilling inscription commemorates the thousands of people who, in 1940 and 1941 were packed into cattle-wagons here and shipped out on a one-way ride to the Gulag camps in Siberia.

I stand and look down the line. There is nothing to see but distance, and no sounds either. In fact, nothing to distract the imagination from what must have happened here. Up to now, I've always found railways inherently friendly. Here at Gulbene it's not so easy.

Sixteen years after Latvia's second independence in 1990 (their first lasted from 1918 until the Russian invasion of 1940) the Russian presence is still surprisingly strong in Riga. The capital, the largest city of the new Baltic republics, is home to as many Russians as Latvians.

There are, on a less permanent basis, visitors from Sweden, Denmark, Finland, Germany, and of course the scorned, but economically appreciated, English, lured over by cheap flights for stag and hen weekends.

Americans have discovered it too, and not just any old Americans. George W. Bush and friends were here recently for a conference and to celebrate our arrival in another new country we eat tonight at the restaurant of the man chosen to cook for the President.

Martin Ritins, a Latvian who's lived in Canada and Corby, Northants, before coming back to his roots, is a celebrity in Latvia. His restaurant is called Vincent's, after van Gogh.

'Any particular reason?'

'Not really,' he says cheerfully.

The foyer of his basement restaurant is lined with photos of an eclectic clientele. Prince Charles and Joe Cocker (not together), Mikhail Baryshnikov and Terry Wogan. Waiters move smoothly by, dressed head to foot in black. Martin, who is engaging and enthusiastic, takes me into his state-of-the-art kitchen to help him re-create the 'Sauce Americaine' he produced for George Bush. A combination of fresh Latvian ingredients, carrots, onions, tomatoes, garlic, together with bay leaf and cognac. It's served with crayfish, summarily executed in boiling ale.

Seeing me wince, Martin shakes his head. 'It's sudden and instant,' he reassures me, without consulting the crayfish. No sooner have they been topped than they're brought out, onto ice, and their heads removed. I'm aware of how slow I am at this job, like someone working on an illuminated manuscript whilst everyone around me is using e-mail.

I must say, it sounds like a nightmare cooking for a President. Apparently Bush's personal chefs had spent three days with Ritins, checking the kitchen, the menu and the food sources. In the end George W., who doesn't drink, ate crayfish with brandy in the sauce, beef with red wine in the sauce, washed it down with Coca-Cola and reserved his most appreciative comments for the ice-cream.

'Wow!' he'd said and asked for more, but the secret service wouldn't let him.

'He's too busy,' they explained to Martin.

Day Eighty-eight: *Riga*

Today we're venturing deep in the other direction of Baltic history. The pagan past still means a lot to these countries who all came late into the European religious mainstream. (So late were the local tribes in converting to Christianity that around 1200 a Crusade to the Baltics was organised, bringing with it the usual mix of missionaries and mercenaries.)

Throughout Latvia tonight they will be celebrating *Jani*, an unashamedly pagan way of marking the summer solstice, and we've been invited out to a party deep in the countryside, some three hours from Riga. Such is the enduring popularity of this ancient animist tradition that traffic on the way out of town is of Bank Holiday proportions. Many of the cars are decorated with leaves and flowers and along the roadside some have pulled up so their occupants can gather wild flowers from the fields.

We find ourselves heading down more and more obscure roads with the forest, which still covers nearly half the country, closing in around us. We park in a field and carry on down overgrown woodland tracks between cow parsley and wild roses until we emerge at a collection of old wooden huts with steep roofs, set beneath a towering maple tree. It looks and feels like somewhere straight out of a children's fairy story, and the sense of time being stretched out only intensifies as our host, an elderly, professorial man with a high forehead and greying hair, tells me one of the cottages has stood here for over 250 years. And they still have no electricity.

Before we can join the fifty or so others present we have to go through the ritual of being teased by the host and having to respond with jokes in a poetic chant. Terrifying really, but as none of us has any Latvian, we attach ourselves to others who do and maintain fixed grins till it's all over.

The Latvian flag is then ceremonially raised and ash tree branches are drawn along the threshold of the property to symbolise, I'm told, the opening of the gates and the disbanding of the evil forces.

The owner of these isolated cottages and most of those he's invited look like well-educated city folk who've chosen to keep *Jani* pure and traditional. Some twenty-five years ago the old folk songs and rituals began to be revived after the communist authorities had tried to ban them. They found 1,200 melodies to be sung on this mid-summer night and 28,000 song lyrics.

'A lot of the people are here for the first time, and they don't actually know what's going to happen,' says Ilge, a woman who teaches courses on how to celebrate *Jani*.

I'm given a garland of oak leaves as big as a lifebuoy, whilst the assembled gathering serenades me.

Ilge explains, 'The oak is the symbol of strength and virility, so you are crowned with strength and virility and they're singing that they wish you will see everything well, hear everything well and film everything well.'

Nigel, without the benefit of a leafy crown, is in fact so confused by the ceremony that he's finding it hard to film anything at all. Meanwhile, I'm trying desperately to stop this oak crown from slipping down over my face and settling round my neck. The women, many in embroidered skirts and white blouses, seem less encumbered by their garlands, in which twenty-seven different varieties of flowers have to be woven.

Yalta, Ukraine Lenin still stands tall in the Crimea. Yalta's visitors take a break on the steps.

Kiev, Ukraine The Great Patriotic War Museum is full of heroic, and unexpectedly moving, Soviet statuary. Independent though Ukraine is now, no-one would suggest relocating them.

Viinistu, Estonia The concrete suitcases of Viinistu remind us of those who had to flee Estonia in the Second World War, including the man whose money created this arts complex.

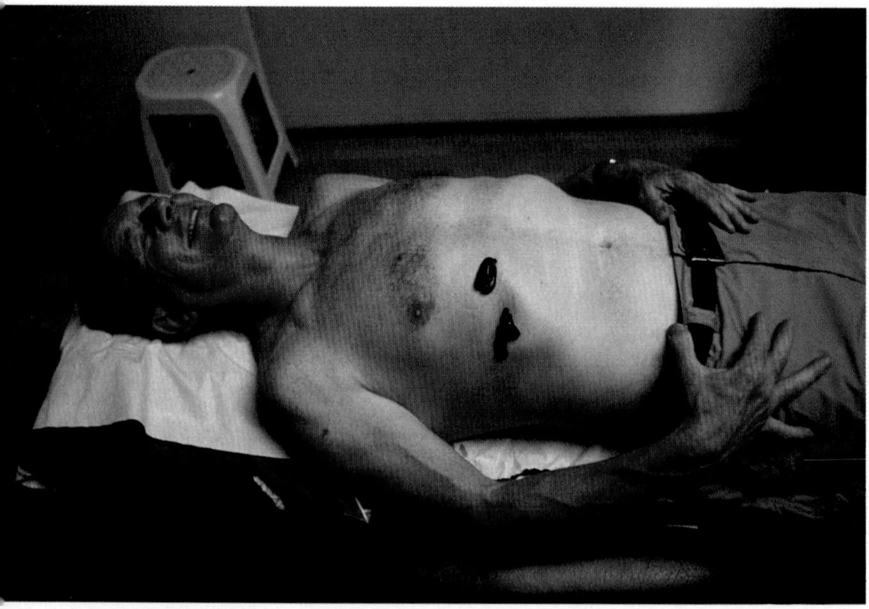

Tallinn, Estonia With three close friends, giving blood at the hirudotherapy clinic.

ABOVE: *Latvia* Celebrating Jani (the summer solstice) in the Latvian countryside. Spectacular effects of the hair tonic.

ABOVE: *Ventspils, Latvia,* The Ventspils radio telescope, through which Soviet Russia listened to the world, was saved from destruction by a dedicated group of local scientists and engineers.

RIGHT: *Ventspils, Latvia* Remains of the revolution. Soviet murals at an abandoned community centre near the Ventspils telescope.

Palanga, Lithuania The Baltic shore from the back of Communist leader Brezhnev's villa at Palanga, Lithuania.

Palanga to Vilnius, Latvia The Hill of Crosses, symbol of Lithuanian freedom.

Kaliningrad, Russia Knights in shining armour at the jousting contest, the fiery finale of National Day.

Gdańsk, Poland The Gdańsk Shipyards, where Lech Walesa worked, are still in business, but only just. Behind me and Andrej, the general manager, their last big contract takes shape.

Auschwitz, Poland At Auschwitz II-Birkenau the railway became a murder weapon; tens of thousands were taken along it straight to the gas chambers. This picture shows flowers on the line with the gatehouse in the background.

The Tatra Mountains, Slovakia Arriving in Slovakia in style. The compact, but breathtaking, High Tatra Mountains. The snow-filled valley leads down to the Slovakian plain.

ABOVE: *Prague, Czech Republic* The magnificence of Prague. The Old Town Square, dominated by the 260-foot twin towers of the Church of Our Lady before Týn. Once associated with the reform movement of Jan Hus, it was taken over by the Jesuits in the seventeenth century.

LEFT: *Czestochowa, Poland* A sumptuous Baroque chapel at Jasna Góra monastery, under whose roof is the Black Madonna, symbol of Polish independence.

RIGHT: *Meissen, Germany* Looking into it. State of the art lavatory production line at Meissen.

BELOW RIGHT: *Berlin, Germany* A DC-3, used in the Berlin airlift of 1948, flies me over Rügen Island. Running along the shore below me is Prora, Hitler's dream of a holiday camp for the Third Reich. It's just too big for anyone to know what to do with it.

BELOW: *Baltic Sea* Journey's end, by the Baltic Sea, full of hope. Could this be the time when a new Europe of co-operation replaces an old Europe of conflict?

There isn't much time for hanging about comparing headgear as we are led in procession to bless the various parts of the property with songs and poems. So we bless the well, the sauna, the bee-hives, the barn and finally gather round a significant oak tree, around which we form a circle. Some of the women toss their garlands up into the tree. Folklore has it that if they stay up they'll be married within a year, if unsuccessful then every time they try again puts the wedding day off for another year.

The culmination of the evening is a Bergman-like procession up the nearby hill. We push through the long grass to a point where we can see the sun go down and welcome the new moon in a celebration of death and rebirth, decay and renewal. As the sun eventually sinks, fires are lit to preserve the warmth and the light, and, in a spectacular climax, a wheel is set on fire and sent rolling down the hill towards the stream.

Only then can we really start tucking into the beer and cheese with caraway seeds. Not an abundant menu, but that's the point. Cheese and bread were all that was left before the new harvest was brought in. Groups sit round the fire, a group of visiting Lithuanians sing softly together, and as we leave to return to Riga around midnight, the purists settle in for an all-night session.

Day Ninety: *Riga*

Yesterday, a refreshing day off pottering round, not the old centre, but the rich heritage of Riga's Art Nouveau architecture, reflecting the wealth and enlightenment of this cosmopolitan port at the turn of the twentieth century. Alberta Street (Alberta *iela*) is a repository of boldly experimental flourishes, the most imaginative of which were designed by a Rigan called Mikhail Eisenstein, whose young son went on to direct films in Russia, producing such twentieth-century classics as *Battleship Potemkin*, *Ivan The Terrible* and *Alexander Nevsky*.

Today, leaving this walkable city behind with some reluctance, we head for Latvia's west coast. This takes us across the old province of Kurland. In the seventeenth century, when the European powers were flexing their muscles across the

Atlantic, their enterprising ruler Duke Jakob struck a neutrality deal with Oliver Cromwell, and acquired the West Indian island of Tobago, which he rechristened New Kurland and which carried on a thriving trade with Europe under his distinctive flag, a black crab on a red background.

Nice to think of Latvia having once been a colonial power.

The nearer we get to the Baltic, the more monotonous become the acres of sand and pine forest. We're looking for something quite unusual, and looming above the tree canopy, some 20 miles north of the town of Ventspils, we finally pick it out. A massive, goblet-shaped radio telescope. In the days of Soviet occupation this was one of the most important of their listening devices, so important that when the Russians pulled out of Latvia at the end of the Cold War, they did their best to make sure it would never be used again.

But they reckoned without men like Juris Zagars.

He has a good story to tell. How what he calls 'one of the most beautiful radio telescopes in the world' was saved from destruction by a group of Latvian scientists, and turned from fighting the Cold War to fighting global warming.

The Russian proposals for blowing up the facility caused an outcry across the scientific community. Juris tells of how the Royal Astronomical Society joined the Russian Academy of Science in protesting that 'to destroy the best radio telescope in northern Europe, only for political reasons, was some kind of vandalism'.

At the eleventh hour, the decision to blow it up was rescinded.

'It was like a fairy tale,' says Juris.

Well, not quite. The Russians sent a crack squad to sabotage the telescope without actually destroying it. In the control room at the base of the telescope Juris explains how they went about it. He shows me thick communication cables into which some hundred nails were driven and their heads cut off. Wires were cut in all but one of the thirty drives needed to power the telescope, and battery acid poured onto them. Hundreds of other vital electrical connections were broken and the paperwork and diagrams that were needed to reconnect them were destroyed.

Juris and a handful of local Latvian scientists and engineers gave up their weekends and holidays to solve the elaborate puzzle of how to get the telescope up and running again. It took four years for them to repair damage that had been inflicted in less than a week.

Juris and I climb up through the innards of the giant frame. It's ruggedly built but with certain flourishes, like round porthole windows, which give it a style beyond the functional.

'This is like in a Russian submarine,' enthuses Juris. And the comparison isn't fanciful. The telescope was built in the naval dockyards in Leningrad, for which Juris is full of both praise and envy. Because it was built for military reasons it was given an almost unlimited budget. No civil government nowadays, he says, would be as generous. It's also engineering of the very highest quality.

At its peak, when it was scanning the Western skies for information, there were 500 people working here under top-secret conditions. A small town of some 3,000 inhabitants had grown up to house families of the scientists. Ghostly remnants of this short-lived brave new world can be found nearby: derelict housing blocks and an abandoned community hall, complete with a stage and Social Realist murals of soldiers at war.

I ask Juris if he knows of any specific surveillance successes of the Ventspils telescope.

'Well, they knew about the death of the Pakistan President Zia ul Haq in an air crash six hours…'

'Before it happened?'

'No…no not before it happened, but six hours before the rest of the world knew about it.'

We're off the main stairway now and swinging high over the ground on a complex and intricate web of steel struts and beams. With a grunt of satisfaction Juris points upwards, and beckons me to follow him. It's a tight squeeze but worth it. The trapdoor opens onto the smooth parabola of the telescope's enormous dish. I feel insignificant, like a tea leaf at the bottom of the cup, surrounded only by aluminium and sky.

A few hours later I find myself down the coast in another relic of the Soviet occupation. Across the border in Lithuania is a garish, brightly lit seaside resort called Palanga, beloved not only of holidaymakers from all over the Baltics but also, once upon a time, of Leonid Brezhnev, the Soviet leader, who for five years between 1977 and 1982 was one of the two most powerful people in the world. And I'm to sleep in his bedroom.

Lithuania

Day Ninety-one: *Palanga to Vilnius*

As we assemble for breakfast it turns out that all of us were told we had Brezhnev's room last night. It's like the scene from *Spartacus*.

'I had Brezhnev's room.'

'No! I had Brezhnev's room!'

The man himself may be long gone, but the Villa, now Hotel, Auska is a testament to misguided grandiosity. The rooms are big for the sake of bigness. Huge doors open onto acres of thickly carpeted empty space. Ceilings are moulded and decorated, colossal fireplaces sit below elaborately stuccoed walls. Armchairs and sofas await vast bottoms. But it's hard to find a hook on the wall and the water emerges from the tap in a trickle.

After breakfast I find my way out of the back of the villa and across a garden with sentry towers rising from the bushes, to a heavy barbed-wire steel door. Pulling it open I find myself in deep, soft sand and a few yards further on I'm looking out over dunes to a wide sandy beach. On the edge of the Baltic an elderly couple, dressed rather oddly, are doing slow but strenuous exercises. I realise after a moment or two that both are stark naked, and what looked like some sort of padded exercise gear is in fact their own bodies.

Lithuania is the largest of the Baltic republics and driving across the country from the coast to the capital one senses a scale absent from its cosier neighbours to the north. It's not only the size of territory that makes Lithuania different. Her history is bigger too. Neither Latvia nor Estonia has known anything to rival the Grand Duchy of Lithuania, a trading empire which stretched as far as Moscow and the Black Sea and was the last pagan state in medieval Europe. In 1569 the Grand Duchy joined with Poland to create the Polish-Lithuanian Commonwealth, one of the most tolerant, civilised and secure of European power blocs, strong enough to inflict defeats on the Teutonic Knights from the west and Ivan the Terrible's army from the east, before succumbing to the relentless growth of a Russian state two centuries later.

Halfway to Vilnius, a small hill stands out from the wide, flat agricultural plain. Every inch of it is covered in crosses, a cruciform forest spilling out onto the fields around. Coaches appear from the middle of nowhere and pull off the road, crunching across the powdery dirt of a makeshift car park. They come from all over Europe and every one is full of visitors who, in one day, can add a few hundred crosses to the collection.

No-one quite knows how long this has been going on, but there is irrefutable evidence that crosses were put here in the nineteenth century to commemorate those who gave their lives in two rebellions against Russian rule. When the Russians returned in 1944, the hill became a rallying ground, not just for Lithuanian nationalists, but for all those anxious to assert their religious loyalties in a godless state. The Soviet authorities were irritated enough to try and clear the hill at least four times and once to divert a sewage outlet across the fields leading to it.

This only encouraged the cross-planters and further enhanced the symbolic significance of the place, and when the last Russian soldiers left Lithuanian soil in 1993 the Hill of Crosses changed from landmark to national icon.

To be honest, I wandered amongst its forest of crucifixes, carved statues of the Virgin and scattering of rosary beads with increasing despondency. What might have been inspiring seems to me to have been tarnished by a sort of quick-fix, off-the-shelf piety. The original, dignified, tall crosses are now just hangers for an awful lot of tat, much of it sold in the stalls at the car park to tour groups who leave their mass-produced knick-knacks and move on.

I was much more moved by hearing, as we reached Vilnius, the capital, a few hours later, that in the summer of 1989 a human chain had linked arms across the length of the Baltic republics, from Vilnius to Tallinn. It was organised to mark the fiftieth anniversary of the infamous Molotov-Ribbentrop Pact of 1939, in which the Germans, in return for non-aggression against their invasion of Poland, agreed to let the Russians occupy Estonia, Latvia and Lithuania.

The line of clasped hands must have stretched some 400 miles. Now that's what I call devotion.

Day Ninety-two: *Vilnius*

Lithuania's long relationship with Poland is the key to what distinguishes it from the other two Baltic states. Estonia and Latvia looked north and west and were very much influenced by Sweden, the leading Protestant power. Lithuania looked to south and central Europe and has been Catholic since Grand Duke Jogaila converted in 1386.

The clean Lutheran lines of Old Town Tallinn are here supplanted by the swirlier, more decorative touch of the Baroque.

One thing all three capital cities have in common is the girdle of colourless concrete estates built by Soviet planners from the 1950s to the 1980s. Politically it was necessary to have these purpose-built blocks to house the vast influx of workers brought here from Russia and ideologically it was important that everywhere looked the same. Today we have the chance to see what life is like beyond the pretty old town centres where few people can afford to live anyway. Albina Takas and Stasys Aukstuolis meet us at the door of one of the blocks and we follow them up a dim, echoing stairwell past scratched and stained doorways. So far so predictable, but once inside their flat everything changes. The rooms are small, laid out on the standard-issue Soviet floor area of 56 square metres but Stasys, an artist, has managed to carve studio space out of a tiny living room. Every inch of the walls not stacked with books is covered in paintings and prints and even on the narrow balcony there are collections of pottery or pieces of driftwood waiting to be turned into something. Albina, short and energetic, with close-cropped peroxide blonde hair, teaches English 'for specific purposes', in her case, medicine. Her desk and computer are in the study which at night becomes the bedroom. From the window we look down on a strip of faded grass around which children play.

Services like water, electricity and heating are still centrally supplied, but Albina and Stasys have been able to buy their flat. For them living here is not some social gesture, it's purely practical. There is very little option. There are no rows of bourgeois houses for them to move into. Many of those were destroyed in the war and never replaced. These blocks are the reality. There is no money to pull them down and they are all over Eastern Europe.

In Tirana, Albania I saw what an artistic eye could do with the outside of these characterless buildings. Albina and Stasys gave me a glimpse of what could be done inside. As I was driven away from their estate, clutching a fine, spare, Japanese-style pencil drawing I'd bought from Stasys, I felt that as well as meeting two talented, energetic, imaginative people, I shall never again look at these blocks with quite the same assumptions of gloom and despair. A small cloud of prejudice lifted.

Recent history permeates Vilnius, not just what it looks like but what it talks about. I have a drink with a local television star, Algis Greitai. He's a charismatic figure, tall, broad-shouldered, with a shaven head and piercing eyes. He could pass for a basketball star. In fact he's a comedian, and, like many comedians, deeply, if a little disappointingly, serious. He makes the point that in 1940 the standard of living in Lithuania was higher than in Finland. After fifty years of Russian occupation the roles were completely reversed.

What riled him most about the Soviet occupation was the attempt to justify it on grounds of houses built and schools and hospitals.

'I mean, fine, but we didn't ask for them. It's a bit like offering a good meal to a condemned man! If they'd let us develop our natural way, things would be much better here.'

'Aren't you in danger of changing one master, Moscow, for another, Brussels?'

He grins, bleakly.

'Moscow was involuntary.'

We talk about national stereotypes and I ask him how Lithuanians see their Baltic neighbours.

'Well, there are Russian jokes about Estonians being very slow, and we call Latvians horse heads.'

He chuckles.

'Which is very offensive as far as I know.'

'And the Lithuanians?'

'Er...well, for some reason we eat terrible food. Our national dish is called *cepelinai*, Zeppelin. It's pork fat covered with potato stuff. Very bad for your stomach.'

'Anything else?'

'Well, people like to whine a lot here. "Things are very bad... blah blah blah." But the Latvians do the same, the Poles do the same. I mean all post-communist nations like to whine.'

During the Second World War, Vilnius was occupied three times, first by the Soviets in 1939, then by the Germans in 1941 and after the failure of Hitler's invasion of Russia, the Soviet troops returned in 1944. Some 30,000 Lithuanian partisans, often students, farmers and teachers, took to the streets and the forests to fight for their country's freedom. Many were imprisoned and tortured in the basement of a big neo-classical building in the centre of the city, which is now open to the public as the Museum of Lithuanian Genocide Victims. Little has been changed. A few display boards, some photographs and background information, but apart from that the flag-stone floors are cold and draughty, the spy holes in the thick doors reveal grey, bleak cells. The occupants were generally political rather than military prisoners. Two archbishops of Lithuania and two bishops were brought in here, one of whom was later shot.

A factual, unemotional commentary, in good English, describes the function of the various cells, the most chilling being what they call 'the ice-pool cells'. A lowered concrete floor would be filled with ice-cold water, from which the only refuge was a small eighteen-inch-square block. Prisoners, wearing only their underwear, were made to stand on the block for hours until sleep overtook them and they fell into the freezing water. There is a padded cell, with puffy, swollen walls that look like ripe bruises, at one end of which hangs a black straitjacket, arms akimbo.

'The walls absorb their cries and shouts for help,' adds the commentary, dryly.

Apart from the callousness of the brutality here, most shocking to me is that the building where it all went on, once a courthouse, once a boys' school, is in the very heart of the city. Surely the most unbearable torture must have been the sight of life going on, people bustling backwards and forwards, bent over bags of shopping or hand in hand with their children, yards away but completely out of reach. In the fifty years that this grim prison existed, only one man ever escaped.

Day Ninety-four: *Nida to Kaliningrad*

From the jetty at the little fishing town of Nida, I look out across the water to what looks like an outpost of the Sahara. A wall of sand capped with pine forest rising sheer from the lagoon and curving south to a distant horizon.

This is the Curonian Spit, the longest and most impressive of the filigree of sandbars strung along the Baltic coast by the tides and winds that scour the unprotected shore. The sun shines brightly on these immense dunes, patterned with the elongated shadows of circling sea birds. Perhaps as curious as a desert on the Baltic coast is the fact that it leads us west, into Russia.

Nearly 62 miles long and never more than two and a half miles wide, the Curonian Spit connects Lithuania with a curious political anomaly, a part of the old German province of East Prussia, ceded to the USSR in 1945 in response to Stalin's demands for an ice-free port. It's now known, after the city at its heart, as Kaliningrad. So it is that, only a few miles south of Nida, we emerge from a corridor of trees to find a sign, half-covered by silver birch scrub, reading 'Welcome to Russia'.

Not a lot changes immediately. The combination of willow, birch and pine planted to prevent further erosion makes the straight road into an arboreal tunnel and the few buildings we glimpse between the trees all bear the same style of rustic red brick from the days when the whole Spit was part of Prussia. Every year vast numbers of migrating birds stop off on the sandbar, and in the 1880s an energetic and committed German ornithologist by the name of Johannes Thienemann set up an observation point at the village of Rossitten, which became one of the pioneering sites for the new technique of ringing birds. Renamed Rybachiy by the Russians, it has survived political change to become one of Europe's most important centres for studying bird migration.

A huge structure rises in a clearing amongst the pines. Developed at Rybachiy some fifty years ago, it's a mammoth bird trap. An entrance 100 feet wide and 50 feet high leads into a 200-foot long net which funnels down to a line of cages. The trap is aligned with the prevailing winds and, during the spring or autumn migrations, can catch as many as 50,000 birds. Mischa, the bird-man who's showing me round, says they once caught 4,000 in a day. This is early summer and there's less activity, but there are a number of crossbills fluttering in the cages, lured by the pine nuts, and Mischa has to ring as many as he can in the hour or so that the birds are kept.

The ringing takes only a few seconds but whilst the bird is restrained they check species, sex, wing measurement, and, by blowing on the breast of each female, they can see from the brood-patch whether it has young or not. While they write up these observations the bird is dumped unceremoniously upside down into a cone-shaped tube with its legs sticking up in the air.

Mischa and his team and their colossal net have had their successes. A swallow ringed at Rybachiy ended up in Durban, South Africa, siskins in Ireland, owls in Central Asia, chiffchaffs in Norway. They've learnt lessons about bird behaviour, as well as conservation, navigation and, more recently, global warming, noting many birds returning much earlier in the spring than they did fifty years ago.

I quite forget I've just crossed a border until I ask Mischa what information a bird carries in its ring.

'Ah,' he says, 'just a code and a number to ring in Moscow.'

We drive on south, to the end of the Spit and onto the mainland. In what was once Prussia, house-proud and efficient, a bumpy two-lane road runs falteringly through run-down villages. A war memorial to the Soviet troops who defeated Germany has storks nesting on top. We ask a local if anyone has tried to move them. He looks up, shielding his eyes and shakes his head. They've been there for the last ten years.

A long stretch of the road is tidily lined with rowan trees, which our Russian driver says were planted by the Germans to prevent their troop movements being seen from the air.

'The last soldiers of Hitler,' he calls them.

Old posters flank the road, put up by the communist administration to celebrate the 750th anniversary of the city of Königsberg/Kaliningrad in 2005. Or more accurately, to celebrate 691 years of Königsberg and 59 of Kaliningrad.

Why rename a city like Königsberg, which had such a long and distinguished reputation for scholarship and enlightenment, the home of Kant and the renowned and respected Albertina University?

Because it was German, basically, and the advancing Soviet army, having lost millions of men at the hands of the Nazis, was hell-bent on wiping out any trace of the hated enemy. The British had bombed much of the old city in 1944 but the Russian troops completed the destruction slowly and methodically. Houses and churches were torched, the population raped, robbed and murdered.

When the rage had burnt itself out the city began slowly to pull itself together, with the Russian settlers and the remaining Germans working remarkably well together to restore the services and clear the rubble.

All went well until, in 1946, the devastated city was renamed after Mikhail Kalinin, a President of the Soviet Union under Stalin, and the whole Kaliningrad oblast was declared a military zone. On Stalin's orders the border was surrounded with barbed wire and the remaining Germans were forcibly removed on special trains.

For over forty years the world lost sight of Kaliningrad. No visas were issued and even supervised foreign groups were discouraged. As my *Bradt* guide observes, 'Lhasa, Pyongyang and Tirana appeared cosmopolitan in comparison'.

The main street is still called Leninskiy Prospekt and our hotel is called the Moskva. Tomorrow we're promised the festivities of National Day, marking sixty years of communist rule. What will there be to celebrate?

Kaliningrad / Russia

Day Ninety-five: *Kaliningrad*

'We are Russians. It's in our souls, in our heart, it can't be otherwise.'

Olga Danilova is a small, bright, voluble woman. In her fifties I should think, with a taut, well-toned physique that makes me wonder if she were ever a dancer. She is a child of the USSR, her parents among those Russian settlers who took this city over from the Germans at the end of the war. With her is her daughter Anastasia, a pencil-thin teenager. She, like her mother, is a Russian patriot. She'd once come home in tears of frustration when a poll she'd run amongst her friends at school showed that seventy per cent would rather work and live abroad. Olga admits that the proximity to Europe makes the people of Kaliningrad very different from what she calls the 'mainland' Russians to the east. The break-up of the Soviet Union only emphasised the isolation of Kaliningrad from her neighbours, but Olga thinks that, with the accession of Lithuania and Poland to the EU in 2004, the situation is changing. The Germans are increasing their interest and investment in the rebuilding of the city, and the prospect of a united free-trade Europe on its borders has reawakened Moscow's interest in their distant colony.

'Because in the Soviet past they didn't care much. There was some Kaliningrad somewhere. Now it's quite a strong involvement. We have a governing team, just for us, in Moscow.'

We're talking beside another memorial to the Soviet dead. In this case to those who lost their lives in the taking of the city in

1945. An eternal flame flutters in the wind. Powerful figures strain forward brandishing rifles and machine-guns. Olga is proud of the memorial.

'It was the very first memorial erected in the Soviet Union after the Second World War, or the Great Patriotic War as we call it in Russia.'

All the more surprising then that the celebrations marking sixty years of Soviet 'liberation' seem deliberately to avoid military bands, march-pasts or rattling of sabres. The first uniforms I see consist of stiletto heels, pleated white miniskirts, ultramarine tunics and white air force-style caps, and the first weapons are white plastic batons with red and blue pom-poms, wielded by a squad of sexy long-legged cheerleaders who seem to be the closest thing to an army I can see in Victory Square this morning.

Nearby, a gleaming new Russian Orthodox cathedral is nearing completion (in the 1940s and 1950s the Russians went about systematically destroying the churches of old Königsberg) and the red marble Victory column has been donated by Yukoil.

At eleven o'clock sharp the thudding, hyper-amplified disco music switches to something in the *Star Wars* style. There is activity at a bland government building from which flutter the flags of Kaliningrad – a blue sailing ship on a white background and the horizontal white, blue and red bands of the Russian Federation. The doors swing open and a delegation of the great and powerful emerges. At the same time the cheerleaders strut out from behind the monument and, having flung their batons about a bit, fall back to allow the hosts of the ceremony to make their appearance. And what an appearance it is too. A man dressed from head to foot in white and a woman in a long taffeta ball-gown. In their attempts to expurgate all military overtones, they've turned National Day into the Eurovision Song Contest.

Pom-poms are shaken, songs sung, red, white and blue balloons are sent billowing skywards. Speeches are made by visiting dignitaries from Moscow, by the governor of the Kaliningrad oblast, the mayor of the city and a general in a peaked cap wide enough to land a helicopter on, but there are few people to listen to them and the words blow away in the wind, chased off by more thunderous music from the PA system.

An hour or so later the Married Couple of the Year competition upstages the opening in two crucial areas. It has a crowd and they're enthusiastic. Meanwhile the Brides Bus cruises the street. All decked out in pink and full of adolescent girls, it rumbles past like a mobile bordello, contributing to an infectious, and quite unexpected, atmosphere of cheerful anarchy.

On my way from the park, after watching men dressed as medieval knights knocking each other about, it's impossible to miss the bright yellow tank of *kvass*, parked up by the side of the road and presided over by a huge woman in a yellow cap.

I ask Olga what it consists of.

'*Kvass*? It's a summer drink, made from fermenting rye bread, sugar, leaves...' Fearing she's not yet made it sound irresistible, she adds, 'It's a traditional Russian drink. A good remedy when you have a headache after taking vodka.'

I try some, ahead of the hangover for once. A curious taste which I can only describe as a mix of Pepsi-Cola and gravy.

We follow the crowds down towards the River Pregel. From a bridge across to an island I can see the two most distinctive, and controversial, buildings in the city. One is the Gothic cathedral, a severe but impressive brick building with tall, unadorned buttresses. Built in the late fourteenth century, it escaped the destruction of the communist years by the skin of its teeth. The story goes that Brezhnev, visiting the city, enquired why this monument to the old Königsberg hadn't been knocked down and was told that it contained the grave of the city's most famous son, the philosopher Immanuel Kant. As Karl Marx had much admired Kant, Brezhnev agreed to a reprieve.

Of course, as Olga pointed out, Kant never went inside the cathedral, and the nearest he got to it was in his tomb, which sits beneath a tree outside. There's a nice story that Robert Motherby and Joseph Green, two grain and herring importers from Hull, had lunch with Immanuel Kant every Sunday for nearly twenty years.

Königsberg's other great building was the medieval castle. Seen as a symbol of Prussian aggression, it was razed to the ground and after much argument a modern concrete block, of huge and lumpen proportions, was built on top of it.

'Why?' I asked Olga.

'Because they called the castle a monument to fascism. And what we got was a monument to communism.'

It's now known, almost affectionately, as the Monster.

There are other traces of the old city. If you look hard enough you might find one of the few remaining Gothic towers. There were twelve of them at one time, guarding the twelve entrances to the city. In most of new Europe they would be tourist attractions, but here they're unlit, neglected and ignored. Kaliningrad is still embarrassed by having been Königsberg.

Olga, broad-minded as she wants to be, is sensitive to slights at her home town. She knows that there are many things that need to be improved. She wants to be able to travel more easily, she can see the benefits of a European Union, and yet she has a deep loyalty to Russia, the country that educated her and brought her up. Whether Russia will reciprocate these feelings is not absolutely clear. At the root of Olga and her daughter's anxieties is that they might yet be sold down the river, and that the Germans may turn out to be better friends to Kaliningrad than the Russians.

Day Ninety-six: *Kaliningrad*

I want to leave Kaliningrad by sea. It seems the right thing to do now I'm up here on the shores of the Baltic. The River Pregel is lined with derelict cranes and huge grain stores, a reminder of the city's history as a Hanseatic port, trading regularly with Britain.

Though most of the wharves and jetties lie idle, awaiting a trade revival that may never come, one of them has been converted into a well-equipped and well-designed Museum of Oceanography.

The centrepiece is the 350-foot *Vityaz*, an elegant vessel with graceful, sweeping lines which between 1949 and 1979 undertook sixty-five scientific expeditions for the Russian navy.

Look a little deeper into her past and you find that there is much more to the *Vityaz* than scientific research. She was built in a German dockyard in 1939 as the *Mars*. In 1945 she carried 20,000 East Prussian refugees safely out of Königsberg before being handed over to the British, who gave her back to the Russians who had by then taken the city.

The energy and imagination behind the Oceanography Museum hints at what Kaliningrad could become with an injection of self-confidence. It's just a question of where that confidence will come from. The museum is courtesy of the Russians, most of the money and the drive behind the restoration of the great cathedral is from Germany.

As I wave farewell to Olga and Anastasia and begin a blustery journey down the Pregel towards Poland I hope that they will have some certainties soon. Kaliningrad may never become Königsberg again, but who knows, it could be Königsgrad. Or even Kalininberg.

Poland

Day Ninety-seven: *Gdańsk*

THE WATERS between Kaliningrad and Gdańsk are awash with the landmarks of history.

On a bitter winter's night in January 1945, a Soviet submarine raced across in pursuit of a German liner, the *Wilhelm Gustloff*, full to four or five times its normal capacity with refugees fleeing from the victorious Russians. Three of its torpedoes hit the *Gustloff*, which sank with the loss of over 7,000 lives. It was the worst loss of life in any marine disaster. Today, the *Wilhelm Gustloff* lies some 150 feet below the surface of the Bay of Gdańsk.

Turning south into the Motlawa Canal, which connects the Bay with Poland's longest river, the Wisła (Vistula), we pass the place where the very first shots of the Second World War were fired. A Polish garrison on the Westerplatte headland was bombarded by the German battleship *Schleswig-Holstein* on 1 September 1939. Less than 200 men held out against the Germans for a week. Today a chunky Soviet Realist-style monument marks their sacrifice (which is a bit ripe considering the Russians had concluded a non-aggression pact with Germany a week before German troops attacked the Poles on Westerplatte).

On the west side of the canal rise the cranes and roofs of one of the most famous shipyards in the world, where an electrician by the name of Lech Walesa (the 'l' is soft, and the 's' has an 'n' sound before it, so he's 'Lek Wayensa') led a strike that was to change the face of communism in Eastern Europe. Now the Gdańsk Shipyards themselves are victims of change. Decayed, dilapidated and struggling to survive in the capitalist world, their fame is more symbolic than commercial.

Once we've landed and settled ourselves in a waterfront hotel, we make a pilgrimage to the shipyard. The famous gates, outside which the world's press camped during the stand-off between workers and the government twenty-seven years ago, are still there, frozen in time. Hanging from their black and white bars are various symbols of Polish resistance: the national flag, a big framed photo of the Polish pope, John Paul II (and a noticeably smaller photo of the current, German, pope), a banner bearing the name of Solidarity, the first trade union in any communist country, bunches of flowers and a likeness of the Catholic icon, the Black Madonna. They reflect the potent combination of religion and politics, priests and workers, that in the words of the historian Timothy Garton-Ash marked 'the beginning of the end of communism in Europe'.

No workers pass through here any more and the gatekeepers direct visitors to the 'Freedom Multimedia Exhibition'.

There is life beyond multimedia exhibitions and some shipbuilding still goes on here, though the workforce has been reduced from 15,000 to 3,000. Andrej Buczkowski, general manager of the yard, takes me in the back door, as it were, past lines of empty red-brick offices, their windows smashed and their walls graffitied, where weeds scramble up drainpipes and onto disused gantries. Andrej is open and candid about the problems. No party line here. The Gdańsk Shipyards went bust in 1996. They are now owned sixty-two per cent by the government and thirty-eight per cent by Gdynia Shipyards, a few miles up the coast. Much of the yard has already been sold off for redevelopment: housing, supermarkets, light industrial stuff.

Then, around the corner, is a glimpse of the old days. A towering steel hull, enmeshed in scaffolding, soars above us, dwarfing man and machines. Its massive bulk rings with the sound of drilling and riveting, and the crackle and flash of welding. Pre-cast steel sections, 30 feet wide, trundle alongside on vehicles piled so high they look as if they're being squashed flat by their load. And dominating everything, the iconic gantry cranes, using their enormous height and power to straddle the ship.

These heavy cranes would have witnessed many struggles, from the strike in the 1970s when some fifty people were killed, to the momentous events of the 1980s when Solidarity was born here, but if the orders don't come in then they too will come to an undignified end.

Andrej blames the situation on rising costs since Poland joined the EU in 2004. With the free flow of manpower the only way they can keep skilled workers is to raise salaries, which raises costs, which in turn can make a big, old-fashioned yard like this as uncompetitive as the British yards it once undercut.

Solidarity is now only one of four unions on site, and Lech Walesa, its legendary founder, who was once an electrical maintenance engineer here, is too busy on the political stage to be the saviour of his old employers.

Andrej is hopeful that the slipways will fill again, and he has no doubt that, in ten years' time, and under new owners, the Gdańsk Shipyards will be more than just a museum of freedom.

I wish I shared his optimism. To me, the shipyards seem to be battling against that inevitable contraction of heavy industry that transformed my home town of Sheffield in the 1980s. To me, there's something sad about seeing heavy engineering replaced by heavy shopping, but it's all part of a process and what comes out at the other end may dismay the sentimentalists, but so it probably should.

Muse about this over *zurek*, a gastronomic first. It's a sausage-based bortsch, served inside a small, round hollowed-out loaf of bread; a sort of edible tureen. Delicious.

Day Ninety-eight: *Gdańsk*

Lech Walesa may no longer have much to do with the shipyards that shaped his career, but he does still live in Gdańsk and he has agreed to meet and talk. He has an office just round the corner from our hotel. Appropriately perhaps, the short walk along the canal passes beneath a crane as iconic as the green monsters that rise above the shipyards. The Gdańsk Crane, with its original timber housing and mechanism largely intact, is the biggest and oldest in Europe. Built in the days when Gdańsk was Danzig, one of the alliance of trading cities of the Baltic and the North Sea known as the Hanseatic League, it stands opposite three long, rather elegant granaries which, like the crane, date from the fifteenth century.

This formidable cluster of buildings provide a taster for what hits you as you walk through the Green Gate (Brama Zielona) and into the Main Town. Long Market (Długi Targ) and Long Street (Ulica Długi), stretching ahead in a gently curving line, must be one of the finest streetscapes in Europe. Dominated by a towering red-brick town hall and lined with houses of all styles from classical to Dutch gabled to Rococo, it is a testimony to the wealth, good taste and richly diverse influences of European traders. A testimony, too, to the skill of twentieth-century Polish builders, architects and craftsmen who have almost totally rebuilt this centuries-old quarter after its destruction in the Second World War.

Above the Green Gate arch is a handsome former royal residence in Dutch Baroque style, now divided up into various living spaces. In one of them, off an entrance shared with Radio Gdańsk, the Nobel Prize-winning founder of Solidarity and one-time President of Poland has a set of offices provided free of charge by the city.

It's airy and spacious with views out over the old docks on one side and on the other the 260-foot town hall tower and the bustle of Long Market. The floors are of exposed oak wood and the furniture is functional, modern and quite bland. The chair behind his desk has a complicated system of cables trailing from it, which hint at orthopaedic problems.

Apart from a big framed map of old Poland most of the walls are taken up with religious images, including crucifixes and a number of photos of Lech with Pope John Paul. On a coffee table are indications of more secular successes: an advert for his wife Danuta's Walesa Pasta and a Globe Award from Nestlé and General Mills for Walesa's 'contribution to the development of the free market economy and widening the boundaries of the free world'. Lech also has some roses named after him, his assistant tells us helpfully.

Everything seems to suggest that there is a substantial Walesa industry centred here, and this is confirmed by the arrival of the chief executive, the man himself. He may be over an hour late but he comes in like a whirlwind, heading straight for his desk, issuing orders as he goes. With his big, mournful grey moustache, greying hair and neat air force-blue suit, he looks like a busy headmaster. Apart from the sandals.

He apologises briefly, he's come from a hospital check-up, but doesn't elaborate on it. He's a few months younger than me and looks quite trim. Now he's here he wants the interview to start right away. Now. He answers my polite questions efficiently enough, but while his answers are being translated back into English he feigns total lack of interest, reading newspapers and letters, fiddling with his computer and generally contriving to look both busy and bored.

He sees globalisation and European unity as the most important new factors at the beginning of the twenty-first century. Having helped dismantle what he calls 'the communist monopoly', he now feels his country must avoid creating any monopoly to replace it.

'We have to create democratic institutions that compete with each other, like in the West.'

He sounds a little disillusioned, or is it just false modesty? 'If I were a capitalist, I would be the biggest capitalist, but that's too late for me. I'm rather poor and frankly I would have to start my business by putting light bulbs in the ceiling again. Frankly, there's no place for me. I'm watching politics. Watching globalisation and peace and how powers interact.'

But a last remark of mine seems to completely change his mood. I'd heard that his daughter is a big success in the Polish version of *Celebrity Come Dancing*, and as we wind up the interview I decide to take a nothing-to-lose gamble with my last throw.

'Thank you very much, Mr President. A privilege to talk to you and may we wish your daughter all the best in her dancing career.'

Suddenly he's all smiles, standing up and reeling off a whole list of reasons why, as he put it, he might have been 'a bit abrupt'.

He's off to Hamburg in the morning. He shrugs and spreads his arms wide.

'I don't know where I'm going or what I'm going to do there,' he laughs.

Then he's due in Italy to talk to 7,000 people.

'A huge gathering!'

Then Portugal. Then the United States.

'It's madness!'

Having got all this off his chest, he shakes our hands and seems genuinely grateful that, just for a moment, he could lay aside the baggage of the Great Statesman and be himself.

Later that night, dipping into a book by Radek Sikorski, a journalist, now Foreign Minister of Poland, I come across his account of a chat with the great man back in 1991.

'I had interviewed Gulbuddin Hekmatyar, the murderous leader of Afghan fundamentalists, and...Jonas Savimbi, the Angolan guerrilla leader accused of burning his enemies at the stake...But I still rate my interview with Walesa as the worst experience of my journalistic career.'

Unfortunately for him, that was before they had *Celebrity Come Dancing*.

Leaving the handsome old city of Gdańsk behind, we head south and east across the Wisła delta, through farming country marked by the odd windmill and clusters of half-timbered houses. This gentle, rolling rural countryside was the stamping ground of the Teutonic Knights. At Malbork there still exists their mammoth fortress, one of the largest in Europe, which this fearsome order of religious warriors made their headquarters after returning from the Crusades. They took the land from the native Prussians and handed it over to Germanic settlers.

From the time they moved into Malbork in 1309 to their first serious defeat by the Poles and Lithuanians at the Battle of Grunwald 101 years later, the Teutonic Order of the Hospital of St Mary, originally set up to give medical and spiritual sustenance to German knights on the Crusades, established a powerful military and commercial machine, using revenue from the Hanseatic traders to fund expansion of their religious and territorial ambitions in the east. Their intense and committed devotion to their order, and the heraldic imagery that went with it, attracted the Nazis, but because of their Roman Catholic affiliations, the Teutonic Order was actually banned in Germany during the Second World War.

The brick-red bastions of Malbork, rising from tranquil water meadows, are hugely impressive and impressively huge. The strength and severity of their fortifications still sends a chill down the spine, and one can only look with wonder at the sheer amount of effort they put into glorifying God, ensuring at the same time that they controlled one of the most lucrative trade routes in Europe, from the bread basket of central Poland to the Baltic ports of Königsberg and Danzig.

Day Ninety-nine: *Elbląg to Warsaw*

Elbląg is another town which was knocked apart in the war. Hitler's U-boats were built at the shipyards here, making it a major target for Allied bombers. It's been restored, but with nothing like the élan of Gdańsk. Cheap, and not very cheerful, concrete caricatures of the tall, thin Dutch-style gabled houses fill the city centre. The grandest building is the Gothic cathedral, whose staggeringly tall tower, topped with a many-tiered stack of balustrades, steeples and subsidiary domes, catches the morning sunlight beside the still waters of the Ostróda-Elbląg canal. On this waterway, opened in 1860 and running for just under 50 miles, we embark on a leisurely cruise south through the wetlands of the Mazurian Lakes.

Conditions are good. The skies are clear and there's not a breath of wind to ruffle the glassy surface of the water.

At eight o'clock, with the cathedral bells tolling, we set off, passing quite soon beneath the bridge of the railway that took away most of the economic justification for the canal trade. Now the waterway is used to take tours through the combination of peaty water, thick reed-beds, marsh and woodland which have been a protected nature reserve for the last forty years. Our boat, the *Labedz* (the 'Swan'), is functional rather than fetching, 100 feet long with a solid, steel-plated hull.

Black-headed gulls, cormorants, grebes, terns, marsh harriers, greylag geese and a white-tailed eagle can be seen scouting the reed-beds as we meander along, being overtaken by the odd vole.

After two hours of this rural ride we come to the first of five quirky feats of engineering that are the real reason why so many people are attracted to this spectacularly unhurried form of transport.

The canal appears to have come to a dead end. A grassy hill lies ahead of us, and that's all. Then, after a certain amount of barked instructions, a bell sounds and the *Labedz* finds herself in the grip of an underwater iron cradle and, gradually lifted from the water on the end of a steel cable, she emerges onto dry land, like some great creature from the deep, dripping slime and weeds. Secured in our trolley, which is mounted on rails, we gather on deck to look in disbelief at our ship's stately progress up the hill. A family working in the fields below barely acknowledge a boat sailing at 45 degrees up a slope above them.

Halfway up we meet another boat going down, and a few minutes later and 42 feet higher than when we started, we're gently deposited back in the canal. Released from our cage, we chug on until the whole process has to be repeated again.

In the next two hours we climb four more of these marvellous slipways, the steepest of which raises us over 80 feet through fields on one side and woodland on the other. The sensation of standing on the deck of a ship whilst rising through dappled beech woods is dream-like, but wonderfully soothing, and when we have to leave the canal and continue by road towards Warsaw I can't help feeling we've exchanged the world of Mole and Badger and are back with Mr Toad.

Day One Hundred: *Warsaw*

Our arrival in this big grey capital coincides with a grey overcast day. The streets are still hung with posters for the Miss World Competition which took place a couple of nights ago at the Palace of Culture, the massive landmark edifice that was Stalin's gift to the people of Warsaw, though if he'd known they might use it for Miss World Competitions he might well have taken it back again.

We're driving through Stalin's other gifts to Warsaw, wide streets flanked with long lines of relentlessly undistinguished housing blocks. They've not aged well and appear to have been ignored in favour of high spending on Old City restoration. One strip is lined with small, seedy sex shops and peep-show parlours. The name on the wall, I notice, is John Paul II Street.

Even though it's over two years now since Poland joined the EU, there are still so many jokes about the number of Poles working in the UK that I'm happy to show that it's not all one-way traffic.

At Warsaw Number 4 Fire Station I meet a Cockney called Kevin, born in Chelsea, who's even named his daughter Chelsea, but who's lived in Poland for fifteen years and is now a section leader in the Straz, the Polish fire brigade. Speaking to him you might think he'd just come over the day before yesterday. His London accent is untarnished and he looks and talks with amiable chippiness as if he's just come out of the Duck and Parrot. In fact, he speaks Polish so well he's written books in Polish, has his own television show, and has just returned from doing stand-up comedy in the tough industrial cities of Silesia, where, he says, German jokes go down very well. Clearly nothing fazes Kevin Aiston.

It's just as well Kevin's amiable, because physically he's quite daunting. Over six foot with head shaved close, he walks straight and tall and fills the space around him like a goalkeeper at a penalty.

He shows me round Number 4 Fire Station, laid out like a stables with the engines housed in long red gabled roofs around a yard.

They have a small museum from which I learn that the 170-year-old Warsaw fire brigade suffered grievously under the Nazi occupation in the Second World War.

'For acts of sabotage, like slowly extinguishing the strategic buildings, many fire-fighters were punished and died in the mass extermination camps,' reads one caption. It reminds me that one in five Poles, twenty per cent of the population, lost their lives in the 1939–45 war, a higher proportion than in any other European country.

When the war ended and the communists took over, Kevin tells me, the country entered a forty-five-year period that Poles call the Deep Freeze. When it was over many were confused as to where they were. As the author Eva Hoffman put it, it was like exchanging the claustrophobia of no choice for the agoraphobia of freedom.

Kevin singles out hospitality as one of the great qualities of his adopted country. 'They'll empty out the whole fridge and knock on the neighbour's door and empty their fridge in order to entertain you,' and he notes their religiousness. 'If a Polish man's on a bus and he's got a hat on and the bus passes a church, the Pole feels an obligation to take his hat off and bow to the church.'

On the whole, the Poles like the British but they do bear grudges over what they see as misapprehensions about the war.

'Twenty per cent of the RAF was made up of Polish airmen, but no-one ever says anything about the Poles taking part in the Battle of Britain.'

The lack of Allied back-up during the Warsaw uprising, when nearly 200,000 civilians died in the unsuccessful attempt to overthrow their Nazi occupiers, is deeply resented, especially by the older generation.

This is not all I learn from Kevin. Before we go, I'm gold-star proficient at sliding down the firemen's pole.

'Lean into it with your shoulder, put your forearms round. Don't hold it with your hands, you'll burn them going down. Leg over leg. Off you go!'

Lunch at the restaurant next door, called Florian's after the patron saint of firemen. It's decorated in a disconcerting butch-bordello style with lacy tablecloths, firemen's helmets and brass-band instruments. A suitable place for my first taste of *smalets*, a delightful confection of congealed lard smeared on bread, a dish for the poor that has suddenly become fashionable. Well, so Kevin says, but then he's a comedian as well as a fireman.

Kevin Aiston is an Englishman married to a Pole and Monika Richardson, who shows me round Warsaw this afternoon, is a Polish woman married to a Brit. She's a wafer-thin blonde with a sharp, acute eye and a good line in well-informed irreverence. She resists my tendency to expect simple answers.

'The Brits in particular have this need to sort everything out and put it in the right drawer, otherwise there's a bit of fear that things might get out of control, and with the Poles...so many things are spur of the moment.'

'D'you think the Poles are a little more spontaneous perhaps?'

'Very spontaneous…more impulsive and unpredictable than the Brits,' she nods as if surprising herself with a simple answer. 'We seem to function OK in the European Union and we do the right thing and progress according to the plans, but it just doesn't seem to be the real us, you know.'

As we're talking we look out over Warsaw from the chilly ramparts on the thirtieth floor of the Palace of Culture. This is a building of massive bulk, heavy-hipped and tall-towered. Stalin gave it to the city in 1952 to show how important Poland was to the USSR.

'Apparently he gave us a choice,' smiles Monika, 'you either get a metro system or a Palace of Culture, and we said, "Oh, can we have a metro," and he said, "OK, I'll give you the Palace."'

'But you've got a metro now, so you're all right.'

'Yes, but not thanks to Stalin.'

This colossus, a gigantic marking of the territory, was much disliked and there was talk of taking it down, but like Ceausescu's Palace in Bucharest, its greatest achievement was that it defied demolition. It was just too big to remove. So now, long after Stalin, the Palace of Culture is reluctantly accepted as a Warsaw landmark, possibly the Warsaw landmark, and everyone is trying to like it and be positive about its theatres and swimming pools and the Congress Hall where interminable political speeches and announcements of Five Year Plans have been superseded by Bob Dylan concerts and Miss World Competitions.

The view from the thirtieth floor is spectacular but there is frustratingly little spectacle to see. Warsaw was once compared with Paris, but after eighty-five per cent of it was destroyed in the war, it never recovered its grace or beauty.

Monika agrees.

'It's not a beautiful city, but it's a brave city, and a working city. A good down-to-earth city of people who have busy lives. I have a lot of respect for it.'

It may not dazzle from a distance, but down at street level Warsaw has some intriguing areas, and the comparisons with Paris become less fanciful when we walk through the squares and cobbled alleyways of the entirely rebuilt Old Town. Suddenly Warsaw becomes less functional and more mysterious. It seems extraordinary that the grey concrete apartment blocks are of the same age as the Baroque and classical façades, re-created from piles of rubble in the 1950s, with the help of drawings left behind by Canaletto's nephew, Bernardo Bellotto.

I ask Monika how much the war still means to young Poles. She's adamant that there is no other nation as conscious of its history.

'You read in your primary school about soap made of people's flesh, and people's hair made into handbags and it all happened to the generation of your parents.'

Then she checks herself.

'But I think it also makes us want to catch up, and show that the potential's still there and we're not slaves of our past.'

'Does anyone in Poland still learn Russian?'

'Not any more. I think the reaction is rather going the other way at the moment, and it's a shame. I mean who wouldn't want to read Dostoevsky or Pushkin in the original. It's a beautiful language.'

It starts to rain. Miss Vietnam, being photographed in a picturesque corner of the Old Town Square, gathers up her shimmering gold *ao-dai* and is whisked away.

'I think Poland in its entirety is now pro-Western, but with certain islands of traditionalism that's not pro-Russian or pro-anything. It's more sort of guarding our identity. This is always a big issue as our identity has been taken away from us on so many occasions.'

A traditional end to the day at a restaurant called, after the mountain region of the south, Podhale. It's a people's palace of a place with lots of old-style beamed rooms and food for those who work in the fields all day. Massive helpings of everything. I have beetroot soup and chicken escalope with *oscypek*, smoked goat's cheese, others have sets of spare ribs the length of a vibraphone. Mountainous beers and two in-house vodkas. All of which just about helped to deal with a tuba and accordion player serenading us with 'Zorba the Greek'.

Day One Hundred and Two: *Poznań*

Poznań is another fine example of an old city centre reconstructed, and the houses around the Stary Rynek (the Old Square) are as handsome as any in Warsaw. There's industry as well as culture here and it was at the Stalin Engineering Works in Poznań that, in 1956, there took place the first ever labour protests in the post-war Soviet bloc. Security forces killed over fifty people in suppressing the protest, which was a forerunner of the later shipyard strikes in Gdańsk.

Despite having been frequently occupied by Germany up till the end of the Second World War, this part of Poland, called Wielkopolska, is considered the heartland of the nation – where Poland sprang from.

I spent most of yesterday's relaxing two-and-a-half-hour train ride here from Warsaw in the dining car. It was of the traditional, and increasingly rare, sort, with lamps on the tables, freshly prepared food, even books on a rack, and no-one bullying you to move on. In this congenial atmosphere I read more of Eva Hoffman's *Lost In Translation*, a finely written memoir of a Jewish girl who grew up in Kraków and eventually, driven by wartime pogroms and post-war anti-Semitism, left her native Poland to live in America.

She's an acute analyst of human behaviour and echoes what Monika was telling me about the Polish temperament. Hoffman was always pleased when her work at school was described as having *polot*, 'a word that combines the meanings of dash, inspiration and flying. *Polot* is what everyone wants to have in personality as well. Being correct and dull is a horrid misfortune.'

In that case, I'm in for a very Polish morning, with *polot* in abundance, for I'm to drive the 8.58 scheduled rail service that covers the 50 miles from Poznań to Wolsztyn (the 'sz' is pronounced as 'sh').

In 1997 a British railway enthusiast, Howard Jones, persuaded the Poles to give him access to some of the last surviving steam-hauled services in Europe, and to let him run a driving course on one of their branch lines. Which is why I'm here on an overcast morning with a bit of bite in the air, changing into overalls and a cap and feeling distinctly nervous, for two particular reasons. One concerns whether or not I shall be able to understand my Polish co-driver and instructor Janos, 'a lovely bloke' according to the compulsively reassuring Howard. He has a few words of English, but once in the cab with all the clatter and hissing and roaring of the boiler could be talking Albanian, or indeed Polish.

Poznań Central is not a station for beginners. For a start, it's on the Paris-Berlin-Moscow main line. Twenty-coach trans-European expresses come through here, and at this time of the morning they're swelled by commuter trains rolling thick and fast into Poland's fifth biggest city. The Wolsztyn train consists of only two coaches, one clean, the other very dirty indeed, but they are drawn by a monster of a locomotive. For those who like these details, it's a 2-6-4, which means it has twelve wheels. It's a menacing sooty-black colour with windshields on either side of the boiler and a freshly filled tender. Its number is 0149 and it bears the white eagle motif of Polish Regional Railways, and, confusingly, the name 'Bob Wyatt'.

My other, more serious, concern is that this isn't just about me and Janos, messing about on the footplate. There are passengers on the train. Good people who only want to get from Poznań to Wolsztyn on time and alive.

I watch them climbing aboard. A sensible woman in a head-scarf and long skirt carrying a bag of shopping. An elderly man with grey hair and a briefcase, and a couple actually running to get a seat.

Howard's reassurance technique merely terrifies me further. Lots of the people who come on this course have never driven a train before, he says comfortingly, then adds that Janos will take over whenever we meet the main line. *Meet the main line?*

I help the fireman shovel some coal into the firebox and Janos who has a big, droopy grey moustache in the Lech Walesa style, beams indulgently down at me. I try hard to impress, so hard that my shovel cracks into the side of the gate and sends coal flying across the floor of the cab. He beams even more indulgently as he watches me clear it up.

The moment of departure comes and as Janos eases us out of the station, and Poznań slowly recedes, I make a mental note of everything he does. Not that it makes things much easier when the time comes for me to take control. Utterly spoilt by power-steering and automatic transmission, it takes me some considerable time to realise that moving the regulator alone requires brute strength. Janos heaves it up and down with one hand whereas I find I have to grasp it like a hammer-thrower. I kick the bar underneath the reverser to release the steam and the engine moves slowly forward with a series of deep throaty grunts. There's no time to sit and enjoy it until the gears are gone through, which requires a series of rolling turns of the reverser wheel as demanding as anything you'll do in a gym. Then comes the moment when everything's in place and, apart from keeping a hand on the whistle and an eye out for any crossings, the great beast is belting along, swaying and shaking like we're in a stampede. An iron horse indeed.

Fifty miles per hour seems awfully fast as the silver birch groves crowd the train so close that you have to pull your head in for fear of a twig taking an eye out, and alarmed deer veer from cover and race away across the fields. In the cab of this great, hot, heaving monster I feel a strange serenity, a sense of power and recklessness at the same time. Pure *polot*. Though we're big and strong and fast, we're completely dependent on those two slim, almost ephemeral rails stretching, dipping and curving into the distance.

An hour and fifty minutes later, I'm just beginning to get the hang of it as we enter the last curve into Wolsztyn station. Janos doesn't, thank God, trust me with the buffers and he brings us to a dignified halt. The remaining passengers disembark without, it seems, a care in the world. I'm happy, grimy and trembling ever so slightly.

More than anything else the experience is a reminder of the physical effort required to drive a steam locomotive. No buttons to push or computers to do the thinking for you. The 8.58 from Poznań to Wolsztyn has only further increased my respect for the engine drivers I watched with such envy fifty years ago.

Howard tells me I've done well. His parting words have an almost Churchillian ring. I will be, he tells me solemnly, one of only a tiny handful of people able to say they have driven a steam locomotive on a scheduled service in the twenty-first century.

Thank you Bob Wyatt, whoever you are.

Day One Hundred and Three: *Częstochowa*

Yesterday it was Wielkopolska (Greater Poland) and today we continue south into Malopolska (Little Poland). In truth, there seems little difference between the two. Rolling farmland for mile after mile with barely a hill to be seen. The flatlands of the Great European Plain, which has through the years made Poland so vulnerable to the invader.

From the late eighteenth century, when an ascendant Russia wiped her off the map, to the end of the First World War in 1918, Poland ceased to exist as a nation. Russia, Germany and the Austro-Hungarian empire redistributed her territory among themselves.

It was a sad time for a country that had been among the most progressive, successful and influential in Europe. One of the great strengths that held the Polish spirit together during these dark times was their Catholic faith. Right down to the Soviet years after the Second World War, it was their religion that proved to be the unbendable backbone of the people. If Lech Walesa's potent strikes had begun the process of bringing down communism he could never have achieved what he did without the moral support of Pope John Paul II.

The unprepossessing city of Częstochowa is the religious capital of the country, and to come here is to understand how profoundly important is the Catholic faith to most Poles. In the fourteenth century an order of monks, followers of the hermit St Paul of Thebes, arrived here and were given sanctuary by King Ladislaus II, who not only let them establish a monastery but endowed it with an icon, a Madonna and Child believed by some to have been painted by St Luke on a table-top from Nazareth. It's been more soberly dated to the twelfth century. As a result of a special varnish applied over the tempera, as well as age and constant exposure to burning incense, it began to turn darker and darker and eventually became known as the Black Madonna.

There seems precious little that is hermitic about the Pauline order today. Their monastery, on a broad hill called Jasna Góra (Clear Mountain), is in a tall-spired complex of buildings, ringed in the seventeenth century by mighty red-brick walls. It is the centre of an enormous commercial and spiritual enterprise based on the growing reputation of her most priceless possession.

In 1655 Jasna Góra withstood a siege by greatly superior Swedish forces and this established the reputation of the Madonna, which came to be seen not just as a miracle-worker but as the symbol of national identity. A presence so potent, they called her Mary, Queen of Poland.

In the years when the name of Poland vanished from the map the reputation of Mary only grew. She was seen as the protector of the Catholic faith against the invasions of Russian Orthodoxy and German Protestantism.

The new Europe, with its secular values and increasing consumerism, has not dented her popularity and between three and four million pilgrims visit the shrine every year. Eighty-five priests and thirty lay brothers are on hand to deal with the tide of humanity that pours through the doors of this great Baroque church. Most are heading for the sacristy, in which the Black Madonna is housed. It's a dark, enclosed little chapel decorated with exquisitely carved wood, but whose few pews can take only the monks and their visitors. The icon is hidden behind a silver screen and there is growing excitement as the time approaches for it to be revealed, as it is with great ceremony twice a day. A stream of devotees make circuits of the chapel on their knees, chanting, singing and supplicating. Worshippers squeeze shoulder to shoulder, desperate for a clear view and those fortunate enough to be in the front have their faces pressed hard up against the iron-work screen that divides off the Chapel of the Miraculous Image from the rest of the church.

The pent-up emotion reaches a climax as one o'clock strikes and, to the sound of a stirring brass fanfare from a band of monks up in the gallery, the silver screen slowly rises to reveal the Black Madonna. It's a curiously unsatisfactory piece of work, not much more than a metre square, with the faces so indistinct and swarthy that they have been augmented by a rich robe of gold, silver and precious stones draped around the figures of the Mother and Child like clothes on a doll.

But its appearance produces near-hysteria. Everyone pushes forward. Breasts are crossed repeatedly, tears roll down faces contorted by agony and joy as the sounds of the fanfare echo and fade into silence. It's a hot day and a rank smell of sweat rises from the body of the church.

My guide, Father Tomon, with big square glasses dominating a round, regular face, shakes his head in wonder at the scene. He remembers the days twenty years ago when the police and the army were a constant threat to any religious display. Now they have special days set aside for them to worship.

We're taken for lunch in a beautiful refectory with a curved stuccoed ceiling. Here we meet Father Tomon's superior, Father Simon, the senior man in the monastery's slick public affairs department.

He's enthusiastic and energetic and talks unstoppably. He stems the flow briefly, to offer us some wine.

Then he looks expectantly towards me.

'I hear you are a comedian.'

I always dread moments like this and mutter apologetically about never being able to remember jokes.

Father Simon's face widens.

'Jokes?' He beams with satisfaction. 'I have 300 of them.'

At that moment a mobile phone rings and he hoicks up his habit and begins to rifle around in voluminous white robes. No-one mentions divine intervention, but there are certainly some sighs of relief.

Two hours south of Częstochowa the small farms and featureless fields give way to a man-made mess of a landscape as we skirt the heavy industrial conurbations of Silesia, which sit on top of huge coalfields, said by some to contain one-tenth of the world's known reserves, and bitterly fought over in the past by Poles and Germans.

We follow the railway, down a side road, and across the River Wisła, which we've followed across Poland all the way from Gdańsk and Warsaw. It's getting towards the end of the day as we reach a threadbare little town, with a BP filling station, five-storey pre-fab housing blocks, a dry-cleaner's, a football pitch, some tennis courts, and a park by the willow-lined banks of a small river through which parents are bringing children home from school. This is Oświęcim, our home for the night.

It's better known by its German name. Auschwitz.

Day One Hundred and Four: *Oświęcim*

It's a little before six o'clock on an autumn morning and a church bell is tolling in the town as I walk in through the surprisingly narrow gate of what was the first Auschwitz concentration camp. Another was built later at Birkenau, just outside the town, where the Nazis committed murder on an industrial scale.

This camp was originally a Polish army barracks. The SS officers who, in 1940, were charged with the task of expanding it into a slave-labour camp for Polish political prisoners wrote in some disgust of the conditions they found here; how smelly and insanitary and dirty it was.

They set about building eight new blocks and adding an extra storey to the twenty that already existed, all in carefully matching red brick. They planted trees, poplars and oaks and silver birches, now tall and mature. They surrounded the camp with double fences of electrified and barbed wire, dug walls 6 feet below the ground to prevent tunnelling, and above the gate they raised a sign with black letters inside an almost jaunty ribbon of ironwork, spelling out the words '*Arbeit Macht Frei*'. Work Brings Freedom. Leaving this ghoulish, apparently un-ironic motto behind me, I walk in among the long, low blocks. There is nothing about the buildings themselves that is particularly menacing. They could be workshops in the Midlands. We had buildings like this at my public school. The green grass is well kept and the trees majestic. The only way to comprehend what happened here is through the imagination. I stop not far from the gate and close my eyes and try to think myself into the mind of someone else standing here, not that long ago, perhaps a year or so before I was born. I can turn round and leave whenever I want, walk back through the gates and have a cup of coffee. The same me, sixty-five years ago would find those gates closed, rifles trained on me by those who despised me and orders barked out by those who knew they could send me to my death without any compunction.

Because the camp is now a museum, there are signs which help the act of imagination: 'The camp orchestra had to assemble here to play marches while the prisoners filed past. This would keep the prisoners in step and help to count them as they went to and from work.' And a little further on, 'If a Polish prisoner escaped, the family members were arrested and sent to Auschwitz. They were made to stand under a sign announcing the reason for their arrest.' In case this sounds brutal but bearable, the next sign by the pathway is uncompromising. 'Within five months of the opening of this camp, some nine thousand had died. Most of them of hunger, hard work and brutality.'

Inside the prison blocks is a series of displays that I find more affecting than any words. Behind long panes of glass are gathered the possessions of those who perished here. I'm grateful to have been here early enough to film the camp before the public come through, for there is something deeply affecting as I walk on through the silent rooms to be confronted in one by a pile of human hair, 80 feet long and 10 feet deep, some of the seven tons shorn from victims and discovered by the Soviet troops who liberated Auschwitz in 1945; in another by the almost unbearable sight of a sea of suitcases in which the inmates had kept their most prized possessions. Battered, squeezed, crushed and tossed onto a pile, bearing the names of their owners, printed, painted or inked on the outside.

'Hann, Irene'…'Coernitz, Francesca'…'Lise Morgenstern'…'Dr Rosenfeldt'. One abandoned suitcase has a name and birth date on it. 'L. Godootkirk, 11.10.05'. A little younger than my mother.

Equally poignant are the piles of children's shoes. One is of red leather, which stands out from the rest and must have been bought and worn with pride. Discarded in death, it lies on the pile, its strap open as if it had just been thrown off at the end of a busy day.

By the car park for the museum is a low building with grass up its side and a brick chimney sticking out of it. This was the armoury of the barracks, converted by the SS into the first gas chamber at

Auschwitz. I walk into it. It's a long low dark space, maybe 150 feet long, 20 feet wide and 10 feet high. The dimensions of a small nightclub. In the next-door room are two of the three furnaces where those who had been gassed could be instantly cremated. Three hundred and fifty bodies could be dealt with daily. By late 1941 it was not nearly enough.

In order to cope with the demands of the Final Solution, the decision was taken to build another, much larger, camp specifically geared to extermination.

The site chosen was the village of Brzezinka (Birkenau in German), less than 2 miles from Oświęcim. Having removed the inhabitants and knocked down their houses (carefully reusing the bricks to build the new camp) the SS and their forced labourers built Auschwitz II-Birkenau, 300 accommodation sheds covering 170 hectares of boggy countryside. Much of the camp has been preserved and the long gatehouse with its pitched and tiled roof and central watchtower with the railway line running through it is grimly familiar from documentaries and films like *Schindler's List*.

I had always imagined this dreadful place to be utterly isolated in some apocryphal landscape, yet there are houses not half a mile from the camp, and quite substantial houses too, with balconies that look out at the evening sun and the perimeter fence beyond which over a million people were murdered.

I walk along the railway line that leads deep into the camp. It comes to an end beside the remains of the five gas chambers, half-destroyed by the retreating Germans. Each one was three times bigger than any at Auschwitz I, and by 1944 they were killing up to 7,000 people a day from all over Europe and the USSR. Today, school parties scramble around over grassy banks whose earth is mixed with the ashes of those who died here. Beyond a line of trees, I can see the roof of a farmhouse.

The fact that the Auschwitz camps remain open as museums is surely right, but to walk through them is still an aseptic experience. The cries and screams of separated families, the visceral malodour of so many people squeezed into such little space, the stench of the crematoria, the sheer corrosive pain of the place, can only be re-created in the mind. Being here shocked and saddened me, and the physical evidence of Auschwitz should be there for ever, but

Primo Levi's *If This Is a Man* told me infinitely more of what it must have been like.

The really troubling thought, that I can't leave behind, is that I was alive when the worst of this was happening. It makes a mockery of civilisation.

Day One Hundred and Four: *Kraków*

Kraków, a mere 40 miles from the obscene ruins of Auschwitz-Birkenau, is one of the most civilised cities of Eastern Europe. The capital of Poland until 1791, it has glorious old buildings and an ancient university, founded by the great innovator King Kazimierz III, of whom it was said 'he found a Poland made of wood, and left it made of brick'. The Old Town was laid out in 1257 and, unlike Gdańsk, Warsaw and Poznań, remained unharmed by the Second World War. The mighty 500-year-old castle on Wawel Hill is the resting place of many of the great names of Polish life and culture, and even when the court moved to Warsaw in 1596, royal coronations and funerals still took place in Wawel Cathedral. It had always been a cosmopolitan city, adorned by Italian architects and builders and home to one of Europe's most thriving Jewish communities. In 1978 the Archbishop of Kraków, Karol Wojtyla, became Poland's first pope, John Paul II. His conservative Catholicism typified the city.

After the Second World War this conservatism put the city fathers in an opposite ideological camp from the communists, who were consolidating their grip on Poland after the victories of the Red Army. The communist solution was to build an entirely new city outside Kraków that would exemplify their new ideals. It would be a socialist workers' paradise, a gleaming retort to the bourgeois traditionalism of the old capital.

It was begun in 1949 and by 1960 a city of 100,000 people had risen from the fields to the east of Kraków. It was called, after its primary means of employment, Nowa Huta, literally New Steelworks.

I'm taken to see it today by Kuba (short for Jakub) Bialach, a twenty-three-year-old student with wild hair and a red goatee beard, who's writing a thesis on Nowa Huta after abandoning his previous one on the sociology of advertising.

'For me communism is history. Maybe for my parents or grandparents it's their life. But for my generation it's history. I can talk with people who are part of this. Nowa Huta is like a living monument.'

Kuba's boundless enthusiasm extends to giving highly individual tours of Nowa Huta in one of the great icons of post-war Eastern Europe, the Trabant, a people's car made in East Germany. (The Polish equivalent was the Fiat Polski.) Kuba's Trabant is a two-stroke, two-cylinder fibreglass box, churned out in virtually identical models for forty years. Although they seem cramped with two big people in the front, they were designed for four or five people and luggage. Like the housing, they were built cheaply and quickly to keep the workers happy.

As we weave out into the traffic along the embankment of the Wisła Kuba runs through some of the eccentricities of the Trabant, to my distinct discomfort. Road-holding is not its strong point. It's better, he says, to have someone else in the car, as the extra weight could be crucial in a strong wind. Over a certain speed, he says, 'it's like being on a dance floor'.

It has no petrol gauge, but if you do run out there's a reserve supply switch, he assures me, as he gropes beneath the dashboard to find it. It has a steering column stick and four gears, but the fourth can be difficult on certain days. And it leaks.

'You always know what the weather's like in a Trabant.'

He tells me all this without rancour, as if describing the vagaries of an old friend.

'Maybe once in a month the wheels may fall off,' he admits, then, catching sight of my expression, hastens to reassure me. 'Not all the wheels. Just the one wheel, you know. But, well, you are without a wheel, in the middle of the road, in the middle of traffic...'

To change the subject I ask him about the dashboard controls.

'This is for the lights, I think,' he says, as a knob comes away in his hand.

'Shall I hang on to this?'

'Yes, please!' says Kuba gratefully as he tries once again for the elusive fourth gear. When he finds it, our progress becomes rapid, and the speed, combined with the feather-light weight, gives me the distinct feeling we might at any moment become airborne. Needless to say, Kuba is on hand to sense my mood.

'The 60s is the killing speed,' he shouts cheerfully.

All I can think of as we race the trams and dodge the trucks, squirting a blue cloud of pollution behind us, is having read somewhere that the German Chancellor, Angela Merkel, was on the waiting list for one of these for twelve years. And she never got one.

As we approach Nowa Huta, now a suburb of Kraków, I notice a shiny new Philip Morris cigarette factory set in green parkland. Kuba tells me this employs 3,000 people. The great Lenin steelworks that gave Nowa Huta its name is now owned by Lakshmi Mittal, the Indian head of the global steel business Mittal Steel. The workforce has been reduced from 45,000 in the 1970s to 8,000 today.

Expecting lines of functional sheds I'm surprised by the eclectic headquarters offices of the steelworks, built in brick with a dash of Spanish Renaissance style. Kuba's explanation is that the style and scale of the buildings were designed as a riposte to Kraków, to give the people of Nowa Huta a sense of grandeur, their own Wawel Hill. Together with parks, sports facilities and good housing it would confirm the ideological point that the old buildings of Kraków were stuck in the past and that the planned proletarian city of Nowa Huta was the face of the future. Now, says Kuba, some sixty-five per cent of the inhabitants of the city of the future are pensioners.

We park the Trabant in a leafy green street and walk into a square surrounded by the stone-faced creamy-white façades of the People's Neo-Classical style. It reminds me a little of what Ceausescu was trying to do in Bucharest, but without the bombast and megalomania. It's actually rather elegant and the Italianate arcades are easy on the eye.

It's a faded Utopia. Whereas in central Kraków a square like this would be ringed with outdoor cafés, there is only one place here for refreshment. It's called the Stylowa (Stylish) Restaurant. As soon as I step inside I sense that I am in a very different world from the international tourist spots. Faces look towards me with more suspicion than interest. The service is polite but a little distant. The tablecloth has a couple of cigarette burns in it and to use the shabby lavatory requires a coin for the attendant sitting outside. A family objects to the presence of our camera.

I can understand how they feel. Life is pretty lousy here and we could easily be representatives from a gloating outside world come to stare. I have very little Polish other than the basics like 'tak', 'nie' and 'dziekuje', and 'yes', 'no' and 'thank you' aren't really enough to convey why I like the Stylowa and its uniqueness in a world where so many places are remorselessly the same. Over big, domestic cups of coffee, Kuba brings out some old maps and photos of 1950s Nowa Huta. In layout and architecture it resembles 'The Ideal City', a classic painting of the Italian Renaissance, a model used by Mussolini for a new city outside Rome. It's ironic that totalitarian architecture, whether communist or fascist, drew such inspiration from the humanist values of the Renaissance.

Kuba points out that the symmetry of the grid plan was good for authoritarian regimes. Observation was easier without nooks and crannies.

'Nowhere to hide,' as he puts it.

The building of Nowa Huta in just one decade was a great source of pride for the new communist leaders. In the early 1970s, when Fidel Castro came to Kraków, he drove straight to Nowa Huta, then flew home again. Black and white photos show happy peasants in fields transformed into happy workers in the great city they helped to build. The hammer and the sickle in perfect harmony. Ploughshares into swords.

It didn't work out. The dream city of the Stalinist planners was built well, with brick and plaster. The second wave of building in the 1960s and 1970s was based on cheap and quick concrete. The brave new world had to be protected from lower steel prices and the collapse of subsidies. Wages were cut and so was the supply of basic goods and foodstuffs.

As the 1980s wore on this socialist paradise saw some of the most violent protests against the pro-Soviet regime outside of Gdańsk. In a bitter irony, the workers of Nowa Huta became the foot soldiers of Solidarity.

Kuba and I walk through the streets. It's not a city for the young, he says, but it's well built and could be turned around, especially as a comfortable flat for two here would cost around 45,000 euros, half that of Kraków.

Turning out of an arcade we come out into the semicircular communal area I'd seen in the plans for the new city.

'This was Lenin Central Square,' Kuba tells me. Then he points to a street sign on the wall above us. It now reads: 'Plac Centralny Ronalda Reagana'.

Day One Hundred and Six: *Białka Tatrzańska*

South of Kraków we finally leave behind the wide, flat plains typical of most of Poland. As the road begins to twist and turn towards the Slovakian border it also starts to rise and fall and after clearing a 2,500-foot pass we find ourselves in Nowy Targ, the last big town we shall see. Lenin was imprisoned here in 1914, in the last days of the Austro-Hungarian empire. This is the start of the region they call Podhale, and all its signs promise a natural wonderland: skiing, walking, canoeing, climbing, a huge national park.

Everything begins to look different. The roofs of the houses grow wider and steeper, wood replaces brick, and the word Tatras keeps cropping up on signs, houses, hotels and villages.

The Tatras or Tatra Mountains are part of the Carpathian chain. They're a small range whose highest peaks are across the border in Slovakia, but the Poles make the most of them.

There's little accommodation to be had and the best we can find in the long, thin, strung-out village of Białka Tatrzańska are modest lodgings at the Pensione Stokrothka (which I'm told, though I'm not sure I believe it, means 'Pensione Daisy'). The people who have lived here the longest, the Górale, have a culture very different from anything else in the country, conditioned by life in the highlands and unchanged for centuries.

The Polish fascination with Górale culture seems to grow largely from a love of continuity in a country that has been conditioned by impermanence.

We're here at the invitation of a young couple, Beata Goryl and Mariusz Budz, both local ski instructors, who are to be married in true Górale style, with a reception at the local fire station (in the absence of village halls they are often the only places that have enough room).

We meet up with Beata at the house of her father, a vet, where she is visited by two men on horseback called *pytaci*, guardians of the ceremonial tradition and ringmasters for the day's events. They are also obliged to keep up a steady stream of observations, verses and general ribaldry in high falsetto voices.

Beata, who is small and lovely in a white dress, patiently bears a cap with a metre-long tail made of plaited pine branches that hangs way down her back, and which she cannot remove until every obstacle to her marrying Mariusz has been removed.

The *pytaci* are despatched to fetch the bridegroom from his house. He's expected to put up a token show of resistance, but within the hour they're back, not just with him but with a covered wagon with a band in it and ten horse-drawn coaches.

If Beata looks long-suffering, Mariusz, in thick woollen trousers, wide leather belt, grey, ermine-trimmed waistcoat and round-brimmed black hat with a white feather in it, looks plain terrified. I'm not surprised. Two fiddlers and a cellist are standing by the fence singing, the *pytaci* are improvising their witty quips and he has to go upstairs to the bedroom for the public removal of his shirt by the bride, and its replacement by a new one. Like much of the ceremony, this little ritual seems to be about renouncing old links and endorsing others.

After all this is completed, a horse-drawn carriage takes the happy couple down the road to the church for the wedding ceremony. This is a comparatively simple matter, though with ten bridesmaids and ten pages the photocall seems to take longer than the service. By mid-afternoon the guests are filing back to the upstairs room of the big, three-bayed, pointy-gabled fire station to eat and drink.

By eight o'clock the vodka, specially distilled for the wedding and bearing the names of the happy couple on its label, is beginning to take its toll, as the final moves of the day's ceremony are played out and the *pytaci* try one last time to keep the bride and groom apart.

Unfortunately they're now a little over-relaxed and losing the plot somewhat.

I feel enormous relief when Beata, deemed to have passed all the tests, is given a bonnet to replace her cap and can at last become Mrs Budz without further interference. The bridesmaids and the pages trade blurrily sung insults with each other, arms linked and weaving about like a rugby scrum on ice. I discover a potently pungent combination of vodka and *oscypek*, the smoked goat's cheese made in heaven, which I first tasted at the Podhale restaurant in Warsaw. The band, two violinists and a three-string cello, then takes over and fast and fierce and slow and decorous numbers tumble over each other in quick succession, and often at the same time. Outside the cold night air begins to tighten its grip and by midnight we're all tucked up in bed at the Daisy, completely and pathetically unable to keep up.

Day One Hundred and Seven: *The Dunajec Gorge*

Leaving Poland on a fresh, bright Sunday morning, I'm struck by the numbers of people crowding into mass. In every village the church seems to be the centre of great activity. A devout country Poland, perhaps the most devout of any we've been through.

What also strikes me as unusual are strips of richly grassed meadow with only one cow in them. I see so many of these that I have to ask someone about them. I'm told that because agricultural collectivisation was never imposed on Poland there are still two million farms in the country, of which one and a half million are smallholdings. I must say the cows look big and happy and not at all lonely. Perhaps herds should be limited to one only.

I leave Poland in style, punted down the white-waters of the River Dunajec (pronounced 'Doon-ah-yets') on rafts of lashed-together wooden pontoons by boatmen wearing black hats with leather bands studded with cowrie shells, and blue embroidered waistcoats. Short Poles using very long poles to guide us down some pretty frisky water.

Above us the jagged limestone peaks of the Pieniny Mountains rise sheer from the water in a 1,600-foot-high wall. Behind them cluster the much taller peaks they call Trzy Korony (Three Crowns) with summits over 3,000 feet. It's both a romantic and a dramatic ending to a southern progress that began in Tallinn and has, up till now, been a largely gentle meander across 700 miles of unremarkable flatlands.

The south bank of the river is in Slovakia. Despite the fact that Slovakian fishermen are allowed to catch grayling and trout from the river and the Poles aren't, the countries by all accounts are good neighbours. A wood-built Polish Catholic church faces its Slovakian Evangelical counterpart across the water. People call to each other from either bank. As we near the border town of Szczawnica, Branislav the boatman flicks his cigarette into the white-water and prepares to serenade me out of his country. Tree-fringed pinnacles tower above us. His voice echoes round the rocks, and on the Slovakian side cyclists on a riverside path stop and wave.

Slovakia

Day One Hundred and Eight: *The Tatra Mountains*

ONCE ACROSS the border the High Tatras present a sudden, precipitous and formidable barrier to further progress. It's not a long or deep mountain range but it is steep and one of the peaks, Gerlachovský, is, at 8,700 feet, the highest point in the whole Carpathian chain. Though distances are short, these craggy passes are dangerous, and the rescue teams are kept busy by those whose mountain walks suddenly become tests of survival. At the mountain hut of Téryho Chata I have a snow-lined corrie of dark and jagged rock behind me and ahead a steep descent opening onto a wide panorama of broad grassland in the middle of which, looking desperately conspicuous, are the concrete blocks of Poprad. Beyond them the Lower Tatra range begins. Not as spiky and pinnacled as the mountains around me now, but it's enough to make me curious to get at Slovakia.

The first village we visit proves that mountains and rivers don't always make hard boundaries. Ždiar, on the eastern end of the High Tatras, is a Górale village, home to the same mountain people we watched getting married in Poland. Both Slav peoples, relations are cordial between Poles and Slovaks. I'm met by Alena, a petite, good-looking Slovak with short chestnut hair whose almost flawless English comes from having spent time in Britain, where she met a Welshman called Rick in Ipswich and married him. They've since come out to Slovakia and bought a house in the village.

Alena learnt dances and folk songs from the age of five – 'something I really missed about the UK' – and this later earned her a special passport to travel outside the country in the days when Slovakia and the Czech Republic were still Czechoslovakia and a satellite state of the USSR.

Since then she has seen the 'Velvet Revolution' of 1989, in which Czechoslovakia peacefully parted from the Soviet bloc, and four years later the 'Velvet Divorce', in which her country parted from its Czech neighbour after seventy-five years of marriage.

Alena felt a bit cheated by the lack of popular consultation over the decision to split. Despite the Czechs and Slovaks having much in common, including a language, the politicians put a fait accompli deal together in 1992. After being cut loose, Slovakia lived very much in the Czech shadow. Its sense of identity can't have been helped by the creation of another new state, Republika Slovenija (Slovenia), not at all to be confused with Slovenská Republika (Slovakia). Recently, though, the Slovak economy has begun to move and opposition to the Velvet Divorce is dwindling.

It's hard to know how politics affects these traditional, change-resistant Górale areas. Wages are low and many need a second job to survive. Since the fall of communism, the people of this struggling rural economy have found fewer jobs in farms and sawmills and more in tourism and the Tatra National Park. They still cling to old ways though, such as slaughtering livestock at home, something that European Union legislation would like to see outlawed, but which has been going on here for centuries.

In a barn attached to a log-cabin home, a very large pig is hauled out of its sty and despatched with a bolt between the eyes from point-blank range. It tips to one side, but doesn't lie still for an uncomfortably long time as the muscle spasms work through the nervous system.

Three men are in charge of the slaughtering. All are into middle age; one is short and portly with a blue cap and little moustache, another has a belly so round and prominent he could be carrying twins. The third is tall, thin and gawky, with the face of a northern comedian of the 1950s. There's no embarrassment about the killing. Indeed, once the throat is cut, two of the executioners, grinning from ear to ear, sit astride the pig to squeeze the blood out.

'Good job I worked in a hospital,' Alena mutters.

The tall one fetches his accordion and plays a tune or two, as children run in and out to take a look.

The pig is carried out by hand, no mean feat as it weighs 240 kilos, and into a hollowed-out wood bath. Then a long and complex shaving process begins. Resin is rubbed into the bristles and water boiled on two wood-burning stoves is poured over the carcass. The hair is further loosened by running a chain beneath the body whilst the boiling water is poured on, after which the skin is scraped with knives and abrasive scrubbers. The pig lies back in the bath, legs akimbo, chalk-white and very naked, like some huge industrialist in a massage parlour.

A bottle of *slivovitz*, the local plum brandy, is passed around as the men take a rest before the next part of what is a very physical process. A triangular scaffold is erected above the tub, hooks are attached to the carcass and it is hauled, with great effort, up into a vertical position. Then the demolition of the pig begins. This is part surgery, part carpentry, part brute force. Hammer, axe and knife are used in equal measure. The head is removed and carefully cleaned, a blow-torch being applied to remove the most resistant bristles. The ribcage and backbone are knocked through with a series of heavy blows.

Soon the whole area beside the house is full of activity as bits of pig are distributed to every available vessel, from huge pots to buckets and bowls. When I go for a pee in the house, I find the bath and basin full of pig parts.

Within a couple of hours almost everything has been processed by hand. Rather too literally, I fear, as I notice one of the men has a small plaster around the end of his finger, which certainly wasn't there earlier.

I rather baulked at scraping the dead pig, but can't resist when invited to help make sausages. This involves attaching recycled stomach lining to a mincer (the only piece of machinery used in the entire process), feeding in the meat and turning a handle. It sounds easy enough but I turn it with such an excess of zeal that my first sausage is over a yard long and the old ladies scream at me to stop.

There is a very good meal at the end of the process. Carvers, carriers, cooks and camera crew sit at tables in a small wood-fenced garden outside the log cabin, with the snow-capped Tatras at our backs, eating liver and pork escalopes that were walking around only a few hours earlier. And as they eat they sing. The leader of the pig slaughterers fancies himself as a bit of a tenor but *slivovitz* has got the better of him by now and he starts songs with violent passion and several keys too high, only to turn bright red with the effort and relapse into surly silence a moment later. Then, just when everyone thinks he's given up, he starts again, this time something low and deeply mournful, which seems to get the mood all wrong. In the end he and the other men are left to mutter blearily whilst the women, gathered together on another table, sing sweetly and gracefully. And they know all the words.

Czech Republic

Day One Hundred and Nine: *Tatra Mountains to Brno*

THE RIDE across Slovakia to the Czech border is along good, almost empty four-lane highway through lovely countryside of low hills and modest, heavily wooded gorges, following the east bank of the Váh River to the town of Trenčín, with a rugged, rambling castle towering romantically above it. Crossing to the west bank we soon reach one of the newest borders in Europe, established after Slovakia parted from the Czech Republic.

We're now in the land of Southern Moravia, once part of the short-lived but resoundingly named Great Moravian Empire, which those ubiquitous Slav missionaries, Cyril (creator of the Cyrillic 'Russian' script) and Methodius reached way back in the ninth century.

Brno, the capital of Moravia, receives apathetic reviews in most of the guidebooks. Some refer slightingly to its part in the Industrial Revolution, when, boosted by coal reserves and water power from fast-flowing rivers, it earned the sobriquet 'the Manchester of Moravia'.

From a distance it has a striking skyline, dominated by the two tall sharp-spired towers of St Peter's Cathedral and the massive Spilberk Castle. It may be a little lugubrious in the centre, but I find it pleasantly free of tourist crowds, and if you look carefully there are surprises.

One is at the little Seven and a Half Theatre, a small functional space saved from closure by the Brno Art College next door and today the venue for, amongst others, Turba's mime classes. Mime was always popular in Czechoslovakia and Turba was one of its finest practitioners. At the beginning of the 1970s he and others were heavily criticised by the Russians for dealing with things like human isolation and solitude, which were considered unnecessarily negative and contrary to socialist ideals. He refused to change and left Czechoslovakia for Denmark, France and Switzerland. Others agreed to change their material and he doesn't blame them.

'They needed money to eat, to…make theatre, to…write, so they made a thousand compromises in order to come closer to their love.'

Turba, a big man with a head of snow-white hair and a ruddy face dominated by a powerful beak of a nose, has now returned home, but his back gives him problems so he performs less and spends more time teaching a class of what he calls movement artists. He asks me to join them for a session. I've always been resistant to mime, admiring it in others but unable to get to grips with it myself, so why I end up impersonating a cockerel in Brno, God only knows, but I put it largely down to Turba's powerful, persuasive, gently applied charisma.

Apart from his intimidating instruction at the start of each exercise – 'Preparation for art – Now!' – I enjoy being drawn in and Turba's authoritative but soft-voiced suggestions create such an intimacy that I forget feeling silly and go for it. We play mirrors and use masks and imitate dogs and farmyard animals, and I find myself thoroughly enjoying the ability to communicate with a group of Czech students without being able to speak a word of their language.

When we go for a coffee one of the students pays me the ultimate compliment.

'We have only seen young people doing this.'

The afternoon train from Brno to Prague is a smart, modern tilting one on its way from Vienna to Berlin. There is some poignancy in all this for Prague was, back in the fourteenth century, the capital of the Holy Roman Empire, a golden city at the heart of Europe, quite overshadowing faction-racked Vienna, with Berlin a mere trading outpost in the distant north.

A combination of poor rulers and being on the losing, Protestant, side in fierce religious wars turned the tables and from the mid-seventeenth to the early twentieth centuries, it was the Hapsburg capital of Vienna that took Prague's place at the hub of Central Europe.

As we glide, tiltless, across the flat plain, out of what was once Moravia and into what was once Bohemia, I think back to the last time I saw Prague. It was in the 1980s and when I asked the friend who was showing me around what was happening in his country he moved me, smoothly but firmly, into the middle of the street where, he told me in a low aside, it was safer to talk. Politics was dangerous then.

Day One Hundred and Eleven: *Prague*

On yesterday's day of rest I saw enough of Prague to be aware of how dramatically it has changed. The architecture is as striking as I remember it, the city as beautiful, but now it is open, welcoming and anxious to please, and you can talk about anything, anywhere. The 'Golden Mile', running from St Vitus' Cathedral and the castle through Malá Strana (the Little Quarter), across Charles Bridge to the Old Town Square, must be one of the most over-appreciated stretches of any capital in Europe. In the high tourist time of day – from nine till five – a thick, slow-moving crowd clogs this lucrative artery, making it impossible to get a sense of anything except other people. Prague is endlessly hospitable and seems as much at ease with the night-time adventurer as the daytime masses. Quite late at night I saw vehicles, looking like converted jeeps, offering rides to the nearest brothel. I also saw a group of medics from Portsmouth, bowling down through Wenceslas Square, all dressed identically in green surgical overalls. They were pissed as newts and yet the Czech people I was with seemed to take it quite philosophically. And they were policemen.

Tour groups generally stick to a predictable route, on either side of which, even a few yards away, all can be quiet. I spent much of my day off, almost undisturbed, in an enchanting courtyard at the back of the majestic Týn Church, with a stack of English-language newspapers picked up from the Big Ben Bookshop. Attuned as I am now to stories from the countries I've just got to know, I'm pleased to read that Poland and Ukraine have been chosen to host the 2012 European Soccer Championships. This is counterbalanced by more sinister news: of bombs thrown at the home of a liberal journalist in Belgrade, and of three people printing and publishing Bibles found with their throats slit in eastern Turkey.

I think of the import of such events as I arrive this morning at the Café Slavia, a time-honoured rendezvous for writers, artists and those of an independent mind, or, as they were known in the old days, dissidents. It's an un-dandified, Art Deco establishment with marble floors, big mirrors, Thonet chairs and rows of banquette seating.

I take coffee with Norbert Auerbach, a clever, charming, combative octogenarian, born in Vienna but brought up in Prague. He left the city, as many of the more fortunate Jews did, just before Hitler moved in, returning to Europe with the American army in 1944. He's now living in Prague again after a lifetime's work in the international film business. I ask him how difficult things were for film production in the post-war period (one of my favourite Czech films, Jiri Menzel's *Closely Observed Trains*, won the Oscar for best foreign film in 1967).

'Prague under the communists was a grey, sad city,' he says, eyes narrowing as he looks over my shoulder towards the river and the green slopes of parkland beyond.

'But for people like film-makers it was a paradise. The communist government subsidised all the films. Profit was forbidden. If you made a profit you were exploiting the proletariat. They were shooting thirty, thirty-five films a year, against ten or twelve now.'

He nods and a smile of recollection crosses his face.

'They had these wonderful things under the communists. In the smaller theatres in the countryside they could only play a film if more than ten people bought a ticket. If they didn't there was no performance and the projectionist didn't get paid, so if there was no-one in the theatre the projectionist would buy ten tickets himself.'

He holds a hand up before I can ask another question.

'Did you hear the story about the Russian projectionist who

got a Stalin Prize? He showed a two-hour picture in an hour and a half!'

He chuckles for quite a while at this, before nodding to himself.

'Yes, the one thing the communists did respect was culture.'

He reiterates the point I've heard so often on this journey, that the nostalgia for communism is still strong amongst the older generation. The Party is alive and well in the Czech Republic, picking up twelve per cent of the vote in the last election.

Norbert cautions against thinking that the EU can ever become the same thing as a United States of Europe.

'Ninety-nine per cent of people who went to the United States wanted to become Americans.' It's different here. 'Most Czechs,' he thinks, 'don't understand what Europe is about, what is a European and what it involves when you start talking about "yes constitution" or "no constitution". Tell a Czech to move to Austria and wear leather pants, he's going to tell you you're completely crazy.'

We order more coffees.

'The French have always wanted to be French because they believe they're the best. The Germans are only now emerging from that guilt feeling of what happened prior to and in the Second World War. The Italians are confused in everything they do, and I think the Czechs are secure in being Czechs with Czech traditions and a Czech way of life.'

I ask him what that is.

'We're a very intelligent, well-educated nation; good workers, not aggressively commercial, like the Americans, let's say. And the weekend is sacred! You tell someone to work on Saturday…'

He waves his hands in mock indignation.

'…Oh my God! Are you crazy?'

In that case, I ask him, who are all these people making money from the tourists on the Golden Mile, seven days a week?

He answers smartly, and with a rueful grin.

'Russians.'

Day One Hundred and Twelve: *Prague and Terezín*

One of the things most Eastern and Central European countries have in common is the disappearance of their Jewish communities as a result of persecution. Prague had a particularly strong Jewish community numbering hundreds of thousands. Now there are perhaps 7,000 in a city of over a million.

Many, like the family of Norbert Auerbach, whom I talked to yesterday, emigrated before the Second World War. Of those who stayed, very few survived the Nazi genocide. Even fewer still are inclined to talk about it. One woman who did, and does, has agreed to meet me today.

Lisa Mikova was in her teens when the German invasion of Czechoslovakia began a sequence of events that led her eventually to Auschwitz. Her experiences are quite beyond most people's comprehension, yet here she is to greet me, a short, composed eighty-six-year-old, very much at ease with herself. Her white hair is perfectly cut and she's dressed with quiet good taste in a stone-coloured coat and silk scarf over a blue cardigan and a crisp white cotton blouse. Her eyes, big and moist, are her most expressive feature. It's as if everything she's been through can be read in them.

Lisa and I walk through the old Jewish cemetery. The gravestones, in weathered sandstone, stand at odd angles, tipping this way and that, crowding every inch of the gently sloping mounds as if about to burst out of the earth. Some are broken and their inscriptions indistinct but they're being restored at the rate of a hundred a year.

Lisa came from an affluent Prague family who thought of themselves as Czechs first and Jews afterwards. They spoke Czech and German fluently. Despite rumours of what was happening elsewhere in Europe, they felt safe in their reasonably well-off, well-educated democracy where Jews were happily assimilated. As soon as the Nazis arrived and started to apply the anti-Jewish Nuremberg Laws everything changed, and changed very fast indeed. Her father's business was confiscated, and he and Lisa's mother lost their jobs.

'We had to leave our schools. We couldn't enter a swimming pool or a cinema or a theatre. Doctors were not allowed to work in the hospital and lawyers could not appear in court. We always thought it can't be worse, and it came always worse, and worse and worse.' She tells me this carefully, with no trace of bitterness or self-pity, but when we go into the Pinkas synagogue which borders the cemetery she finds it harder to keep her emotions in check.

On the walls of what has been a place of worship for over 500 years are marked the names of all those Jews from Bohemia and Moravia who perished in the concentration camps. Seventy-seven thousand, two hundred and ninety-seven names.

I ask her how different this is for her from the cemetery outside. She stops at the end of one wall and looks closely.

'Here are my parents. Only their names. They have no graves.'

Twenty of her close family are listed on the wall, including a brother shot in Dachau three days before the Americans liberated the camp.

She sighs.

'I don't like it very much to come here. It's too emotional for me. I really don't like it.'

She straightens up and takes a deep breath, and we walk outside again.

Two years into the war the Nazis began moving the Jewish population out of Prague. They established a ghetto in the old garrison town of Theresienstadt, or, in Czech, Terezín, an hour north of the city towards the German border. Dominated by two long, low brick fortresses, built by the Hapsburg Empéror Josef II in 1780 to defend his northern borders, it was cleared of its civil population in mid-1942 and replaced with 50,000 Jews from all over Europe, among them Lisa, her new husband and her parents.

She arrived here in the depths of winter, on her twentieth birthday, and today, sixty-six years on, she's returned.

At first glance Terezín seems pleasant enough. The town is laid out in a typical neo-classical Central European pattern. There is a large central square full of sweet chestnut trees and, amongst them, a statue of Jan Hus, the early-fifteenth-century religious reformer and Czech national hero, burnt at the stake for criticising the Catholic Church. There's something wrong with the place though. The atmosphere is odd. It's almost empty for a start.

There are plans, I'm told, to try and revive it by locating parts of Prague University out here, but for now it remains a ghost town, cursed, perhaps, by its past. As a transit point for Auschwitz and the extermination camps of the east, 144,000 people came through Terezín; 33,000 died here and of the 88,000 sent on to the camps, just under 5,000 survived.

'There was no railway station here,' Lisa remembers, 'so we had to go by foot about 4 kilometres, with all our luggage...and the German SS was always around us with dogs.'

Families were split up, men in one part of the camp, women in the other. The men's quarters are now a Ghetto Museum, over whose entrance is inscribed the word 'Remember', in Hebrew. The walls of the stairwell are covered from top to bottom with paintings by inmates of the Terezín ghetto. A snowman, a vase of flowers, a queue at a soup kitchen. As painting was forbidden, these seemingly innocuous works represented acts of considerable defiance. Lisa tells me that during the war some of them were smuggled out of Terezín and published in a Swedish newspaper. The artists were identified, rooted out and had their hands crushed.

There is a cinema in the museum which shows a Nazi propaganda film made in Terezín to fool the Red Cross into thinking that this was, as the commentary has it, 'Hitler's City for the Jews'. Before the Red Cross arrived the place would be cleaned up, football matches and concerts encouraged and everyone ordered to smile. And it worked. Not once, but twice. The Red Cross left Terezín alone, and the 'transports' resumed. In 1944 Lisa's husband was put on one to Auschwitz. A few weeks later the womenfolk were given the chance of 'joining their families'. She agreed to go, but never saw her parents again, and never met her husband in Auschwitz.

She survived the death camp and was removed to Dresden to work in an aircraft factory, witnessing the great raid of February 1945 from the factory, in which all the workers had been locked whilst the bosses fled to shelter.

'We were so happy when we saw the English planes, even though they could also destroy the factory where we were! For us it was a wonderful feeling, but it's terrible when I say this to a German, he looks at me as if I'm not normal.'

She was moved in a cattle truck from Dresden to Mauthausen concentration camp in the Austrian mountains. There they would all have been murdered had not the Allied advance reached so close that the incriminating gas chambers were destroyed by the SS. Emaciated, riddled with typhoid and weighing less than 40 kilos, Lisa was liberated by the Americans on 5 May 1945.

The happy ending to her ordeal was made even better when she realised her husband had also survived.

Lisa tells me her story on a bench as the wind sways the trees around the square in the town that brought her so much pain. Recently, after the death of her husband, she joined with one or two of her fellow survivors to tell their story to the teenagers and sixth-formers of today.

'Because we are the last ones. We are the last generation whom they can ask.'

Day One Hundred and Thirteen: *Prague to Karlovy Vary*

On my last morning in Prague I walk down to the end of Charles Bridge, marvelling as I go at the flamboyance of detail wherever I look in Prague. A bench in a park is not just a bench, it's a work of art, its arms a pair of wrought-iron silver serpents entwined around the wood. Passing the grand late-nineteenth-century National Theatre, I glance up at the sky-blue roof with a pattern of stars painted on it and wonder at the enormous amount of sculptural activity that's going on up there. Gold chariots and angels seem poised to leap over the edge and no end of statues stand precariously along the balustrades. At any excuse the people of Prague stick eagles or sunbursts on their turrets and towers. Crouched lions can be tripped over almost anywhere and even the circular guards around the base of street trees are lavishly patterned. The main railway station is an Art Nouveau masterpiece and it doesn't surprise me to read in my *Time Out*

Guide that Prague boasts the world's only Cubist lamp post.

Charles Bridge, perhaps the best-known landmark in Prague, was originally quite severe. Built in the 1350s from blocks of stone, now blackened with age, it's sturdy and elegantly functional. What makes it so distinctive and memorable is Prague's restless tendency to embellish; 320 years after the bridge was built the first statue appeared (of St John Nepomuk) on its parapet. There are now nearly fifty of them, all religious, running the length of the parapet.

Descending from the sublime to the ridiculous, I walk down some steps at the end of the bridge and there, in the shadow of a tall and imperious Gothic tower, is a line of yellow pedalos.

I meet up here with Bára Vaculíková, a twenty-eight-year-old, whose light, loose clothes and hennaed hair give her a vaguely New Age demeanour. She's one quarter of a group called The Yellow Sisters, who are playing later today at a castle outside Prague, at a special event to mark Witch-Burning Day. It's a pagan celebration in origin, when effigies are burnt in fires at the top of hills and high places. Bára tells me that it's more about fire and its power, and most people quite like witches.

We pedal out into the gentle flow of the Vltava. Apart from the odd warning blast from a tourist boat, it's a peaceful way to take in the sights.

Bára is easy company. She takes her music very seriously, but doesn't make a living out of it, and next week she'll be starting part-time work as a tourist guide. The Yellow Sisters' music is heavily influenced by what they've seen and heard in Africa, especially on the west coast in countries like Gambia and Guinea. At the same time she worries about the effects on African music of what she calls a Euro-American culture.

'I think we spoil it. It'll soon be gone: most of the Africans that you meet will be wearing football dresses.'

I like that phrase so much I feel a bit sour about correcting it.

'Football shirts?'

'Football shirts, yes. From David Beckham and Ronaldo.'

To counter what's happening she and her friends try very hard to bring traditional African musicians to Prague, but the immigration policies are very strict, so it's not easy. I realise that throughout my journey I've seen only a handful of Africans, and Bára is the only one who seems to have any personal experience of, or indeed any interest in, the growing numbers of young Africans trying to get into Europe. When they get here, I ask her, what do they find?

'Loneliness. They find loneliness, and they find people very strict and unfriendly. They get the material world, but they don't get the emotional world. It's impossible because people don't chat on the street here.'

She's angry, and right to be so, because I think it offends her own sense of tolerance. She was brought up in the Czechoslovakia that I remember from twenty years ago. Everyone being watched, friends informing on each other. Then came the Velvet Revolution, which she remembers as being very much riskier than it sounded. More recently she saw the Czechs and Slovaks split, which she was against. She desperately wants to bring people together rather than keep them apart.

Despite her disillusions, Bára is optimistic. She likes Prague for its culture, and the Czechs for their humour.

'It's dark humour. We are very ironic and sarcastic. We can get used to everything, you know. Even though we don't have much to offer we can somehow take it.'

As we come back to our pedalo port the Charles Bridge is heaving with people, and I've no wish to join them. My short voyage with a Yellow Sister has given me an insider's view of life here which you'd never get in a month of tours.

I shall look out for the fires on the hilltops tonight.

Due west of Prague the road dips and twists as it enters the foothills of the steep mountain range beyond which lies Germany. It's a famously disputed area, rich in coal and other minerals, known to the Germans as the Sudetenland. Hitler grabbed it back from Czechoslovakia in 1938, but at the end of the war the German community was expelled. However, their influence is still pervasive. Nestling at the confluence of two rivers and tucked discreetly into their wooded valleys is Karlovy Vary, known for most of its history by the German name Karlsbad. The therapeutic effects of its twelve world-renowned springs were apparently first noted by the man whose bridge we pedalled under this morning, Holy Roman Emperor Charles IV. Though a predominantly German clientele has been replaced by one predominantly Russian,

Karlovy Vary has retained pride of place among the spas of these mountains.

The official guide to the town proudly lists all the famous people who've come here to take the waters, and in case you don't know who they are, their profession or occupation has been helpfully added. So, along with 'R. Strauss, Composer' and 'A. Tolstoy, Russian Writer', we have 'C. Cardinale, Italian Actress' and my favourite, 'A. Hitler, German Politician'.

With big, lushly painted chocolate-box houses and stucco-covered hotels, it's a suitable venue for some of the most unreal experiences on this entire trip.

Most of the accommodation seems to be taken up with an event called the Aristocrats Ball, to which I've been invited. A helpful Czech friend has suggested that I might like to accompany one Tatana Kucharova, not your average date, but the current Miss World. She is, as you would expect, a beautiful girl, and though she speaks excellent English she is only nineteen years old, and as neither of us is an aristocrat, she, like me, is more than moderately baffled by being sat in the sumptuous ballroom of the Grand Hotel Pupp, in the company of Swedish diplomats wearing the regalia of an ancient Spanish-Sicilian order. However, we do get to be formally announced as 'Miss and Mr World', and meet up with the odd deposed king and even the occasional Burmese prince.

Tatana and I talk about travel, it being one thing we do have in common. She's on a world tour, having been chosen to be Miss World some six months ago. They work her hard. Official duties have already taken her six times to China and three times to America.

A very friendly Scotsman in full Highland dress invites us to come and meet Baron von Frankenstein and a lady called Ulrika Hapsburg.

'I mean you don't find people like that at your table very often.'

The dull and prosaic facts of the matter are that I've ten more days of filming ahead and Miss World has university exams in two days' time, so we withdraw from this glittering throwback to the nineteenth century, and leave the massed aristocrats to trip the light fantastic to a twenty-piece orchestra, complete with harp. We agree to meet up tomorrow and test the curative credentials of this shiny little town, grown rich on hypochondria.

Day One Hundred and Fourteen: *Karlovy Vary*

Miss World and I take the waters in the very elegant neo-Renaissance Millspring Colonnade, one of the few restrained buildings in the town. The coffered ceiling of the 430-foot gallery is supported by 124 slender columns and five separate spring outlets spout into carved stone basins, each one progressively hotter than the other. The last one is 62° Centigrade, which somehow makes the unpleasantly sulphurous taste more bearable. We drink out of traditionally designed ceramic mugs, with a long thin spout at the side, presumably the same as those used by A. Hitler, German politician and C. Cardinale, Italian actress.

Around us the streets are beginning to fill with visitors. Coaches with plush velvet interiors are hauled around town by ponies wearing little red caps over their ears.

Tatana is the first Czech girl ever to be crowned Miss World, but despite the grandeur of her status her feet are remarkably close to the ground, and she's more worried about her exams tomorrow than what make-up to wear.

But before we go our separate ways, we're both given the once-over at a clinic in town where we meet the human dynamo that is Milada Sárová.

Milada is the very personification of good health. Her skin exudes a warm glow, she has a head of thick red hair in mint condition, and as she gives me a preliminary examination her enveloping smile never falters.

'I want to know about your water,' she asks, with such intimate jollity that I find myself desperately anxious to please her.

'Your stool is normal?'

'Oh yes, yes.'

'Your legs are not inflammated?'

'No, no!'

'Please take your clothes off. I control your liver.'

'I wish I could!' I find myself replying, dry-mouthed. She looks down at me indulgently but without laughing, as one might look at a puppy that's just farted.

The waters are the bedrock, as it were, of Karlovy Vary's fame, and Milada recommends a course of one litre a day for twenty days to clean out the body properly, but more sophisticated treatments are available for those with the money to pay.

I have a hot-stone massage on my back, immerse myself in a mud bath and, in one quite surreal treatment, Miss World and I are put into long white plastic bags which are sealed around the neck then filled with carbon dioxide.

Milada stands over us, gazing down and smiling as if this were the best party ever.

'When you are in the pack twenty minutes, your inner organs are without hypertension. It's good for your heart, for your blood pressure, for circulation, for people who have problem with...'

I lose my concentration. So bewildered am I by this whole Karlovy Vary experience that I look across at Miss World, lying, like me, in a long white bin-liner, the pair of us like those stone carved effigies of medieval couples you see in church, and for a moment I do think I've died and gone somewhere very strange.

Germany

Day One Hundred and Fifteen: *Karlovy Vary to Dresden*

IT'S ONLY 16 miles to the German border, through foothills which rise to become a small range, the Krusné Hory, 'Ore', mountains. Most of the mineral wealth has been exhausted now and Jáchymov, the last Czech town before the border, once a valued source of uranium, looks a little down at heel.

The transitory nature of border towns, their listlessness and decay, is depressingly similar the world over. As we drive up the last hill out of the Czech Republic, houses are dilapidated, roofs missing here and there, everything could do with a coat of paint. Some of the houses are scarcely disguised brothels with scrawled signs offering 'Erotic Car Wash' and 'Streep Club'.

At the top of the pass the mountains change their name to the Erzgebirge and the country changes its name to Bundesrepublik Deutschland. Eighteen years ago the name at this border would have read *'Deutsche Demokratische Republik'*, German Democratic Republic or GDR, the eastern part of Germany that fell under Soviet influence after the war and whose leaders declared an independent state in 1949.

In 1961 the Cold War, that era of institutionalised mistrust between Russia and the West which lasted for most of my lifetime, turned distinctly chillier as East German troops and engineers erected a barrier along their borders. It remained in place until young Germans took sledgehammers to it during the extraordinary events of November 1989 when the GDR, quite suddenly, imploded.

The German side of the border is neat and tidy. We're in

what they call Saxon Switzerland, a landscape of Alpine forest, meadows, ski-lifts and tight-packed villages with steep-gabled roofs nestling in the valleys. Gradually this gives way to a spread of rolling uplands covered with a mixture of conifer plantations and fields of glaring yellow rapeseed in the midst of which wind turbines whirl around, looking like lines of giant Mercedes stars.

Of all the countries I've visited on this journey Germany is the one which resonates most personally with me. I was born in the Second World War and many of the books and films I was brought up on replayed that war, telling and retelling tales of the bravery and tenacity of our boys, and the inhumanity of the enemy.

There was, however, always one episode of which no books ever boasted, something that was spoken of in subdued voices, if at all, a tale to which heroism just wouldn't stick. It was the Allied bombing of Dresden in February 1945. An estimated 35,000 people died, many of them refugees fleeing the Russian advance. Some of the finest buildings in Europe were destroyed overnight.

The single word Dresden is a chilling symbol of a peculiar horror, the aerial bombing of civilians. Both sides had been doing it throughout the war. The citizens of London, Coventry, Hamburg and Berlin knew what it was like to be terrified from the air, and yet it is Dresden, the capital of Saxony, the city we are approaching in low sunlight on a fast autobahn, which stands, alongside Hiroshima and Nagasaki, as a synonym for the worst and darkest excesses of aerial destruction.

It isn't the easiest place for an Englishman to spend his first night in a new country.

Day One Hundred and Sixteen: *Dresden*

The associations with that apocalyptic night of 13 and 14 February 1945 are everywhere. Not so much in people's eyes or the way they talk to you, but in the fabric of the city. The great feats of rebuilding that characterise Dresden cannot be understood without first understanding the scale of the destruction. In the wide space of the Neumarkt the nineteenth-century city is being re-created, punctiliously, rows of housing as well as public buildings. There's been controversy over the plans, some complaining that they're building a Disney World, a façade of old Dresden; a cloak for covering state-of-the-art modern interiors. In a temporary hut on the site a display charts progress. The black and white photographs taken shortly after the Allied raid are a revelation. The Frauenkirche, the Church of Our Lady, is reduced to two or three tottering strips of wall. The rest is rubble.

Yet, when I step out into the Neumarkt again, there it is, as big and confident as ever. What's more, the few walls left standing can still be seen. The black stones are what was left, the pale stone is new. In an extraordinary feat of restoration every single scrap of rubble was marked and sorted and, if possible, put back in its original position. Forty-five per cent of the new Frauenkirche was at one time part of the old and the reconstructed walls carry a dome weighing 13,000 tons.

The work on the Frauenkirche was not authorised until the early 1990s, after the fall of the GDR, which didn't care much about churches. Its reconstruction, completed in 2004 at a cost of 132 million euros, is seen as a symbol of reconciliation. Much money and support has come from the countries which carried out the raid in the first place, and the 20-foot-high globe and gold cross that crowns the dome was made by the son of one of the British bomber pilots, something which Felix, my young guide to the church, tells me was particularly appreciated by the people of Dresden.

Felix, studying at the University of Technology here, is understandably more keen to talk about the Dresden of his generation, the city that has risen from the ashes. '"Silicon Saxony", we call it,' he tells me proudly, as we take in the dizzying panorama from 225 feet up on the dome of the Frauenkirche, 'more than 760 companies. We're the centre of micro-electronics in Europe.'

He points enthusiastically out towards a green sward of public park.

'The Grosser Garten. Bigger than Monaco!'

There is undoubted beauty out there, but from our lofty viewpoint I can see that most of Dresden is not beautiful; largely rebuilt in the communist style, with the familiar swathes of concrete blocks, it looks like anywhere else in the east. I ask Felix what his parents' generation make of all that.

'They tell me that not everything was wrong in the German Democratic Republic. There was a larger community, everybody was helping each other, and yes, not everything was wrong. That's what they always tell me.'

Firmly grasping the balustrade, we move round till we're looking down over the Elbe, running from the mountains of the Czech Republic to the North Sea, winding its way through Dresden, dividing the Altstadt, the majestic complex of Baroque buildings on the west bank, from the lively student quarter of the Neustadt to the east.

Felix frowns, as if still thinking of his parents and their very different way of life.

'We say some people still have the Wall in their heads…that even seventeen years after reunification there is still segregation between the eastern part and the western part, and it will probably take another generation to get rid of that Wall.'

Today's Friday, the day of the week when they have a special service of remembrance in the Frauenkirche and prayers are exchanged for the people of Coventry and Dresden. Fifteen minutes before the service starts it is almost impossible to find a seat. The place is packed.

Inside, the church is a riot of Baroque overstatement; marble columns, plaster clouds, sunbursts, grottoes with landscapes carved inside, buckets of gilding and a ceiling painted with glowing rose and salmon pinks. The service is, by comparison, a little colourless. The church organ thunders out some fine Bach fugues, but the address is muted and the congregation never gets to sing. Maybe this has more to do with the legacy of that stern black figure who stands on a plinth outside: Martin Luther.

Day One Hundred and Seventeen: *Dresden to Meissen*

The Elbe is very low at the moment and there is a real worry that Europe's oldest regular steamboat service, the Elbefahrt, may have to be suspended. It's been plying between Dresden and

Meissen for the last 150 years, with a fleet of paddle-steamers that can usually cope with a shallow draught. We climb aboard the *Krippen*, named, I'm assured, after a local town rather than a foreign murderer. After some initial groaning and grinding the *Krippen* raises her retractable funnel and heads out into the stream before turning and giving us one last look at the dark, ornate and powerful group of buildings so immaculately restored along the Brühlsche Terrace. We pass under the Augustsbrücke, the bridge that bears the name of the seventeenth-century Elector of Saxony, King of Poland and Lithuania, Augustus the Strong, who was responsible for the grandeur of Dresden, despite being, according to my guidebook, 'an exceptionally loathsome figure, as well as a disastrous political operator'. Ah, well, you can't have everything.

It being a peach of a morning, the tables on deck are soon full of bread, bratwurst and even a few beers, though it's just nine o'clock. The only seat I can find is next to a lady engineer from Lake Constance, way down near the Swiss border. She's an independent traveller, in her thirties, and although she's from the depths of West Germany her opinion on how things are going seems very similar to those of East German Felix. What she calls 'the forty years of separation' are not yet overcome and she thinks that a sense of unity will have to wait for a new generation.

'But I'm a little worried about the teenagers of nowadays,' she confesses. 'We call them the fun generation. They aren't interested in history.'

Our big red paddle-wheels chug round, smoke drifts from the newly painted black funnel. Green fields and distant low hills slide by, gentle riverine scenery reminiscent of the Thames valley. Those who aren't tucking into picnics are taking photos, or checking their hiking gear, whilst a number of sun-reddened figures, leathery and lean, tinker with their bikes. A cycle path runs the length of the Elbe and you can, if you like, pedal all the way to Hamburg. Not a bad way to see Germany.

My companion and I talk about Europe. She is oddly evasive when I ask her if Germany, as the biggest economy in Europe, feels the responsibility of leadership. To her generation, the words 'German' and 'leadership' still raise uncomfortable spectres. She shies away from politics, and thinks that the best results from Germany's up-coming Presidency of the EU will be on the less controversial ground of climate control. She expresses polite doubts about further expansion of the European Union, worrying that the rich countries will have to pick up a big bill, and is confused about Turkish membership.

'I don't know how to think,' she says, spreading her arms, 'it's half in Asia and half in Europe.'

There are vineyards close to the river now, small plots on hillsides divided up by drystone walls and the occasional red-topped dovecote.

'What is the end of Europe?' she asks. 'Is it in Egypt? Is it in Syria? What's the definition of Europe?'

This is exactly what I've been puzzling over these past few months, but further discussion is pre-empted as a shrill whistle from the *Krippen's* bridge announces the approach of Meissen, a jewel of a town built around a colossal fortress, precariously and most skilfully poised on a steep and rocky prominence.

Meissen made its name from porcelain, and the tourist trail is flanked with shops selling the curiously fussy bits and pieces which people collect for enormous amounts of money. A less well-known spin-off from Meissen's traditional skills is the relocation here, from western Germany, of one of the country's largest manufacturers of bathroom appliances. This, strangely, is not on most tourist itineraries.

It should be, for the Duravit factory production lines are something of a work of art in themselves. They make 400,000 units a year, most of these toilet bowls. In one enormous shed, as hot and humid as a tropical rainforest, rows of drying lavatory moulds stretch far into the distance, looking like a lot of open-mouthed, recently caught, deep-sea fish.

The glazing ovens are dramatic, with lines of appliances, like some porcelain army being marched slowly down a 50-yard tunnel towards a distant blazing fire. But nothing in the process is more weird and wonderful than the robot in the paint shop. Every now and then the doors slide open, offering a brief glimpse of an electronic scarecrow, all in white, flinging itself about like a whirling dervish as it sprays another pan.

Isabella, my guide to this all-white world, tells me not only about the process and the product but also answers my more prurient questions, such as the reason for the German preference for flat pans in the bowl as opposed to the straight drop. This, I'm told, is called the 'wash-out' model and has practical and medical advantages.

'You can examine your business when you've made a number two,' she tells me, adding rather sweetly, 'as we say in Germany.'

I ask her views on the current controversy gripping middle-class Germany. Should men sit or stand to pee?

'It's a very new thing,' Isabella tells me, briskly. 'In every German family it's a big discussion point for the housewife, who has to keep the house clean, and yes, it is true that a lot of German men have decided to sit when they pee. They don't like to speak too much about it because they still consider it not very masculine, but young men of my age very often sit.'

She concedes that this may be because of strong women, which backs up what I've heard about it being more of a female emancipation issue. Whatever. In polite German society it's now something of an insult to be a *Stehpinkler* in a world of *Sitzpinklers*.

And when you think about it, it is less selfish than spraying the surrounding floor. Who knows, this conversation could be something that changes my life in the way visiting Japan stopped me from using pocket handkerchiefs to wipe my nose. And put the filth back in the pocket? Disgusting. (I now always use tissues. Thank you, Japan.)

Nowhere seems very far from anywhere else in Germany, thanks to the fast and ubiquitous autobahns, and we're in Leipzig in time to catch an evening show at the Academixer, one of the many satirical cabaret clubs in this big working city, which at first glance is dowdier than Dresden, but seems a lot more lively.

It was here, in October 1989, that the first unauthorised protests against the GDR took place, which led, with startling rapidity, to what became known as the 'Peaceful Revolution', what they now call *'die Wende'*, the turning point, and led, within a year, to the reunification of Germany.

Gunter Böhnke is an actor and comedian who was one of those who closely watched Leipzig's transition from GDR to

Bundesrepublik, and he's asked me along to his club for 'Seventies Night', a nostalgic look back at what made them laugh in the good old days of the police state.

Gunter's in his fifties, short and with a perfect comic combination of serious face and huge moustache. He was born in Dresden but has lived in Leipzig for forty-two years. For him, Leipzig had the advantage of being the city where the international trade shows were held. Gunter made friends with people in Scotland, and although he was not allowed out of the GDR to visit them, they could come and see him. 'Leipzig is an open city, you see. In East German times it was called the secret capital of East Germany.'

Dresdeners, by contrast, were seen as a bit out of touch, cut off physically by the hills around them and mentally by their conservative, plutocratic attitude. There was a satirical description of Dresden and Gunter struggles for a moment to find its English translation.

'Ah yes. Valley of the Clueless. That's what we called Dresden!'

When I ask him how Dresdeners, and indeed people like himself, felt about the Allied destruction of the city, he says that people have come to terms with it now, and there's little animosity, but the unveiling of a statue to Sir Arthur 'Bomber' Harris in London in 1992 reopened a lot of old wounds and caused considerable resentment.

The Academixer Club, where he's been putting on a show since 1967, is a comfortable and inviting combination of a well-appointed 250-seat theatre, with plenty of ancillary space in which to hang out, including a clubby bar, and a restaurant serving excellent food. I don't know anywhere quite like this in London. And it's not the only one in town.

'This is the city in Germany,' Gunter enthuses, 'within one square kilometre you have eight cabaret theatres. It's the capital of satire.'

Tonight's nostalgia show has brought a full house, but Gunter tells me that this is quite rare. In the GDR days they always sold out, as if there was a desperate need for laughter then. Now there's so much to choose from people can take it or leave it.

I can't understand the finer points of the show, but I laugh a lot. The cast look good, and underplay very effectively.

I ask Gunter who they were allowed to make fun of in the communist days.

'We were allowed to make fun of everything,' Gunter begins breezily, 'except the Party line, the Party leaders, the top leaders of the trade unions, the Stasi and the National People's Army.'

I feel I've a lot to learn about eastern Germany, and Gunter agrees to help teach me.

Day One Hundred and Eighteen: *Leipzig*

We meet up for a coffee in St Nicholas' Square, beside the Nikolaikirche, the church which during the 1980s became the focus of opposition to the socialist regime, which had demolished another church nearby. On 9 October 1989 the congregation came out and instead of going home, remained in the square. Anti-government banners were unrolled and, very rapidly, people began to join them. Gunter says he feared violence, there were plenty of tanks nearby, but thinks that the sheer size of the protest took both sides by surprise.

'If it had been 7,000 they would have opened fire, but when they saw there were 70,000 the order wasn't given.' The turning point had come, and nobody was quite prepared for it.

In the square today a discreet little plaque set into the cobbles shows in children's shoeprints the significance of that demonstration, when the people of Leipzig voted with their feet.

The GDR was never overtly sustained by military force, relying instead on an intense and comprehensive surveillance system run by the Ministerium für Staatssicherheit, the Ministry of State Security, known to all as the Stasi. They operated a network of informers so extensive that estimates say one in every sixty inhabitants of the GDR was informing on someone else.

We walk down towards the old Stasi headquarters, passing on the way a series of condemned housing blocks which the city, unable to afford to demolish them, has wrapped in huge sheets and commissioned an artist to decorate with a series of massive murals.

The offices from which the Leipzig Stasi kept an eye on the two and a half million people in their district was built for an insurance company just before the First World War, and during Stasi days was known and feared as the Runde Ecke, the Round Corner. It's a self-important building on a busy corner opposite the Felix Mendelssohn High School for Music and Theatre.

Inside is a museum run, not by any tourist board, but by a serious-minded Citizens' Committee who, in their own words, 'want to sensitise the young generation, who no longer know about life in the GDR from their own experience, to the dangers of dictatorship'. There are no expensive hi-tech displays here; indeed, the name of the permanent exhibition, 'Stasi – Power and Banality', says it all. The lino, the yellow wallpaper, the cramped little office of a typical employee, with most of its space taken up by a filing cabinet, a shredder, a tape recorder and shelves full of ring files. A display of wigs used in surveillance, jam jars full of 'smell samples' taken from suspects, everything perfectly captures the small-minded drabness of this bureaucracy of oppression. A system created, as someone observed, to protect the government from the people.

When demonstrators stormed the Runde Ecke on 4 December 1989, the Stasi began desperately trying to destroy the vast amount of information they had secretly acquired, but there was so much that it proved impossible. Now the Stasi files are public property and anyone can have access to them. Those from Leipzig alone stretch for 6 miles. Shredded material is being sorted by the 'puzzle women', a team of ladies near Nuremberg, who physically go through the sacks and piece the remains together. It's estimated that, working at their present rate, it will take them 350 years to complete the task. Computers are now being used, though it's expensive. This admirable accessibility of information has painful consequences. People are now discovering that their close friends and acquaintances were informing on them.

Gunter, who realised then that his phone was being tapped and that every letter to a foreign country was opened, now knows that an acquaintance of his, faced with the evidence, has admitted he was an informer.

'At one point he said, yes, I know you know, but I must tell you Mr X and Mrs Y were much worse.'

Truth and reconciliation in the former GDR clearly has its limits.

'Nobody came and said I just want to tell you I was an informer, nobody.'

It's tempting to see all this stuff on display at the Runde Ecke as small-minded, petty, even weirdly comic. There is a growing phenomenon known as *Ostalgie*, typified by an increasing interest in the paraphernalia of the GDR, which is seen as fashionable and trendy. But this was an oppressive, ruthless system. Many thousands of lives were ruined, destroyed, or physically ended by people working here. As Gunter the satirist reminds me before we part company, 'We never ever did jokes about the Stasi. That was taboo.'

Day One Hundred and Nineteen: *Bitterfeld*

Someone who had more than his fair share of Stasi files is Hans Zimmerman, a big barrel of a man with deep blue eyes and a long grey beard who looks like a cross between Father Christmas and Bismarck. He lives just north of Leipzig in Bitterfeld in an industrial town whose name he made famous across the world. In the late 1980s Hans, unable to tolerate the permanent cloud of pollution that hung over his town from the chemical and pharmaceutical works, co-operated secretly with a journalist from the West called Margit Miosga to make a television report on conditions in Bitterfeld. It had such impact that it was shown far beyond the borders of Germany, prompting visits from all sorts of concerned parties and the eventual closure of many of the most polluting plants.

Margit recently returned to do a 'twenty years after' film, and I meet up with them both at the Zimmermans' busily furnished top-floor flat in a modest block opposite a shopping mall.

They're an odd couple, the big, hairy, provincial Hans and Margit, a bright, energetic, chain-smoking urban intellectual, but they've clearly struck up a close rapport over the years.

Hans' wife Inge has made us one of her apparently legendary cakes. Hans beams and recommends a piece. Margit translates for us.

'He says it's good for sweaty feet and a broken heart.'

In a bedroom-study at the back of the flat, on whose shelves are a series of ring binders containing all 3,228 pages of the Stasi's files on Hans Zimmerman, they tell me their story.

Margit, alerted by an environmentalist friend in the GDR, came to Bitterfeld in 1987 and Hans took her out on his motorbike for a 'Stinketour', as he called his introduction to the mess of evil, bubbling waterways and yellow-belching chimneys of Bitterfeld. Margit had never seen anything like it and set about planning to make a report for a TV station. It wasn't easy. She couldn't telephone Hans, as all calls from outside the GDR would be tapped, but plans were made through intermediaries and Margit cleverly suggested they shoot on the day of the European football final, when most of the male population would be indoors in front of their televisions.

With a cameraman on the back of his bike, and the camera hidden in a shoulder bag, they successfully filmed the Stinketour. Hans was never seen or heard on the finished film.

I ask him what his penalty would have been had he been found out.

'Fifteen years,' translates Margit, 'and not in one of the comfortable jails.'

The footage was shown in a ten-minute clip on a popular political programme.

Margit reaches for a cigarette.

'Two days later a bus from Berlin came, from the big shots. They cleaned the whole factory, and they brought loads of sand and soil and filled in the dirt lakes we showed.'

Hans interjects.

'Yes, the policy was at that time to cover everything and to change nothing.'

After the Wall fell Margit and Hans suddenly found themselves the subject of enormous international interest, with visits from TV crews, American senators, German chancellors, and Jane Fonda.

'The bad thing, of course,' says Hans, 'is that now the factories are closed down, so people are unemployed.'

The estimated figure is staggering. Some 30,000 jobs were lost. People retired or went to work in the West, but though Hans was blamed by some, others saw him as the man who saved their town from being slowly poisoned.

His Stasi files, which Margit collected for him, show that the security police were aware of Hans and his activities and had plans for him. His marriage was to be destroyed, and it was to be made impossible for him to get a job. He was to be labelled a criminal and locked away.

Ironically, despite being a hero of the environmental movement, and having achieved far more for it than most, he's now living on the dole.

At the end of the day, after Margit has caught her train back to Berlin, I climb on the back of his latest bike and he re-creates some of the Stinketour for me. Hans, wearing a specially light motorcycle helmet so he can hear the wildlife, instructs me where best to hang onto him. He's a big man and it's a small bike, so I grasp his left shoulder and right breast and hang on for dear life.

The skies are bright, the air's clear as we drive down what was once 'the street of a thousand smells'. The chemical complexes are still there, all clean lines and futuristic shapes. A soaring brick chimney still puffs out a trail of smoke, but there were once thirty-nine more like it. Now when Hans stops, it's to point out a nature reserve, or a stream to which fish have returned, or to listen for the sound of a woodpecker.

Day One Hundred and Twenty: *Bitterfeld to Berlin*

There is a temptation to see Germany only from the autobahns, so quick and comprehensive is the system, but after a diet of cities, it's a relief to pull off the E55 and take in the last stretch of relatively unspoilt countryside before we reach Berlin.

The Spreewald is an area comprising 1,200 miles of waterways radiating out from the River Spree over an area of 300 square miles. I learn all this from my authoritative boatman, Herr Marx, a punctilious man in his late fifties with an obsessive interest in the locally born explorer Ludwig Leichhardt, who disappeared, presumed dead, crossing the Australian outback in 1848. I happen to be fascinated by him too, after reading Patrick White's epic novel *Voss*, which was based on Leichhardt's short life. The lean, earnest Herr Marx makes me feel a complete dilettante, for he has actually been to Australia and wandered the bush in the footsteps of his hero. And can't wait to go back.

The water meadows and languid waterways of the Spreewald couldn't be more different from the hard-baked desert where Ludwig Leichhardt (probably) met his death, but Herr Marx is just as keen on them.

We pass under a railway bridge.

'Built in the year 1866 by a British company,' he shouts, disturbing a pair of waterfowl that clatter up into the sky and wheel steeply off across a waterlogged field.

'A wonderful area for nature. Fifteen thousand flowers, animals and birds. A wonderful area.'

He used to work as an engineer in a local power station which was closed down in 1996, part of the price paid when the centrally planned economic system he'd grown up with was subsumed by the capitalist, competitive West. Many people left the area, and often Germany itself.

'In the town of Lübbenau lives, in 1990, 25,000 people. Today, 10,000. Big problem.'

Herr Marx, it turns out, is not actually German. He belongs to a minority nationality called the Sorbs, a Slav people from the east, of whom he estimates there are some 40–50,000 in the country. They have their own language, which for most of the twentieth century was banned in churches and schools. Teachers, he says, were given money for every Sorb child they taught to speak only German.

In 1941 the Nazis decided that the Sorbs were not true Aryans and plans were drawn up to remove them all to Auschwitz. Thanks to Hitler's invasion of Russia these were never carried out, and the Sorbs survived until their fellow Slavs in the Red Army liberated them in 1945. 'Today no problem. No problem.'

We glide into one of the small, attractive Spreewald villages with wood-built thatched cottages and green lawns coming down to the water. Their owners, probably weekenders from Berlin, keep these little communities spick and span. The barns and fences give off a satisfying smell of freshly applied creosote, and the banks are secured by stout wooden pilings.

Herr Marx points out things for me: the two entwined snakes with crowns that mark each end of the rooftop and are supposed to bring good luck; a 300-year-old house, half-hidden behind an orchard of cherry blossom; the way they use plaited wheat stalks for the topmost row of an otherwise straw-thatched roof; a restaurant called the 'Funny Halibut'; a museum entirely dedicated to gherkins.

'The speciality round here is cucumber, asparagus and gherkin.'

By now the mosquitoes are biting hard and the *Wind in the Willows* world is becoming more like Leichhardt's last journey, but when we eventually disembark the hospitable locals have prepared a wild boar barbecue for us. Hunting is an important part of the Sorb way of life, which explains all those wooden platforms with steps up to them, in the fields by the river.

'The hunters shoot 20,000 animals in one year,' says the ever-helpful Herr Marx, with a bit of pig in one hand and a Krombacher beer in the other. A man of serious enthusiasms. Just like Ludwig Leichhardt.

I learnt from Herr Marx that the Spree is one of the most placid rivers in Germany, dropping a mere 150 feet over its 310-mile course, and if he'd gone on punting (and I'm sure he would have done) he could have deposited me in the heart of Berlin.

So is it sheer coincidence or part of some higher plan that two hours later when I open the window of my hotel room off the Alexanderplatz I see people dining below me, on the banks of the River Spree?

When I was last in Berlin, the Wall still cut off one half of the city from the other. The welcome was all in the West, which is where the hotels, shops, restaurants and foreigners were, while, frustratingly, the finest buildings were in the East. Tonight, my first in reunified Berlin, I walk, scarcely able to believe the difference, from my modern hotel in what was the grey socialist heart of divided Berlin, along the glorious Unter den Linden (literally 'Under the Linden Trees'), which had also been on the GDR side of the Wall. The cluster of imperious monuments to monarchical power, built to glorify the ambition of Frederick the Great, Brandenburg-Prussia and the Hohenzollern dynasty, remain not only intact, but in pretty good shape. One major building, larger and more modern than any of the rest, remains an ugly, abandoned eyesore. This was once the Palace of the Republic. In it were bowling alleys, theatres, restaurants, dance halls, libraries, 1,500 seats, 20,000 light bulbs, wardrobes for 5,000 coats, and the Parliament of the German Democratic Republic. It represented everything the socialist government was proud of. Some three years ago, the authorities of a reunited Germany decided to knock it down. Like many relics of the communist years, it wouldn't go quietly. Riddled with asbestos, it's having to be dealt with carefully and painstakingly slowly. The authorities, doubtless embarrassed by the brooding hulk in their midst, have drawn attention to their environmental sensitivity. Attached to the fencing around it is a large sign which perhaps says more about post-war Germany than the problems of asbestos.

'Palace of the Republic,' it reads, 'Dismantled, not Demolished.'

On the other side of the road, by contrast, is a tidy, well-patronised, green and pleasant space with a fountain playing in the middle. This is the Lustgarten. One of the Nazis' favourite rallying places.

Day One Hundred and Twenty-one: *Berlin*

The choice of Berlin as capital of the new Germany is geographically interesting, as it orients the centre of German government firmly to the east. Thanks to Stalin's insistence that after the war, Germany's eastern border should be pushed back to the Oder-Neisse line, Berlin is far closer to Poland and the Czech Republic than it is to Munich, Cologne, Frankfurt or Hamburg.

The city, which stood for so many years as the emblem of divided Europe, now signifies the healing process, not just of Germany, but of Europe as a whole.

There are so many symbols here, from the Brandenburg Gate to the Holocaust Memorial, the new Reichstag and the Wall itself, that I feel in danger of being overwhelmed by Significance. What I need to do before I go is to unfreeze history and meet and talk to some people who live and work in Berlin.

Two young actors, Olaf Rauschenbach and Jörg Pintsch, give me a whistlestop tour of east Berlin in an open-top stretch Trabant (which could be another metaphor for reunification – the ultimate socialist car given the ultimate capitalist treatment). Both men are married with three children each. They still see Berlin as a city of two halves and Jörg, particularly, finds the east 'more authentic', and preferred by a lot of younger Berliners to the comfortable conservative consumerism of the west. He was in London recently and not enchanted.

'Eight pounds to go in Saint Paul's Cathedral!'

With one of them playing the 'Westie' and the other the 'Eastie', they perform a dialogue, interspersed with song and poetry, about the two sides of their city.

As we drive past a preserved strip of the Berlin Wall on Mühlenstrasse, covered in graffiti, and photo opportunities for tour groups, they tell the story of the barrier that the GDR called 'The Anti Fascistic Protective Wall'.

'Just imagine, in 1960 alone 200,000 citizens from the GDR left their home country on a 20p train ticket for the golden West.'

'And that's what you call a haemorrhage, and the loophole has to be closed up tight.'

'At one o'clock at night, Central European time, 13 August 1961, workers start to erect the installation for democratic Berlin.'

'On the eastern side, a 3-metre-high border fence, and a death strip, meticulously raked and smoothed over in order to make footprints clearly visible, and then the Wall itself, 4 metres high with a round tube on top.'

'Just imagine you are eighteen years old, liable for military service and also convinced that socialism is the right thing for a young GDR.'

'Somebody comes stumbling over the wire towards the Wall, directly towards you. You have three possible ways to react. The first is, put up your gun and shoot the guy dead. The second is, you put the gun aside, risk the contempt of the working people, and believe me, an officer's standing behind you who will take the necessary action. The third is to try to do your duty. You call to the runaway, no reaction. You give a warning shot. No reaction. You take aim and you shoot him.'

Two hundred people from the East were shot trying to cross the Berlin Wall, and there were around 1,000 casualties along the rest of the border.

Jörg and Olaf have some good insights.

Jörg, as Westie: 'In my country we think of war as something resembling a natural catastrophe. We don't do it ourselves. It just happens to us.'

Their dialogue also deals with painful issues currently facing Berliners, like the controversy over the number of memorials and who should be remembered.

'The country that started both world wars has a very strong tradition in memorial sites. There will be a memorial for all the nations suffering in war.'

'All dead soldiers.'

'All the Jews that have been murdered.'

'All the Roma Gypsies that have been murdered.'

'Homosexuals, deserters.'

'Civilians killed by bombs.'

'SS soldiers killed by partisans.'

'Them too?'

'Yes, of course. Democratic memorial.'

It's a bracing run with Jörg and Olaf, and their funny and sometimes moving banter raises a few questions which I talk over later with the author of a book called *From Max to Monty*, which compares German and English humour.

We meet at the terrace café of the Opera House. I'm half-expecting someone with a red nose and a fright-wig, but Hans-Dieter Gelfert is a bespectacled academic. Amusing, but cerebral.

The difference between German and British humour is, he says, down to priorities.

'The top priority for the British, from Magna Carta to the present day, has always been individual freedom, and the top priority for the Germans had to be security and safety. I call the English humour a "bottom-up" humour, and the German humour a "top down".'

The fact that he can say this without a trace of a smile perhaps makes his point.

But his view that the English mock order and the Germans mock disorder is echoed by Anna Funder, who wrote in her excellent book on the Stasi that the Germans tend to be over-respectful of authority because of their complicated and unsettled history – as she puts it, 'the mess that gave rise to all that order'.

I ask Hans-Dieter about the new Europe. Does he think Germans will make good Europeans?

Yes, he thinks they will, as the Germans were until very recently a combination of little units, used to interacting with each other.

Does he believe they can be leaders of Europe?

No, he believes the Germans are 'hesitant' about themselves as leaders.

'There is still far too much shame about what Germans have done under Hitler, that they are now so modest in their attitude and have so little national pride.'

He reckons the only events which trigger outbreaks of German national pride these days are things like football championships.

'I don't believe they will ever again feel really proud and strong.'

Looking out from where we are having a beer I see a statue of Frederick the Great, and right beside us is August-Bebel-Platz, formerly Opernplatz, where Joseph Goebbels organised the infamous book-burning ceremony in 1933.

We're surrounded by so many reminders of what Germans could do when they feel insecure, that I only hope he's right.

Day One Hundred and Twenty-two: *Berlin*

We drive east towards the Polish border to investigate another example of post-socialist enterprise. Like Herr Marx's Spreewald boat trips, Jörg and Axel Heyse's tank-driving school, or, as they call it, 'Panzer "Fun" Fahrschule', is a small triumph of local initiative in a world where all the best jobs have gone west.

Axel Heyse, a short, compact, middle-aged man with thick, swept-back dark hair and Latin film-star looks, was, like his brother, a tank commander in the GDR. At the height of the Cold War his was one of 7,000 Warsaw Pact tanks facing 1,500 NATO tanks with only flat, sandy heathland between them. Axel said that their T-55s could have reached Marseille in five days.

Though he left the army in 1988 and became a police officer, tank-driving was in his blood and after the collapse of the GDR he saved pieces of old tanks from scrap and reassembled them. Their appearances were so successful that three years ago they opened the school and now employ fifteen people.

I'm given the chance to drive a T-55, an opportunity that probably won't come my way again, and about which I have extreme misgivings. I sign a form absolving the 'Fun' Fahrschule from all responsibility if I turn one over or inadvertently crush the reception area and am given a balaclava to wear with a tight cap over it with a headset inside. Axel, muttering encouraging words like 'This is Russian technology, it's indestructible, do what you like with it', directs me towards the dusty olive beast about 30 feet long and 10 feet high that I'm to take control of.

And I will indeed be in control. There's no dual steering here. I'm given the briefest of briefings by my instructor, a fair-haired young man of Slavic features called Mischa. Even without the engine running I find it hard to understand most of what he says, so I'm not at all a happy boy as I lower myself into the driver's seat. Somehow I'd expected the interior to be more like a ship's bridge, or at least a flight deck, with two or three seats, control panels, even a cup of coffee and a biscuit. Wrong. There is no room at all beside me, and barely any behind. There are cables and all kinds of incomprehensible entrails of which, I realise, I'm one.

The technology is more farm tractor than armoured cavalry, with a brake, accelerator and clutch pedal and no wheel, but two vertical levers on either side with which to steer.

Mischa starts the engine for me, then climbs out to sit on top. Through the narrow letter-box slit in front of me I can see the small sandy hills, then a green field and some houses in the distance. Mischa shouts something incomprehensible, which I take to mean let the brake off, and we move ponderously forward. His voice rises.

'Guess,' he shouts. 'Guess.'

'Guess what?' I want to shout, but don't have the German.

'Guess!'

The engine rumbles and dies.

Mischa's face appears and points at the accelerator and the RPM counter beside me.

'More guess,' he says, and now I can hear him I know what he's actually saying is 'more gas'.

He restarts the engine and I give it maximum wellie. But it's still not enough and the engine stalls again. Fat lot of good I'd be at invading.

Softened up by years of automatic gearbox and power-steering, I try to remember my train-driving lesson in Poland and all at once everything clicks, or in this case grinds, into place. This is heavy equipment and it needs hard work. Once I and the tank have got our relationship right, I'm rewarded by a remarkably springy performance. These T-55s may look big and bulky but they can hit a top speed not far short of 40 miles per hour. Though I get nowhere near that, I feel as if I could reach Marseille eventually, and steep slopes and precipitous drops are no problem.

Extracting myself from the tank is the final challenge to overcome before I'm awarded my tank driver's certificate and christened 'Panzer Palin' by Basil.

We drive back to Berlin. This area, Brandenburg-Prussia, once the powerhouse of Germany, is not quite what I'd expected. There's no sign of great estates or country houses and Tamsin, our English translator and fixer, confirms that this is a pretty depressed area. A now-familiar landscape of wind farms and endless fields of rapeseed (grown for bio-fuels) gives way to the suburbs and the mile upon mile of rectangular modern blocks in which most of Berlin's population lives. And likes to live, according to Tamsin. Unlike the British, the Germans are perfectly happy to live in high-rise apartments, most of which are rented.

They're adaptable too, and if, when the family moves out, they no longer need a three-room flat, they'll happily downsize. In fact,

Tamsin thinks, it's very 'East Berlin' to make do, to be seen not to be extravagant. That goes for the older population in the housing estates and the young professional families in the city. It's chic to be shabby, to reuse, never to throw things away. If this is true, then the inheritance of the GDR may not be all bad. It might be better attuned to the present mood of environmental responsibility which the Germans, who like to get things right, are taking more seriously than most.

Day One Hundred and Twenty-three: *Berlin to the Baltic*

Tempelhof Airport is a traveller's dream, even if it was originally built by the Nazis. It's in the heart of Berlin and used by only a few local and international flights. This morning its uncluttered central hall reminds me of how American airports used to look in the 1950s. Outside, a single, long crescent of a building with the terminal in the centre and hangars, stores and workshops on either side, embraces the field, in the centre of which, and looking not a bit out of place, is the dream-like shape of a silver DC-3.

This is an aircraft that knows Tempelhof well. In 1948 the Soviets, in disagreement with the rest of the Allies, set up a road and rail blockade of West Berlin. The blockade lasted eleven months before being broken by an American, British and French airlift which had kept the city supplied by 270,000 flights, some coming in only five minutes apart. The DC-3 was the workhorse of this extraordinary siege-busting operation. Today this historical curiosity will take me to another, Hitler's holiday camp on the Baltic Sea.

Berlin, a city in ruins sixty years ago, now reincarnated as the capital of the most powerful economy in Europe, slips away below us as we head for the Baltic at a steady 120 knots, just short of 150 miles per hour.

Landing at an airstrip near Stralsund, we drive on through the Mecklenburg countryside (which feels familiar, not unlike East Anglia) and onto the last lap of a journey that's taken us more than five months and through twenty different countries.

Rügen is a pretty, amoeba-shaped island, its beaches always popular, especially during the GDR, and here, on a wooded bay at a place called Prora, the Nazis planned a People's Resort (the language of the National Socialists was uncannily similar to that of the Democratic Socialists who replaced them). It was part of what was known as *'Kraft durch Freude'*, 'Strength through Joy', a policy of organised leisure which would offer lucky workers a carefully regimented holiday of relaxation and indoctrination.

'Organising one's free time privately has no value to the German people,' claimed Robert Ley, the alcoholic with a severe personality disorder whom Hitler put in charge of the programme.

All Nazi buildings had to be monuments to the thousand-year Reich, and a holiday camp was no exception. Work began in Prora in May 1936, and by the summer of 1939 over 3 miles of five-storey accommodation stretched along the coast, enough rooms to take 20,000 people at a time. But no holidaymakers ever came here. The outbreak of war brought other priorities, and the People's Resort became a hospital for evacuees from the bombing of Hamburg, and a hostel for forced labour squads from all over Nazi-conquered Europe.

Now under federal ownership, there is a museum here, and one or two well-intentioned educational projects, and some talk of a hotel, but its scale is so daunting that, sixty-eight years after it was built, it's still here, a long, dusty-white concrete skeleton between the pine forest and the sand. I walk through it and onto the beach. A few boys are playing football. A crisp, cooling breeze comes off the Baltic.

I look behind me at the wreckage of a dream. A dream of a Europe united by force.

I've seen a new Europe these past five months, a Europe which could be united, for the first time in history, by co-operation rather than conflict.

If it happens, and the signs are hopeful, it will be a mighty achievement.

Acknowledgements

IMMEASURABLE THANKS, as ever, to my two series directors, John-Paul Davidson and Roger Mills, who not only dreamt up the project with me, but provided me with places to go and people to see.

A huge thank you to Nigel Meakin on camera, ably assisted by his son Peter, and John Pritchard on sound, fellow travellers of many series' standing – well, staggering anyway. A special thank you to Pete for mending my glasses so often. Jay Jay Odedra and David Wright stood in as assistant cameramen. To Alex Richardson who edits all the material we bring back, and still speaks to us. To Sue Grant our production manager, who said goodbye to us so many times, but we still kept coming back, and to Michelle Hanley who stood, and sat, by her, on the top floor at Prominent Towers. Thank you for looking after us all.

Thanks to Lyn Dougherty, for being un-flapped by twenty different currencies. To the redoubtable trio of Vanessa Courtney, Claire Houdret and 'Miss Vicky' Bennetts who not only set up stories, but guided us to, through, and safely out of dozens of locations with amazing grace. To Mimi Robinson for not only listening to all my voice-recorded ramblings, but writing them down as well and to Mike Griffin who made departures and arrivals so easy, but couldn't save Sheffield United. Richard Klein at the BBC was sympathetic, encouraging and constructive throughout.

In the Prominent Office, thanks to my two indispensable stalwarts, Paul Bird, tireless organiser who makes my life much easier than it should be, and our executive producer Steve Abbott, who has guided my affairs for over a quarter of a century, and who has kept *New Europe* on course since it was a glint in an old presenter's eye.

In many ways this was the most complicated series we've done and relied on the generous help of friends in twenty different countries. Some are mentioned in the book already, but there are many unsung heroes who worked behind the scenes. So a big thank you to Vanda Vucicevic, Sandra Ovcina, Ardi Pulaj, Riina Sepp, Divs Reiznieks, Darius Ross, Olga Danilova, Gyorgy Paraszkay, Igor Khmarsky, Witold and Basia Starecka, Mira Staleva, Maya Vitkova, Jordan Topkoski, Tatiana Tibuleac, Olga Maxim, Ionna Abur, Bogdan Stefanescu, Bogdan Petrovic, Funda Odemis, Selen Korkut, Jano Gordullic, Michael Havas, Ondrej Strejceck and Tamsin Walker.

At Weidenfeld & Nicolson, I must thank my editor, Michael Dover, for keeping a cool head and guiding me through an uncompromising timetable with his usual good grace and good humour and David Rowley for conjuring up such a handsome book, against the clock as usual. Thanks to Linden Lawson, my copy editor, for ploughing through a minefield of fine detail, to Justin Hunt for helping to pull the book together, and Angela McMahon and Katie Hambly for alerting the world to its existence.

Special thanks to photographer, friend and foodie Basil Pao for continuing to be the best in the business and for showing how enticing, intriguing and downright good-looking Eastern Europe can be.

Rough Guides, *Bradt* Guides and *Time Out City Guides* were my staple references, as well as *Lonely Planet*'s indispensable *Moldova* and *Ukraine* Guides. I learnt a lot from the following: Misha Glenny's *The Balkans*, Dervla Murphy's *Through the Embers of Chaos*, Janine de Giovanni's *Madness Visible*, Robert Carver's *The Accursed Mountains, Journeys in Albania*, Robert Kaplan's *Balkan Ghosts* and *Eastward to Tartary*, Patrick Leigh Fermor's *A Time of Gifts* and *Between the Woods and the Water*, Orhan Pamuk's *Istanbul*, Victor Sebestyen's *Twelve Days, Revolution 1956*, Anna Reid's *Borderland*, Radek Sikorski's *The Polish House*, Norman Davies' *Heart of Europe, The Past in Poland's Present*, Eva Hoffman's *Lost In Translation*,

Timothy Garton Ash's *The Polish Revolution* and Anna Funder's *Stasiland*.

Among fiction that brought places vividly to life, I particularly enjoyed: Andrey Kurkov's *Death and The Penguin*, Ismail Kadare's *The General Of The Dead Army* and *Three Elegies For Kosovo*, Dubravka Ugresic's *The Ministry Of Pain* and *The Radetzky March* by Joseph Roth.